The Memoirs of Jin Luxian

The Memoirs of Jin Luxian

Volume One: Learning and Relearning
1916–1982

Translated by William Hanbury-Tenison
With an Introduction by Anthony E. Clark

HONG KONG UNIVERSITY PRESS

Hong Kong University Press
The University of Hong Kong
Pokfulam Road
Hong Kong
www.hkupress.org

Original Chinese text © Jin Luxian 2012
English translation © William Hanbury-Tenison 2012

ISBN 978-988-8139-66-8 *(Hardback)*
ISBN 978-988-8139-67-5 *(Paperback)*

All rights reserved. No portion of this publication may be reproduced or transmitted in any form or by any means, electronic or mechanical, including photocopy, recording, or any information storage or retrieval system, without prior permission in writing from the publisher.

British Library Cataloguing-in-Publication Data
A catalogue record for this book is available from the British Library.

10　9　8　7　6　5　4　3　2　1

Printed and bound by Condor Production Ltd. in Hong Kong, China

To Reverend Peter Lefebvre S.J.

I dedicate this book to my benefactor, the exemplary missionary Reverend Peter Lefebvre S.J.

My revered teacher Peter Lefebvre[1] was born in France in 1883. As a young man he was impelled by his love of China to leave his native land and cross the broad oceans to work in my country as a missionary. First he learned Chinese, then completed his theological studies and became a priest, serving the Tangmuqiao parish in the Pudong district of Shanghai. Later on he served as rector of Aurora University, father superior of the Society of Jesus in Shanghai, auxiliary bishop of Shanghai diocese, vicar general of Yangzhou diocese, rector of the Xuhui School of Theology and professor at the Xuhui Major Seminary. During his life he often expressed the wish to die in China. The Lord answered his prayer. In 1955 the military authorities in Shanghai ordered his immediate expulsion from China, but he died suddenly while under escort and was buried in Guangzhou by Bishop Deng Yiming. May his soul in heaven bring yet more grace to the Church in China.

---

1. Peter Lefebvre S.J., author of *A Guide to Catholic Shanghai,* Shanghai, 1937.

And we know that all things work together for good to them that love God, to them who are called according to his purpose.

Romans 8:28

Deus, cuius providentia in sui dispositione non fallitur, te supplices exoramus, ut noxia cuncta submoveas, et omnia nobis profutura concedas

Collect for the 9th Sunday of Ordinary Time

Contents

List of Illustrations	xiii
Introduction by Anthony E. Clark	xv
Translator's Note	xxi
Preface	1

Part I Family

1.	Youth	7
2.	Pudong	15
3.	Going to School	19
4.	The Chinese Catholic Church in Those Days	21
5.	St. Ignatius College (1926–32)	25
6.	Great-Uncle Jin Fushan	29
7.	Two Elder Sisters: Lu Naying and Rong Dexian	31

Part II Seminary Life

8.	Seminary of the Sacred Heart of Jesus (1932–35)	37
9.	Seminary of the Sacred Heart of Mary (1935–37)	43
10.	St. Ignatius College (1937–38)	47
11.	Joining the Society of Jesus: Two Years of Novitiate (1938–40)	51
12.	Taking First Vows: Juvenate (1940–41)	57
13.	School of Philosophy (1941–42)	61
14.	Studying Theology (1942–46)	71
15.	Subei (1946–47)	75

Part III   Life as an Overseas Student

16. Travel to Europe — 87
17. Tertianship in France (1947–48) — 93
18. Learning English — 105
19. Gregorian University — 113
20. Two Eminent Persons — 117
21. A Few of My College Friends — 121
22. Archbishop Paul Yu Bin — 127
23. Necessary Measures in the Society of Jesus: Visitor Burckhardt — 131
24. Vacation in Switzerland, Austria and West Germany — 135
25. My Second Year in Rome — 145

Part IV   Returning Home

26. Acting on Orders — 151
27. Reporting to the Diocese — 157
28. The Shanghai Diocese after 1949 — 161
29. Various Political Movements — 165
30. Xuhui Seminary — 177
31. Anti-Imperialism Patriotic Movement — 181
32. The Four Roles — 187
33. Gong Pinmei — 199

Part V   Life in Jail

34. My First Sight of Prison (1955–60) — 205
35. Public Trial and Sentencing (1960) — 225
36. Jail in Shanghai (1960–62) — 229
37. Foreign Language Translator, Qincheng Prison (1963–67) — 235
38. The Fushun War Criminals Management Centre (1967–73) — 247
39. Return to Qincheng and Resumption of Translation Work (1973–75) — 255

40.	The No. 4 Re-education through Labour Camp in Henan Province (1975–79)	259
41.	The End of the 'Great Proletarian Cultural Revolution'	265
42.	Hebei No. 1 Jail (1979–82)	269
43.	Friends Come from Afar	277
44.	My Return to Shanghai	283

Index of Names 291

List of Illustrations

Photos

1. Jin Luxian (second from right in the second row) as a choir boy at St. Ignatius College. The accompanying priest is Rev. Vincent Zi S.J.
2. Jin Luxian as a young man
3. Funeral portrait of Mary Jin Weixuan
4. Rong Dexian
5. Family of Rong Dexian and Zhu Yisheng with Bishop Walsh
6. Lu Naying (third from right in the back row) with the family of Lu Bohong
7. Jin Luxian in Rome
8. Donate Seeger
9. Jin Luxian as a young priest in Beijing
10. Shanghai Jesuits with Bishop Gong Pinmei. Jin is at Gong's right. Rev. Peter Lefebvre is fourth from right in the first row.
11. Jin and Edeltrud Meistermann-Seeger 'Mami'

Maps

1. Map of Xujiahui Jesuit buildings
2. Map of Catholic Shanghai
3. Map of China showing Jin's travels

Introduction
By Anthony E. Clark

They must often change who would be constant in happiness or wisdom.
—Confucius

During my most recent visit with Bishop Jin Luxian I gave him several rare photographs of himself and other Jesuits in Shanghai before his arrest in 1955. I had not yet read his memoirs, and only after reading them did I realise why he was so moved by this gift; he had not seen images of these 'old beloved friends' since the 1950s, six decades ago. At 96, Jin is one of the last remaining persons to have witnessed the turbulence of China's Republican Era (1911–49), the capriciousness of the Maoist era (1949–76) and the precipitous rise of China in the Deng Xiaoping era (1980–present). Few people today can retrospectively recount personal encounters with so many historical people and events that altered the trajectory of China's modern history.

Jin Luxian has lived through China's war with Japan (1930s); the violent conflicts between his own countrymen as the Nationalist and Communist forces vied for China's future (1920s–1949); the Maoist victory in 1949; the Hundred Flowers Movement (1956) and the subsequent Anti-Rightist Campaign (1957–58); the Great Leap Forward along with the bitter famines that followed (1958–61); the chaos of the Cultural Revolution and the Red Guard attacks on the 'Four Olds' (1966–76); the 'Lin Biao Incident' (1971); the fall of the Gang of Four (1976) and the post-Mao period of reconstruction (1989–present). He experienced much of this tempestuous history, however, while serving a jail sentence as a 'dangerous counter-revolutionary', imprisoned because of his alliance with an 'imperialist power', the Roman Catholic Church. And I still have not mentioned the upheavals and reforms that transpired in the Catholic Church during Jin's lifetime, such as the Second Vatican Council (1962–65) and the sweeping reforms that changed the landscape of Catholic Christianity.

In short, Jin's autobiography provides historians an extraordinary personal glance into one of the world's most extraordinary periods of transformation.

Jin Luxian's memoirs are as complex as Jin Luxian himself; they reveal a life of remarkable experiences that were also survived remarkably, and any well-informed historian who is honest to his or her sources cannot help but wonder at the enigmatic nature of Jin's choices, alliances and remarkable longevity. In turn he has been accepted and rejected by the Communist party, his friends and family and his order, the Society of Jesus. He has been labelled a dangerous political element by his government and a traitor by his Jesuit confreres, only to be later embraced by both as a model member of each. Despite the multiplicities of Jin's character, the constant strand in his life, woven through his entire memoirs, is his personal identity as a member of the Catholic Church and the Jesuit Order. In one of our meetings he exclaimed: "I am both a serpent and a dove. The government thinks I'm too close to the Vatican, and the Vatican thinks I'm too close to the government. I'm a slippery fish squashed between government control and Vatican demands." No matter what one's opinion of Jin is, he has been and remains one of China's most powerful Catholic bishops, and has lifted the Catholic Church in China out of ruins and into a growing religious community.

History

In both academic and ecclesial circles, Bishop Jin Luxian is known for his arrest and long imprisonment by the Communist party, and his later rise to prominence as China's leading Catholic prelate. It might thus be disappointing to some that his memoirs comment more on the people involved in the arrests of 8 September 1955, than on the circumstances of the arrests. Despite the fact that fewer than 1% of Shanghai's population was Catholic at that time—around 110,000 out of six million people—the news of State–Catholic conflicts in 1950s Shanghai and reports of widespread arrests of the Catholic faithful reached a global audience. Jean Lefeuvre's account of these conflicts, *Shanghaï: les enfants dans la ville, chronique de la vie chretienne a Shanghai 1949–1955*, became a bestseller when it was published in France in 1956. Once Premier Zhou Enlai had become aware of Lefeuvre's derisive criticism of the party's behaviour in Shanghai, he invited Simone de Beauvoir to China to write a more flattering view of the Chinese Communist Party. Her work in support of China's new Marxist leaders, *The Long March: An Account of Modern China*, was published in 1957, though Lefeuvre's book had already left a permanent impression on Western views of China's government. More recently, Paul Mariani, who, like Lefeuvre, is a Jesuit, has published a more academic study of the events that precipitated Jin's arrest. Mariani's work, *Church Militant: Bishop Kung and Catholic Resistance in Communist Shanghai*, published in 2011, and *Shanghaï: les enfants dans la ville*, provide an alternative view to those held in these memoirs. Jin's recollections are given additional flesh when read in conjunction with these other two books, written by his Jesuit confreres, Lefeuvre and Mariani.

Jin Luxian was a Roman Catholic priest in Shanghai on the eve of China's communist revolution, and both the Church and the party had drawn a clear battle line. Pope Pius IX's 1937 encyclical, *Divini Redemptoris*, clearly defined the Church's position: "The militant leaders of Catholic Action thus properly prepared and armed" will be the first "to save these ... our beloved children, from the snares of Communism", furthermore calling for a "vast campaign of the Church against world Communism". China's party officials justly viewed the Catholic Church among its enemies—had the Church not called itself a 'military'?—and, thus, set about orchestrating an Anti-Imperialist Patriotic Movement directed against the Catholic faithful and activists. In this movement, as Jin recalls in his memoirs, "the government Propaganda Department used novels and films to great effect to spread the news of the crimes of the missionaries, utilising every means to thoroughly blacken the name of the missionaries and thus attack Catholicism." While he was completing his doctorate in Europe, the conflict between the party and the Church intensified, so that when Jin returned to his native Shanghai in 1951, Sino–Vatican relations had reached a breaking point. For most Chinese at this time, to be authentically Chinese was to set oneself against anything 'imperial' and 'foreign'; Catholicism was decidedly both.

By 1950 Shanghai's Religious Affairs Bureau remarked in a document concerning Christianity that: "Marxists are fully atheist, and we believe that religion is an obstruction to the people's awakening."[1] Since the leader of Shanghai's Catholic resistance was Bishop Gong Pinmei, the government initiated an intense campaign against the 'Gong Pinmei counterrevolutionary clique', to which Jin Luxian was, perhaps unwittingly, connected. On the evening of 8 September 1955, the Shanghai police made a massive sweep through the city, arresting roughly 100 Catholics (some accounts say hundreds were arrested),

---

1. Shanghai Municipal Archives, B22-2-1.

followed by several thousand faithful who were accused of membership in the 'Gong clique'. Jin was reading in his room when at 9:30 p.m. plain clothes policemen charged into his room and arrested him: "I was pushed into a small motor car and driven away." He was held in various jails around China from then until his final release in 1982, when he ended his "27 years of lost liberty". Indeed, among the more compelling portions of Jin's memoirs are those that describe his time in prison, when he was rebuked for being a "stinking old nine intellectual", and a "parasite".

The morning after Jin's arrest, Shanghai's *Liberation Daily* newspaper heralded the "eradication of the counterrevolutionaries concealed in the church and their leader, Gong Pinmei", and the *Daily* accused these Catholics of providing "vital military, state, and economic secrets to imperialist spies". That Jin survived this episode to later become a government-sanctioned bishop in China—China's most powerful bishop—has not passed without a large number of Catholic detractors who have rejected him considering him a Communist collaborator. As Jin laments, even the deputy superior general of his own order stated, "that I was a traitor and no longer a Jesuit." His memoirs are, in his own words, a response to "certain accusations" that "have been mischievously" made: "after struggling with my conscience several times, I have decided to write this memoir and thus provide the reader with some knowledge of the period of history I have lived through." Indeed, his memoirs may be compared somewhat to John Newman's *Apologia Pro Vita Sua*, though in Jin's case his critics come from within his own Catholic community.

One of Jin Luxian's chief detractors was Laszlo Ladany, also a Jesuit, who accused Jin of promoting unorthodox views in order better to collaborate with the Communist government and position the Chinese Church to be independent from the Roman Church. Among other allegations, Ladany accuses Jin of being duplicitous, complaining that Jin expresses his "admiration for Rome", while asserting that, "the papacy was not established until the 5th century. It has no authority over other churches. All local churches are equal", and that Vatican II was a "victory of the bishops over the pope".[2] More critics followed Jin's 1988 profession in support of the Catholic Patriotic Association, which outside of China, Jin believes, is largely reviled and misunderstood. In an address to the Catholic Patriotic Association in Shanghai, he broadcast: "I solemnly declare in the name of the Shanghai diocese that the Patriotic

---

2. László Ladány, *Meditation on the Church in China* (Hong Kong, 1988), 13.

Introduction xix

Association is our most important helper," and he exhorted: "The more enemies of the Patriotic Association, the higher we should raise the banner of the Patriotic Association."[3] Statements such as this have engendered a string of criticisms, but few of these critics have attempted to explain Jin's assertions from Jin's point of view.

Bishop Jin's reasons for maintaining a collaborative relationship with China's authorities are at last enumerated in his memoirs; those who are well-informed regarding the post-1949 history of Catholicism in China will perhaps either side for or against Jin's justifications for conciliation. Many view Bishop Gong Pinmei, who refused to concede to government regulations vis-à-vis Catholic activities in China, as a foil in contrast to Jin; it is evident that Jin himself views Gong as a foil, for in his memoirs he reproaches Gong Pinmei for, essentially, abandoning his sheep. "Good pastors remain with their flocks," Jin asserts, "but after six months [in America] Gong did not return to China … living a comfortable life and making many anti-communist speeches." Jin Luxian decided to remain in China.

As Paul Mariani has noted, "Even Jin's detractors call him 'brilliant' and are forced to concede his impressive accomplishments."[4] Jin has managed to re-open more than 100 Shanghai churches. He has also established China's pre-eminent Catholic seminary with a remarkably well-appointed theological library, opened a diocesan publishing house and a popular retreat centre, and has commonly sent seminarians abroad to prepare for priesthood. Shanghai, as of 2004, boasted 110 churches, 130 seminarians, 30 novices, 80 nuns, 70 priests and 140,000 Roman Catholics.[5] Near the end of his prison term, the party invited Jin to lead Shanghai's Catholic community, encouraging Jin to consider that: "In another twenty years, you will go to heaven and Catholicism will simply die out in China. You will bear the responsibility for that … You should take responsibility for the Church." Jin accepted this invocation and was able to restore the Church in Shanghai after 27 years in prison, and this was accomplished after his 66th year; since then he has remained tireless.

---

3. Address to the Shanghai CCPA on 1 December 1988, published in the *Sunday Examiner* (Hong Kong, 10 March 1989).
4. Paul P. Mariani, *Church Militant: Bishop Kung and Catholic Resistance in Communist China* (Cambridge: Harvard University Press, 2011), 217.
5. Jean Charbonnier, *Guide to the Catholic Church in China 2004* (Singapore: China Catholic Communication, 2004), 548–49, 567.

Faith

Jin Luxian was born, raised and educated in China's most Western-influenced city and baptised a Christian in one of the world's least-Christian countries. Jin is thus often discussed in conjunction with remarks about the Chinese government's modern history of religious suppression, especially the suppression of Catholic Christianity. Reading Jin Luxian's memoirs might cause one falsely to assume that China's Communist leaders invented anti-Christianity. Long before Karl Marx was born, however, China had a popular saying, 'one more Christian means one less Chinese'. Both Jin and Chinese Communism were born into China's long history of antagonism with foreign religion. That said, Jin's memoirs deal surprisingly little with Communist anti-Christianism; rather, his memoirs are principally an exercise of spiritual devotion, perhaps even more than they function to exonerate himself under the long scrutiny of his critics. For the historian, Jin's remarks provide significant and novel insight into China's transition into its modern identity, but for the religious reader it is Bishop Jin, rather than counter-revolutionary Jin, who speaks loudest.

In his personal narrative, Jin reminds his reader that through the many vicissitudes of his life he found solace in the statement of Blessed Elizabeth of the Trinity, who said, "Heaven is the Trinity; with the Trinity in my heart, I am as if in Heaven." His memoirs are likewise punctuated with aphorisms that have sustained the Jesuit Order in its mission to educate and evangelise the peoples of all places, such as the central motto of the Society, *Ad Majorem Deo Gloriam*, or 'all for the greater glory of God'. The individual complexities of Bishop Aloysius Jin Luxian S.J., woven through his memoirs, vacillate between political reflection, personal recollection and self-justification, and are all sustained by his abiding confidence in God's assistance. Jin Luxian has been identified as a politician, protector and prisoner, but he would simply refer to himself as a priest; and in a final word, Jin has always been, and remains, a priest.

One of the profound marks of Jin Luxian's memoirs is his witness to personal growth in a world of hurried change. If John Henry Newman's remark that "Growth is the only evidence of life" may be taken as true, then it may be said that Jin Luxian has truly lived.

Translator's Note

I first met Jin Luxian in 1995 at his residence at Sheshan next to the basilica on the hilltop outside Shanghai which Jin had chosen as the location for his new seminary.

Having lived in China on and off since the mid-1980s I was already fully aware of the situation of the Catholic Church in China, divided between an underground Church of fiercely traditional families and persecuted priests and an official Church that seemed on occasion no more than a means by which the authorities could squeeze what life was left out of a bitter enemy of the Chinese Communist party. In a country where every person is compromised by the demands of the secret police, most of the official priests I had met seemed glad simply to be out of jail and willing to do whatever the government asked of them.

Jin was completely different. Here was a man who demonstrated his spiritual authority in his words, in his actions and through his very considerable achievements. Practising my religion in Shanghai was completely different from what I had experienced in Beijing or other major cities. In Shanghai foreign Catholics were able to establish their own parish; a vibrant seminary was educating a new generation of deeply committed priests; young people in Shanghai were discovering the religion of their grandparents; the sermons in the local churches were socially relevant and gripping. Given that the activities of the Catholic Church continued to be monitored with an obsessive paranoia it was clear that we Catholics were operating under a protective umbrella established at the highest levels. For this we have Jin to thank.

Over the years I got to know Jin better, spending time with him, doing what little I could to explain to the outside world what he was doing and why I felt that his choice was the right one. The longer I knew him the greater my respect and love for him grew.

Two years ago I attended early morning mass at Jin's private chapel. After mass he showed me a copy of a translation of his memoirs that had been done by a Chinese translator and asked me whether I could polish it. Having compared the original text with the translation I realised that it would be much easier simply to start afresh. I suggested this to Jin and he asked me to do the work.

During the year that I lived with Jin's memoirs I gained an even deeper understanding of this extraordinary man and of the world that made him. There were moments when I was overcome with emotion and had to rest from my work to regain my composure. At all times I kept in mind Jin's own personality and tried as best I could to replicate his voice in the English text.

A work of this nature is written without self-glorification, either of the self-promoting or the self-denigrating kind. The purpose may be one of self-justification in the face of criticism, but even then serves simply better to hone the essential evangelical message. Jin's life has been led in the service of God and his memoir also serves God's purpose.

I would like to thank those who read manuscript versions of this translation, not least Jin Luxian himself (who checked every page), but also Richard Rigby, Warren Kinne and my mother Euphan (to whom I owe my Catholic faith). My wife Mina and our children Alexander and Clovis share my devotion to Jin and have supported me throughout the long process of translation.

William Hanbury-Tenison
Shanghai, September 2012

Preface

In 1933 when I was 17 years old I was given an introduction by friends to the aged patriot Ma Xiangbo,[1] who was then 94 years of age. He was wearing a long black gown over which he had on a mandarin jacket and he was sitting straight up in a formal chair. I offered my respects and congratulated him on his great age. He replied: "Ninety-four years have passed by in an instant." I wondered how 94 years could pass by in an instant. Now I too have reached my nineties, having frittered away 92 years.

When I close my eyes and think back, those years have truly passed in an instant, but on close examination this instant was full of hardship. Having been born into a moderately prosperous family, I, from the age of ten on, met with repeated misfortune. My mother and father died and my elder sister passed away. In a short period of time I lost everything, found myself both without close relatives and as poor as a church mouse. In the prime of life I even lost my liberty for a period of not less than ten thousand days. Only on reaching my seventies was I able to practise my vocation, although I was assaulted by groundless accusations on every side and subjected to slanderous attacks in the face of which I found it hard to establish my innocence. The ancients opined that human nature is inconstant, that gossip is a terrible thing and that the resulting wounds are deep indeed.

As things turned out, every time I thought that I had reached an impassable section of the road, I would come across the shelter of yet another village to which the angels would guide me by their invisible hands and the Lord's

---

1. Ma Xiangbo S.J. (1840–1939) was the most prominent Chinese Jesuit in late Qing and early Republican China. He was involved in the founding of Aurora Academy, Fudan Public School and the Catholic University of Peking (later known as Furen University).

assistance would come just in time, leading me to the inevitable conclusion that in life one could overcome all difficulties. When my father and my mother had both died, the family property had been lost and I had no home to return to, my great-uncle arrived on the scene, carried my siblings and me to his own home and treated us as if we had been his own children. When my great-uncle died and my elder sister's life ended prematurely, Lu Naying and Rong Dexian both said to me: "From now on I will be your elder sister; please don't worry." They both treated me with the love of an elder sister until the day they left this world. While I was at the prison in Baoding, the most painful period of my reform through labour,[2] the parents of my German friend Donate came from afar to find me and thereafter looked after me until they died. My road was replete with perils, but I travelled in peace and overcame all the dangers that beset me.

Born into a Catholic family, educated at a Catholic school and then joining the Society of Jesus, I was at every stage guided by the Holy Spirit through the medium of the Bible and prevented from stumbling. When beset by challenging circumstances I recalled the phrase: 'All is Vanity; vanity of vanities' (*Vanitas vanitatum, omnia vanitas*). While I was doing my novitiate in the Society of Jesus I was made miserable by the attitude of the master of novices, but found solace in the words of the founder of our order: "Rejoice in the slights and neglect of others" (*Ama nesciri et pro nihilo reputari*). When in jail and having lost my liberty, I recalled the words of Blessed Elizabeth of the Trinity: "Heaven is the Trinity; with the Trinity in my heart, I am as if in Heaven." Thus I made of jail my heaven, never ceasing to praise the Trinity, forgetting all pains and living replete with joy.

After completing my sentence I returned to my diocese, first as rector of the Sheshan seminary and then later I was chosen to be auxiliary bishop. I always made use of the following phrase to remind myself who I was: 'He should grow and I should shrink' (*Oportet illum crescere, me autem minui*).

Life is but a string of choices. On the basis of what principle should one then chose? As a Jesuit my principle was always: 'To the greater glory of God' (*Ad majorem dei gloriam*). As long as my actions served the greater glory of the Lord, I went ahead in confidence.

---

2. Otherwise known as *laogai* or 'imprisonment in correctional facilities where hard labour is intended to bring about reform of the politically deviant individual'.

Preface

'The setting of the sun is a great good; it is simply the time of the dying of the light.' My good friends have one by one predeceased me and it will soon be my turn. Thus I now ceaselessly say to the Lord: "Oh Lord, permit your servant to depart peacefully." To depart peacefully is my wish.

Since I sincerely believe that all in this world is but vanity, why should I concern myself with writing my memoirs? In recent years more and more foreign articles have been written about me and been widely disseminated. In many details these articles do not accord with the facts and certain accusations have been mischievously included. This matters little to me, but has had some surface impact on the Church in China and has not been helpful to the work of the Holy Spirit. If I do not stand witness, uninformed people may take these accusations as fact. After struggling with my conscience several times, I have decided to write this memoir and provide the reader with some knowledge of the period of history I have lived through.

When I was arrested on 8 September 1955, the Shanghai Public Security Bureau seized all my belongings, including my diaries, my correspondence, all my photographs and personal effects; none of these remain today.

On my release and return to Shanghai, my heart was full of lingering fear and I kept no more diaries, wrote no letters. Thus I have written this memoir purely on the basis of my memory; there must be errors, for which I beg understanding and ask that they be pointed out to me.

Jin Luxian
30 August 2008
Written on the 70th anniversary of my reception into the Society of Jesus

Part I

Family

1
Youth

My name is Jin Luxian.

I was born in Shanghai's Nanshi District[1] on 20 June 1916. In 1916 World War One was raging in Europe, without any sign of a clear outcome between the two sides. China's government declared war on Germany and Austria and, to assist the allies, many young people were sent to France to provide additional labour power in the support areas, as all available Frenchmen were at the front. The then leader of China's Beiyang clique, Yuan Shikai, signed the treacherous 'Twenty-One Demands' treaty with Japan to meet the demands of Japanese militarists and to further his own ambitions. Japan planned to colonise China and seized the opportunity to occupy the Jiaozhou Peninsula. Yuan Shikai's attempt to revive imperial rule met with the opposition of all Chinese, with the result that as the self-proclaimed Hongxian Emperor he became panic-stricken and met with an early death. After Yuan Shikai's death his subordinate generals used the support of various foreign powers to seize political control and natural resources, setting up a series of semi-independent and internecine states, bringing the people to the depths of disaster. When in 1919 the victorious allies (the United States, France and Britain) organised the Paris Peace Conference, they decided to pass Germany's confiscated colonial possessions in Shandong Province to Japan, causing unprecedented anger among the Chinese, leading to the May Fourth Movement and forcing the Beiyang clique delegation to refuse to sign the Treaty of Versailles.

I was born at a time when the people of our country were suffering from the chaos of civil disorder and foreign occupation, so during my youth there was no National Day and only national disgrace.

---

1. The Chinese city, formerly walled, to the south of the Bund and the foreign concessions.

The day after my birth was the saint's day of the young saint Aloysius Gonzaga so I was christened Louis in French, while my father gave me the name *Luyi* in Chinese. Later, when I was in middle school, the class supervisor said that Luyi was meaningless in Chinese and changed my name to *Luxian* (which has a similar pronunciation to *Luyi* in Shanghai dialect). I have used this latter name throughout my life.

My father was silent at home; he went to work in the morning and came home in the evening. On Sundays he stayed at home reading, preferring novels, especially detective stories. He smoked incessantly and only rarely talked to his two sons. When I look back, it seems as if he never spoke to us at all. He had an illness that prevented him from taking communion more than once a year, because of the requirement to purify the body by not taking food or drink from midnight on the day before mass. My father was a most generous man. I remember that before Chinese New Year he would sort through the IOUs people had given him and say to my mother: "This person and that person have still not paid, let's not ask them to pay us back." He then burnt the IOUs. My mother always agreed with him.

Many visitors came to our house, especially from my paternal aunt's family. Among them I remember Zhang Dengtang (aka Thaddeus Tsang) who became a priest and his younger brother Zhang Dengyin who came often. After my family went bankrupt and my parents died, I once met the latter in the street and called out to him warmly, but he ignored me. I suffered from this slight for many years, thus learning a lesson in the cold ways of the world.

I've never seen my family tree, but suspect that my ancestors were peasants for generations back, that they were poor people without any social status and thus never had a family tree. I am very hazy about my ancestors and just remember my grandfather.

A village elder showed me the ring of seven tombs and told me: "Jin Family Village had seven brothers named Jin. A few hundred years ago they came to this wasteland, established boundaries, married, raised children and grandchildren, all staying in one place until it became a village of Christians where most people had the family name Jin. So it was called Jin Family Village." Strangely enough, when the seven tombs were dug up during the 'Cultural Revolution', one of the tombs was found to be empty.

In the middle of the village was a small stream that bisected it: the two sides being named Xinan (south of the stream) and Xibei (north of the stream). Our ancestral home was in Xinan and the church was in Xibei.

Everyone in the village was Catholic, but I have no idea when they had converted. Even the village elders could not say for sure, having no reliable records. The Jin Family Village church had at one time been a cathedral. A Korean named Andrew Kim Taegon (Jin Dajian) went to Macau to study for the priesthood. He set out for Korea from Macau with the French priest Jean Joseph Ferréol (the first Bishop of Korea), passing through Shanghai. On 17 August 1845 Andrew Kim was ordained by Bishop Ferréol at the Jin Family Village church. He said his first mass at Huang Tang church and then returned to Korea via Beijing, losing his life after two years at the age of 26. On 6 May 1984, Pope John-Paul II, on a visit to Seoul, canonised Andrew Kim and his 102 fellow martyrs. Andrew Kim is the pride of the Korean Catholic Church and this glory is reflected on Jin Family Village.

The first priest of Jin Family Village was named Joseph Jin. He was the first priest in the Jiangnan region to be sent to Italy for higher formation; the second priest was named Jin Wenqi, who was ordained in 1931. He was sent to be vicar in Zhang Jing and met his death at the hands of the Japanese invaders in December 1937. The third priest was I myself; the fourth was Jin Heting, who has already died; the fifth was Jin Zhenqi; the sixth was Jin Chongwei, who was a member of the Salesian order and worked for the Congregation for the Propagation of the Faith (*Propaganda Fide*) in Rome until his death in July 2009.

My grandfather was named Jin Xinheng and christened Paul. He was a devout Catholic, born in 1844. When he was a child the armies of the Taiping rebels, also known as the *Chang Mao* (long hair) on account of their troops' distinctive hairstyle, sacked Shanghai. Grandpa always said that he was press-ganged by the Taipings and had to work for them in the logistics corps. He named his first son Jin Xinde (virtue of faith); the second, who became my father, Jin Wangde (virtue of hope). He had hoped to father a third son so that he could have sons named faith (*xin*), hope (*wang*) and love (*ai*), but he had to settle for two. Later on my grandfather moved to Shanghai as an apprentice and opened his own grocery store on the corner of Edward VII Avenue (today's Yan'an East Road) and Henan Road. His grocery store sold beef and mutton, imported wines and spirits, imported canned foods, butter, milk products, etc. and specialised in supplying the foreign community. He also traded in cattle and used the money he earned to build and rent out houses. He was a good businessman. In 1925 he had a stroke and fell to the ground dead—he was 77 years old.

My father was born in 1885 and named Wangde, with the style name Zhongchao (second supernatural virtue, i.e. hope) and the saint's name Luke. My mother was one year older than my father. She was born in 1884 and named Zhang Yunzhen and christened Lucia. Her hometown was Zhangjialou in Pudong, about two kilometres away from Jin Family Village. My maternal grandfather was Zhang Zhitang, also known as Lianghai. As a young man he came to Shanghai a total stranger and became a comprador to the British Chamber of Commerce and to Shun Chang Co., Ltd. Later on he went bankrupt speculating in foreign exchange (he had bought a position in Russian roubles before the October Rebellion in 1917 and lost everything). My mother was the eldest of two sisters, the younger being named Zhang Wangzhen, who, after graduating from Changde Girls Middle School, entered the Society of Helpers of the Holy Souls and became a nun. The Helpers of the Holy Souls is a very strict French order. On joining the order one has to pay a lot of money, which my father provided for her.

My grandmother died early on and my grandfather married a woman named Cao to look after him in his old age. She gave birth to two sons and four daughters, of whom one son died in childhood.

After my father graduated from St. Ignatius College, he became a schoolmaster, but later on joined a foreign firm. My father's Chinese, French and English were all excellent; he was a rare commodity in those days. The British company Hutchison hired him to work in Nanjing as a Chinese manager or comprador. When he returned home to tell his father that he was going to work in Nanjing, his father was not pleased, saying: "When the filial son's parents are still alive, he doesn't stray far from home." The Confucian rule was that children should pay daily visits to their parents to ask after their health and to show their respect. My father insisted on going because of the large salary offered in Nanjing. My grandfather said that if my father went, then he would disown him. My father went anyway, so my grandfather left all his money to my uncle Jin Xinde.

When my parents had been married for a year they had a boy, but he died after only a few months. My father wanted other children, but had to wait nine years for the second, who was my elder sister. My father thought that she had been sent by God to comfort her parents and so named her Mary. My elder sister was very clever and went to board at Xuhui Girls Middle School at the age of only ten. She was loved by her teachers and by her fellow students and also by me.

When my sister was three years old, my mother became pregnant again with me. But I arrived at a bad time, since after giving birth to me, my mother fell gravely ill and nearly died. My mother insisted on returning to Shanghai, saying that if she had to die she wanted to die at home. Although my father was doing very well in Nanjing, he didn't want to make my mother unhappy and had no choice but to resign his position, causing bad blood between him and his foreign employers. My parents returned to Shanghai, but never had such an easy life again. On first returning to Shanghai my father could not find a good job and, while I was crawling on the floor babbling, the mood at home was gloomy. According to what I have been told, when my father was asked to hold me he would pay no attention, saying that I had brought him bad luck. Of course he later on accepted me. Because my mother was sick and could not feed me, we hired a nurse. The nurse liked me very much and after I was weaned came to visit every year, getting clothes, money and even jewellery from my mother. Later when our business failed and we lost our home she was no longer able to come and see me. I still remember that she was taller than my mother and the same age as her.

When I was two years old my younger brother came into this world at the right moment as my father had already found a very good job with the Belgian Congregation of the Immaculate Heart of Mary, which had set up an office in Shanghai and hired him at a very good salary. My whole family especially loved my younger brother. He was born in mid-November, close to the Feast of St. Stanislaus, so he took that as his Christian name. His Chinese name, given by my father, was Dayi. We didn't fix our names according to the prescribed names in the family tree. In contrast my cousins were named Guangsheng, Rensheng, Zhisheng and Lisheng. My father stuck to Christian names, calling me Luyi (Louis) and my brother Dayi (Stanislaus).

My father smoked tobacco, preferring large Havana cigars. He also grew a moustache that flew up on either side of his mouth like the number eight (八) in Chinese. He wore both Western suits and Chinese gowns, but his trousers were always Western style and for those days he was very Westernised. My father had many friends. I remember his best friend, a man named Chen Yide. When he learnt of Chen Yide's death my father cried, which was the first time I had seen him do so. After a gap of 80 years, Chen Yide's granddaughter was kind enough to bring me a photograph of their ancestor, after learning of his friendship with my father. I was deeply moved by her kindness.

I have a full memory of my childhood, even recalling my brother's birth. My mother cradled him while he slept and asked me to sleep at her feet, about which I was not at all happy. I still remember my mother used a string to restrain me, with the other end in her hand. If I strayed too far, she pulled on the string to bring me back.

When I was born our home was in the Chinese city next to the City God Temple in a street named Fangbang Road. Our lane was called Lin De Li (Linde Terrace) and was close to the Little East Gate. In those days the busiest street in Shanghai was Nanjing East Road, after which it was Little East Gate and then Gong Guan Road (now known as Jinling Road), then North Sichuan Road. Huaihai Road had not yet become fashionable.

After a while my family moved to San Pai Lou in Tou Sha Chang where we lived in a little alley, in a *shikumen*,[2] known as Shan De Li (Shande Terrace). There were three families there—we lived in No. 2. In No. 1 was the Ye family whose father was an itinerant salesman, while in No. 3 there lived a family named Wang from Anhui Province: he was a dealer in tea. I remember our house there with nostalgia because it was the only habitation in my whole life that I could call my home. When I was twelve my father's business failed and he fell ill and died soon after. Thus we lost the house. We were then compelled to live under the roofs of others and even at times had nowhere to stay. After that I entered the seminary, took instruction from my superiors and never had my own home—to this very day. During that time I even made my home in prison for 27 years and since then the Church has been my home. I remember that the house in Shan De Li had a small sky-lit courtyard where we could grow a few bonsai trees. It was also a space in which we could play. We played with marbles and kicked shuttlecocks. Behind the courtyard was a very square reception room, next to it a living room. Above the reception room was a small dining room. Above the living room was my father's study. My sister slept in the wing-room below. When I was old enough a bed was put above the reception room for me and I got a room to myself—my own universe. In the evening I could read many books, which in truth meant novels.

In the passage above, I have written of my warm feelings for No. 2 Shan De Li. In 1951, when I returned to China, I went back there to have a look. In 1982 when I was permitted to return to Shanghai, I went there once again. Nothing

---

2. A traditional style of housing that recreated the Chinese courtyard-style house in a constrained urban setting.

had changed; even the owner remembered me. In 2004 I went back one more time and found a building site where they planned to build a high-rise. Shan De Li had disappeared before my eyes, but its image remains stored in my heart.

In my childhood the place we visited most often was the old church and the school which was right next to the church. The church was in the Chinese city of Shanghai next to the City God Temple. To go to school at the church we had to go past the City God Temple, around which there was always a very lively scene with small shops or market stalls. My brother and I frequently went to the places that sold snacks such as grilled squid, sugar candies, etc. In those days the City God Temple was the playground of the ordinary people. Today the same area has become an expensive and high-class tourist destination.

The old church was really old. According to tradition it had been erected by Xu Guangqi's granddaughter. It was 400 years old, a real heritage building. The church was built in palace style, which could also be termed temple style. I liked that church a lot. Just as the church was old, so were the resident priests. I remember one named Ni who was 80 years old: his given name was Ximan (Simon). He sat throughout the mass, even during the consecration of the gifts. His successor was Jin Matao, also 80 years old. The old church had been through many turbulent times. When the Qing dynasty banned Christianity it had become a Taoist temple dedicated to Guandi, the god of war. After the Liberation in 1949 it was used as a school. The school moved away, but the old church has still not been returned to the Catholic Church. Let's hope this policy will change one day. In the Shanghai diocese several priests, including Bishop Aloysius Tsang (Zhang Jiashu) and myself, were all baptised in this church, which is of great historical significance.

My mother did not have much education, only studying at home with tutors. She never attended a regular school. She was a devout Catholic, taking us every day to attend mass. At home she directed us to say the rosary and our evening prayers. In those days we had two servants, but my mother would still cook supper for my father herself in the evening (he didn't come home for lunch). I remember that when she had some free time she would sew cotton shoes for her children or patch up our soles. I still remember when once my brother and I damaged shoes that she had just mended a few days earlier, she lost her temper and said: "I am not going to make shoes for you anymore; let's get leather shoes for you to wear." After that we never again wore cotton slippers made by her. I remember that every day a woman came to do my mother's hair (we called her 'hair-comb auntie'). I used to stand and watch. In those days hair was washed in a shampoo made by boiling water with the wood chips left by carpenters. What a contrast to today's foundation, powders, scents and the like—so many cosmetics.

My mother was hospitable. Whenever people came from the village she would welcome them warmly, always asking them to stay a few nights. On their departure she would always give them money or clothes. My brother and I always loved it when visitors came. Whenever guests came we would run and jump. My mother would say that we had got 'guest fever'. I remember once when my brother was chasing me I tripped up and struck the corner of the bed with great loss of blood, leaving a scar. Luckily the scar was hidden by my hair and didn't damage my looks. Whenever I would fight with my brother, my mother would say: "They are still immature; it'll be better when they grow up."

She always forgave us and never beat us.

2
Pudong

I was born in Shanghai, but because of my family background, have always spoken with a Pudong accent. As soon as I open my mouth people know that I am from Pudong. I should explain that Shanghai is divided into two districts by the Huangpu River—the east bank is known as Pudong and the west as Puxi. After the First Opium War (1839–42), Shanghai was opened to foreign residents. When the foreigners came they established their presence in the concession areas in Puxi, so that bank of the river developed very fast. Pudong remained agricultural, its residents mainly peasant farmers, its produce mainly paddy and cotton. The river acted as the divide between the two worlds: to the west, the Paris of the Orient; to the east, backward villages. When I was small and the Lantern Festival came around (on the 15th day of the Lunar New Year), I would run down our alley with my lantern, singing songs expressing wishes for a good harvest taught to me by my mother. We prayed for good harvests of both rice and cotton—reflecting the desires of the Pudong farmers.

In those days only a slip of land in Pudong called Lujiazui (opposite the Bund) was built-up at all. Here were found the British–American Tobacco Factory and some textile mills—that was all. There was no ferry across the river. If we wanted to go to Pudong, we had to crowd into a tiny sampan with about 20 people aboard and be rowed across the river. On the other side there were no paved roads, just a few narrow mud tracks known as *yang chang* (sheep's gut) roads. Naturally there were no motor vehicles, nor any horse carts, not even any rickshaws (which were pulled by humans)—there were only single-wheeled barrows on which three people could sit on each side while the driver puffed and grunted as he pushed the barrow slowly forwards.

Jin Family Village was about six kilometres from the river. Everyone in the village was a farmer, 80% with the surname Jin, the other 20% named Tang. The village didn't even have a shop. To buy things the villagers were dependent on itinerant peddlers who carried basic items such as oil, soy sauce, vinegar and salt as well as needles and thread. When the peddlers came they rang bells and shouted out calls that brought people out to buy things. Some people used eggs as currency. To buy anything significant people had to go a couple of kilometres to Yangjing township, so it seems that our village was quite underdeveloped. The people worked in the fields during the day and at night spun cotton or flax. Others wove a cloth that was very durable, using simple looms. After the foreigners came they brought in cotton piece goods and there was no longer a market for the country cloth.

For lighting there was of course no electricity, not even paraffin, nothing but rapeseed oil lamps, where the wick floated on a round plate, giving out very little light. In the novel *Rulin Waishi* (The Scholars),[1] a man, just before his death, sticks out two fingers to let his wife know that using two wicks was too wasteful—one was enough. In those days material life was pretty simple in Pudong, but the Catholic Church was very developed, with churches every couple of kilometres and next to them presbyteries known as *yang fang*. Our village church had been the cathedral and next to the modern church was a smaller church that we called 'old church'. It was the old church that had been the cathedral, while the bigger church had been built later, when the bishop still lived in Jin Family Village. Several times when it had been damaged, the faithful had raised funds to have it rebuilt. In those days every church had nuns or consecrated virgins looking after it. There were no Chinese religious orders so chaste women took an oath of virginity to serve the Church. The priests had to look after several parishes, for example the Jin Family Village priest was responsible for about ten parishes including Xiaotangkou, Yangsiqiao, Yanjiaqiao, Jiegouwan, Tangjiahong, Nanhuang, etc. The priests toured the parishes and the consecrated virgins managed everything. The consecrated virgins served the Church with total commitment, taking no salary, working as volunteers, doing handicrafts to support themselves; sacrificing their lives for the Church. They have made a huge contribution to the Shanghai diocese and the Church should never forget them.

In those days Pudong parishioners had good reason to be proud of themselves. Pudong produced many priests and even more nuns. Pudong's parishioners considered, even in the 1920s, that they could form their own diocese. They joined together to write a letter to Rome to petition the Pope to form a

---

1. 儒林外史 (Rulin Waishi), or *The Scholars*, by 吴敬梓 (Wu Jingzi), completed 1750.

Pudong diocese, with a Pudong priest as bishop. This issue irritated the then French Bishop of Shanghai, so he ensured that the letter never received a reply from Rome and instead was passed to him to handle. When he saw the letter, the bishop was very angry and called in several of the leading signatories of the letter for a dressing-down. He furthermore required them to make a public confession, saying that they had sinned, or else he would excommunicate them.

The Lord works in mysterious ways, so that after the Liberation in 1949, the first Bishop of Shanghai was the Chuansha, Pudong native Gong Pinmei (1901–2000). After Gong Pinmei was arrested, the acting bishop was Zhang Shiliang, a native of Zhangjialou in Pudong. Later on another Pudong native, Rev. Aloysius Tsang, became bishop and he was succeeded by me. Thus did the Lord make allowance for the desire of the Pudong faithful for a Pudong bishop. The sad thing is that the Church is not well established in Pudong today and very few Pudong people study for the priesthood. Today only a few aged Pudong priests survive, with just a single young one named Huang Zhenping. I have prayed to the Lord to permit the Catholic Church to revive in Pudong and to change the current situation where there are so many old people, but so few young people, let alone children.

When I was a child, Pudong was not only economically under-developed, but Pudong people were also less well educated, with many being illiterate. In the 1920s the Chinese government did a survey and found that among the counties of China with the highest rate of illiteracy was Nanhui in Pudong. The lowest rate of illiteracy in the nation was at Yancheng in northern Jiangsu Province. Pudong people not only farmed but also did handicrafts. Many were tailors, cooks, carpenters—very few were white-collar workers. Pudong also had very few famous people—the most famous among them was Zhang Wentian (aka Lo Fu, 1900–76), who was at one time general secretary of the Chinese Communist party, making a great contribution to the Chinese revolution. He never struggled for power or personal benefit; he was an admirable revolutionary, worthy of the respect of later generations.

When I was a child, my father and grandfather both worked for foreign companies and were thus influenced by colonialism. In those days the Manchus had just been overthrown and the 1911 rebellion had only just succeeded when Yuan Shikai seized power and feudalism once again controlled the people's minds. Radio and television had not been invented. In the house there were one or two magazines and a subscription to *Shen Bao* (Shanghai News). In the church school there was no politics class and no class on patriotism, so people's minds were politically unenlightened. As a child, all I knew of the affairs of the world was gained from overhearing snippets of conversation between my father and his friends, which I committed to memory without fully comprehending. In those days the country was divided by warfare and the people were oppressed. My father and his friends discussed the warlords after dinner, condemning them as running dogs of the imperialists. They only respected Marshal Wu Peifu (1874–1939), saying that he was uncorrupted, without any personal assets; that he was a patriot; that all the other warlords had bought houses in the Tianjin foreign concession so that when they were overthrown they could hide in the concession under the protection of the imperialists. Only Wu Peifu had never entered the foreign concessions. They did not like the warlord Feng Yuxiang (1882–1948), saying that had Feng not opposed him, Wu Peifu could have taken control of the whole country. Later on events proved that Wu was a patriot. When Japan invaded China and conquered the north, many politicians became traitors. The Japanese invited Wu many times to join the puppet government, but Wu resolutely refused and requested that the Japanese leave China, including the three north-eastern provinces. In the end he was assassinated by the Japanese. When I was a child I heard this news and remember it to this day, reminding me of my family's influence on my thinking.

3
Going to School

At the age of six I went first to a girls' school to do my basic education. There were two female teachers, one named Shou, the other Gu, who were both very patient. I remember one of my fellow students was a girl named Xu, who came from a wealthy family and was very well mannered. She later became a nun and entered the Congregation of the Presentation of Our Lady to the Temple. She says that she never forgot me.

In the second year I transferred to a boys' school. I remember only two teachers, named Zhu and Hu. Because we went to mass every day I had to eat my breakfast and lunch at the church. Another student named Ni Linxiang, who lived at Dongjiadu and attended the elementary school at the old Catholic church because of the influence of his great-uncle Rev. Simon Ni who was the pastor of that parish, also took his breakfast and lunch at the church. My deskmate was the grandson of Mr. Du Zishan, who was responsible for renting out the diocesan properties in the Old City. Later on Ni Linxiang and I entered St. Ignatius College at the same time, graduated in the same year (1932) and went together to the minor and major seminaries. Later on he contracted tuberculosis and died an early death. His niece Ni Yao married a cousin of mine named Wu Zuxiang, with whom I have remained in touch.

On the subject of life at elementary school I have few memories, apart from Teacher Zhu who used to walk about while we were studying calligraphy and grab our writing brushes from behind. If he could take them from us, he happily taught us a lesson. On the rare occasions when he could not remove the brush, he would praise us for holding it firmly. I also remember writing my essays with some precocity, always beginning with phrases such as "Into this world a human being was born" that had rather an adult tone.

I also remember on one occasion my brother and I made a plan to play hooky on the way to school. We at once returned home and told my mother that the school had closed temporarily and my mother believed us. Who could have expected that after dinner Teacher Zhu would come to our home, worried that we two brothers had been prevented from going to school by some accident or illness? As soon as he arrived my mother knew that we had skipped school and had lied about it. Once my parents had seen the teacher to the door, my father became angry and told us to kneel on the floor. He picked up the badminton racquet, threatening to beat me. He said that I was the elder brother so I must have led my younger brother astray. Fortunately my mother used words to dissuade him. Naturally we never tried to skip school again.

At the age of ten my father sent me to board at the elementary school of St. Ignatius College. This school was very strict. After the beginning of term there was no vacation and we could not go home. I still remember that after I had been enrolled for about a month my mother came to see me. She went to the headmaster, a foreigner named Rev. Yves Henry. The headmaster called me to his office and said that my mother had come to collect me to attend my grandfather's 70th birthday and that he permitted me to go. Later on my mother told me: "That was very first time I saw a foreigner with such a long beard. I was very scared of him." My mother also told me: "Today I told a lie for the first time. It was because I missed you, wanted to see you, couldn't manage without you and wanted to bring you home for a couple of days. So I told him that your grandfather was celebrating his 70th birthday, which is in fact an untruth. This is the first time I have told a lie in my life." Young children are not very aware, so I was of course happy just to get some time at home. Now that I think about it, I realise that my mother truly loved me. She was a very good person. She never told lies; but on this occasion, for my sake, she told a lie. I am very moved by this thought.

4
The Chinese Catholic Church in Those Days

The Shanghai Catholic diocese was a missionary district of the province of Paris of the French Society of Jesus. In Shanghai the Jesuits set up many charitable and educational activities, including middle schools, universities and so on. Their main geographical area of activity was the French concession.

In those days Shanghai had concession areas. The notion of 'concession' is not well understood among Chinese today. When I was a child and a young man, I lived in the concession. The so-called concession was a piece of national territory that was ceded by our government, under the intense pressure of foreign imperialism, through the signing of unequal treaties, to a given foreign country to constitute a state within a state. In the concession, the administration, security, taxes, financial administration and legal system were all run by foreigners. Those Chinese who lived in the concession were obliged to pay taxes to that country and obey the laws of that country. The police were nationals of that country, with most policemen being sent from their colonial possessions. For example many policemen in the French concession were Annamites (Vietnamese), while in the British concession the policemen were Sikhs from India. Although they were from colonised countries, they despised us Chinese. The concessions were a humiliation to the Chinese. The French concession stretched from the Huangpu River, with Renmin Lu as the southern boundary and Edward VII Avenue (today's Yan'an Lu) as the northern boundary, all the way to Xujiahui. From the north side of Yan'an Lu to the north shore of the Suzhou Creek was the British concession. Hongkou District was controlled by the Japanese, while Yangshupu District was the American concession. Later on two of these concessions merged to become known as the International Settlement, but the French concession remained French, with French administration, while the International Settlement was run by the British, Americans and the Japanese.

In those days the Catholic Church operated mainly in the French concession and did not allow in any other churches. In those times the Shanghai faithful had a branch of Action Catholique. This society was very well organised. It was led by Lu Bohong and Zhu Zhixiao, among others. They set up charitable activities such as schools, missions, etc., but the Catholic bishop did not permit them to operate in the French concession. Action Catholique's activities such as St. Joseph's Hospice and Yixin Middle School were in the Chinese city. They also opened hospitals, all outside the French concession. In Yangshupu District there was the Sacred Heart Hospital, in Beiqiao the Puci Rehabilitation Centre—a specialised mental health centre. In Zhabei District was the Sacred Heart of Mary Hospital and, in Songjiang County, the St. Joseph Hospital, among others. Nonetheless, the Society was not allowed to operate in the French concession, which was reserved for Frenchmen. Mr. Lu Bohong noted that at the French concession's St. Ignatius College lessons were taught only in French and that English was becoming more important in Shanghai, so, when on a trip to the United States, he invited the California Jesuits to come to Shanghai to set up a middle school, thus angering the French bishop, who opposed the plan. Mr. Lu immediately travelled in person to Rome to petition the Pope, who authorised the plan so that the French Jesuits in Shanghai could resist no longer. Nonetheless they insisted that the school be located in the International Settlement, where it was established with the name Jinke Middle School.

In those days the whole Chinese Catholic Church was divided up according to the missionary countries and orders. Thus, what was then known as Jiangnan Province belonged to the French Jesuits. Later on Jiangnan was divided into Jiangsu and Anhui Provinces with Jiangsu still in the hands of the French Jesuits and Anhui given to the Spanish Jesuits. The southern half of Hebei Province also belonged to the Jesuits with Xianxian given to the French, Daming County to the Hungarians and Jing County to the Austrians. Inner Mongolia was the territory of the Belgian Scheuts. Most of Shandong Province belonged to the Germans. Since the Americans arrived late, they got the Jiangmen diocese as well as Meixian County in Guangdong Province. The Lazarist order came early on and so had Beijing, Tianjin, the northern half of Hebei Province, and Zhejiang and Jiangxi Provinces. The Franciscans were partly in Shandong and partly in Shanxi. The French Paris Overseas Mission was allocated north-east China and the provinces of Sichuan, Guangdong and Guizhou. The Augustinians were in Hunan Province. The Irish Columban

Missionary Society was in Hanyang (Hubei Province) and Nanchang (Jiangxi Province). The Divine Word Missionaries arrived rather late in the day and so got the provinces of Shandong, Henan and Gansu as their territory.

The Chinese missionary districts were divided up by missionary orders. Thus, Church affairs were governed by each order, with decision-making outside China. Every nation put the needs of its own citizens first and gave them the administration of each diocese. The French government used the Defender of the Faith status granted by the Pope to interfere even more. The Chinese Catholic Church was not in the hands of the Chinese people. There was no overall planning, as each missionary society administered its own affairs, so that efficiency in spreading the Gospel was compromised. Pope Benedict XV tried to rectify this situation and issued the papal letter *Maximum Illud* in 1919, emphasising that the main role of the missions was to cultivate the clergy of every nation and to ensure that the native people could eventually assume the administration of the Church in their lands. The response of the bishops in China to this letter was glacial, both holding up and preventing the dissemination of the letter. Only the Bishop of Jiangchang in Sichuan, Monsignor de Guebriant (1860–1935) gave an enthusiastic response so that the Pope made him apostolic visitor to the Church in China and he was called to Rome to make his report. As a result the Pope decided to send a permanent representative to China, which led to the translation of *Maximum Illud* into Chinese by Ma Xiangbo and its dissemination.

5
St. Ignatius College (1926–32)

In September 1926 I entered the elementary section of St. Ignatius College (later registered as Xuhui Middle School by the KMT[1] Bureau of Education). The principal of the elementary school was Rev. Aloysius Tsang S.J. He was later dean of my high school and eventually Bishop of Shanghai when I returned to the city after my long stint in prison. Thus he witnessed all the major turning points of my life. In those days school discipline was very strict.

In 1927 when the KMT Northern Expedition reached Shanghai, the school was temporarily closed and the students sent home—and from that moment my luck began to change. On Saturday 8 April my mother felt unwell and took to her bed. In fact she had had a brain haemorrhage and after a while became paralysed on one side and could no longer speak clearly. My father sought the opinion of a Chinese doctor and he gave her a few injections. On Sunday he came to see her again and said that she was a bit better. On Monday morning he said that she was on the mend. My father then sent me to the church to ask the priest to say a mass for my mother, but when I returned to the house all I could hear inside was moaning and crying so I knew my mother had died. I had not been able to be present at the time of her death.

A year later, while I was at school, my father came to see me, bearing a box of chocolate candies. Apparently my father had had a setback in business and had been obliged to sell his home in the village and all his rosewood furniture. He said that he wanted to go far away and not return for several years. So he left enough money to permit me to finish my middle school studies at St. Ignatius College. My mother died on 10 April 1927, when I was not yet 11 years old. On this day I was also to lose my father. My father patted me on the head and went

---

1. The KMT or Kuomintang ruled China from 1928 to 1949.

away. I stood there like a wooden statue watching his back slowly disappear. Then I returned alone to the study room and lowered my head to hide my tear-filled eyes.

In this manner my childhood days came to an end—so brief, a mere ten years more or less. Nonetheless my mother's deep respect for God, her warm and affectionate character, as well as my father's reticence and generosity have left a deep impression on me.

When it came to the vacation, the other students went home, but I had none to return to, so remained alone at school. When my family had been prosperous, relatives frequently came with food to visit me; after my father's bankruptcy nobody ever came again. After one year, my father reappeared. He had found new work, but not as good as before, with a lower salary. He lodged at the company, leaving me, my sister and younger brother at the school. When it came to the winter and summer holidays he rented a room at an inn and had my brother and me stay there. The inn provided food and once a week we would go to see my father at the company to collect our pocket money.

Then in 1931 my father got ill with pneumonia. Today this disease is not so serious and can be cured with an injection of penicillin, but in those days there was no effective medicine. He first went to what was in those days called St. Mary Hospital, but when they could not cure him he discharged himself and lived for a while with my maternal grandfather and consulted a doctor of Chinese medicine. I knew that my father was gravely ill and asked Rev. Tsang for furlough to be able to visit my father, but he would not permit me to go. Later on that day, just as I was about to go to bed, Tsang suddenly let me go because my aunt's husband had arrived to tell me that my father was critically ill. He took me to my grandfather's house where I found my father had already died. I had not been able to attend the deathbed of either of my parents, a source of unremitting grief. After one day we asked our vicar Rev. Baumer to do the obsequies. There was a photograph of my father hanging on the wall, but the priest said this was not permitted and ordered us to take it down, saying it was contrary to the regulations of Rome. Truly bizarre!

That was 11 April 1931 and on that day my siblings and I became orphans. When my father died he left us some money, but not much. I remember that my grandfather borrowed 2,000 yuan from my sister and that my aunt's husband and my maternal uncle told my sister: "If you put your money in the bank the interest will be very little. Give it to us and we will invest it for high interest." I remember my sister took 3,300 yuan from the bank and handed it over to these men. Who could have guessed that they would take the money straight to the casino and gamble it away? Thus, instead of low interest, we lost all our capital. Many years later, another aunt told me that when my father was dying, she took advantage of the chaos to take 1,000 yuan. In 1945, on the eve of my admission to the priesthood, my older uncle came to me saying that my father had left 4,000 yuan with him for safekeeping. At the time he had feared that I would waste it and so had held it back. He said: "In those days you were all young. Four thousand yuan in 1931 money is only worth 2,000 yuan today, which is what I return to you." He also said that in 1931, 4,000 yuan could buy 800 tables of wine that would stretch all the way from the Huangpu River to Jin Family Village. In 1945, 2,000 yuan could at most buy you a rickshaw ride up and down Sichuan Road. "So we are settled," he said. My aunt sought out my sister and said to her: "In your home are buried two ingots of gold that your grandfather gave to me and are not yours." My sister and she went together to dig under the bed and found the ingots, which my aunt took with her. After which my sister said to me: "If the gold had been given to her, how come she didn't come to fetch it while father was still alive?" I said: "Why are our relatives all so heartless?" In this manner we became as poor as church mice. My sister had to abandon her studies, our house was gone and we had no money left at all.

6
Great-Uncle Jin Fushan

At this time one of my great-uncles Jin Fushan appeared on the scene. He was similar to my own grandfather in that he had opened a joint-stock company supplying food to foreigners. The company was known as Tong Mao, or Dombay & Son in English. It was a large and prosperous concern. He was always open and generous in spirit, once making a large donation for scholarships at St. Ignatius College in order to assist those children whose families had fallen on hard times. He was also truly God-fearing, belonging to Action Catholique and spending his vacations proselytising in the suburbs. He felt pity for us three orphans and told us: "Come and live with me." So we went and he treated us as if we were his own children. We had a safe refuge for which I am grateful to this day. When, during the mass, I remember the dead, I always think of him and his two daughters who raised us. One was named Jin Yingxiu, a nun of the Presentation of Our Lady to the Temple, who had at one time been headmistress of Fangde Middle School; the other was called Jin Dexin—she never married and raised the two small children her deceased younger sister Jin Huixiu had left behind.

When my sister was going through my father's papers she found an IOU for 600 yuan signed by a cousin of my father's. This man had opened a lumberyard in Yangjing village. My sister took the IOU and visited him to collect the money, but he chased her away. My sister told Jin Fushan, whereupon he asked his own lawyer to write a letter to chase the debt, with the result that the man immediately sent over 600 yuan. Jin Fushan saved the money for us so that we had a small amount of capital. Later on my sister was introduced to a job at the Cathay Mansion (now the Jinjiang Hotel) to manage a small library that provided books for the residents to read. It was an easy job with a monthly salary of 70 yuan, which was not bad at all. Thus she had yet more resources with which to look after us. My elder sister loved me very much. She always told me: "Big brother is good." She said that when I had become a priest she would enter the convent and become a nun.

In 1935 Jin Fushan went to Dachang to spread the Good News. After mass, when he had had breakfast and was walking to the car, a sudden gust of cold wind blew him to the ground. By the time they had taken him to hospital he was already dead and beyond resuscitation. He was only 53 years old. His saint's name was Joseph. I remember him every time I say mass. Such a good man as he must surely have already entered heaven in the eternal presence of the Trinity.

7
Two Elder Sisters

Lu Naying and Rong Dexian

My aunt was a nun in the Congregation of the Helpers of the Holy Souls and taught mathematics at Qiming Girls Middle School and Xuhui Girls Middle School. She had one favourite student named Lu Naying. After my father's death my aunt very much wanted to help me, so she summoned Lu Naying and told her: "My favourite nephew is now an orphan. Why don't you take him to be your younger brother and your mother can make him her godson." After Lu Naying went home and talked to her mother, she took me home to pay my respects to Mrs. Lu and to address her as 'mother' for the first time. Thereafter Lu Naying always watched out for me, visiting me at the seminary and making clothes for me up until the day I entered the Society of Jesus.

Lu Naying was born in 1908 and was christened Catherine and took the Chinese name Naying. Her father was named Lu Bohong with the saint's name Joseph. He was a famous businessman. He had been general manager of the Nanshi District Electricity Bureau and of the trolley bus company as well as of the water supply company and the Zhabei District Electricity Supply Company. Outside the foreign concessions he was responsible for all the electricity and water utilities. He had also set up the Hexing Steel Co. and the Datong Steamship Co., where he served as general manager. He was furthermore a great benefactor, overseeing the Xinpuyu Hall orphanage, old people's home and hospice which catered to more than 2,000 people. He set up the Puci Hospital especially for people with mental illnesses, helped set up the Sacred Heart of Jesus Hospital in Yangshupu District, the Sacred Mother Hospital in Zhabei and the Joseph Hospital in Songjiang County. He was also an educator, setting up the Dongjiadu Action Catholique Elementary School, the One Heart Middle School in the Chinese City and the Mingde Middle School in Jiaxing County. He also constructed the Yangshupu Girls Technical Middle School. Most outstanding was his deep Catholic faith, attending mass every day at the

Dongjiadu Road church. Whenever he passed a church he had to go in to pay his respects to the divine presence. In his car he had a copy of the *Imitation of Christ* from which he would read a passage whenever he had a free moment. At one point he was the chairman of Action Catholique in China and spent his vacations spreading the word in neighbouring counties and villages, constructing many churches. He was connected with many Shanghai hospitals where he would go after work to talk over the Catholic faith with the sick, encouraging them to be baptised. The Pope made him a papal knight. Unfortunately he was assassinated on 30 December 1937 during the Japanese invasion of east China.

After Lu Naying graduated from Xuhui Middle School, her father sent her to be headmistress of Mingde Girls Middle School, which he had set up and that was run by nuns. Lu Naying felt that her level of education was insufficient and asked to be permitted to continue her studies at university. But in those days the Bishop of Shanghai had ordered that any of the faithful who allowed their children to attend non-Catholic schools should be refused communion. This was a very big error since in those days there was no Catholic university for women. Aurora University did not yet accept female students. Families with girls in public education could not arrange for them to get higher education, which was very unfair. Lu Naying took up this cause and decided to challenge the unjust regulation. Her father, who was a committed believer, did not feel able to defy the bishop's instruction. So Lu Naying went on her own to visit the bishop and with the force of her argument obtained his consent. She matriculated at Suzhou Protestant University's law school and after four years' hard work obtained her degree. By this time the girls' school set up by her father was already in operation and she was named headmistress. In the same year the Japanese invaded our country. Shanghai was overrun by the enemy, her father was assassinated and Lu Naying, overcome with grief, went to Belgium to study sociology before returning to China to devote herself to education. During the 'Cultural Revolution' she was tortured to death. After Mao Zedong died and the Gang of Four was overthrown Lu Naying's reputation was rehabilitated. That such an exceptionally talented person was unable to fully demonstrate her abilities during her lifetime is a tragic thing.

My aunt, Sister Zhang Wangzhen also greatly liked one other female student named Rong Dexian. Rong and Lu Naying became close friends while studying at school in Xujiahui. Lu was older than Rong so they called each other 'older sister' and 'younger sister' respectively. They were also both friends with my elder sister. I met Rong at Lu's home. She was from Wuxi and her father Rong

Ziwei was a merchant in Shanghai. Rong Dexian first graduated from the Qiming Girls Middle School in Xujiahui and was then accepted into the trainee course at the Shanghai Commercial Bank established by Chen Guangfu (aka K.P. Chen 1880–1976). She was introduced to a husband from the Zhu family named Zhu Yisheng who had studied engineering in the United States.

While in America Zhu had met the young Maryknoll priest James Walsh (1891–1981) and had frequently been a guest in his home. Walsh was later posted to China where he worked as a missionary in the area of Meixian in Guangdong Province and later was made Bishop of Jiangmen. He returned to the US before the Pacific War broke out. In 1948, after Cardinal Spellman visited China, Walsh was left behind in China where the papal nuncio Archbishop Riberi established the Catholic Central Bureau (CCB) and appointed Walsh as secretary general to coordinate and direct all Catholic activities in China. The offices of the CCB were in Yueyang Road, Shanghai. In 1951 the Shanghai Military Committee ordered the CCB to cease all its activities in China and arrested several people. Walsh stayed in China, since by that time there were no longer any exit permits available. From then on his life became very difficult. Since Rong Dexian's husband Zhu Yisheng lived nearby on Yongjia Road, he frequently took food and visited Walsh; these actions drew the attention of the authorities. In 1958 the People's Government arrested Walsh on charges of espionage. At the same time they arrested Zhu as Walsh's contact and put him in Tilanqiao Prison. Zhu was later seen in prison by Rev. Jiang Weilin, who had been sentenced to reform through labour. Walsh was sentenced to 20 years in prison and only released on the eve of President Nixon's visit to China in 1972. As for Zhu Yisheng, he died in prison.

Zhu Yisheng's father Zhu Shishao was in business the equal of Lu Bohong. He established the Hengtong Textile Works, the Qiuxin Shipyard, the Hezhong Wharf and Warehouse Company, etc. He was also a philanthropist and the people who benefitted from his generosity throughout his life are beyond counting. On one occasion Zhu Shishao made a large sum selling a piece of land in Pudong and immediately gave it to the Church and to charitable organisations, saying to his children at the time: "I've bought you a big house in heaven." He was a model Christian, using all his resources to support the Shanghai Church and his brother, Bishop Zhu Kaimin (aka Most Reverend Simon Chu) of the Haimen Church, and other dioceses. He also acted as deputy head of the Shanghai Action Catholique. The Vatican made him a papal knight. He died in 1955 aged 93. People as dedicated as him should be counted among the saints.

Rong Dexian and Zhu Yisheng had one son and five daughters. Their son, named Zhu Enrong, asked permission to enter the seminary and his mother allowed him to become a Jesuit. Later he became a priest and did youth work in Taiwan where he earned the love of his students. The respect for God of this couple and their love for humankind left a deep impression on me.

In those days going to school wasn't as tough as it is today. We had less homework and lots of time for leisure. I have a good memory, so when the teachers required us to learn our lessons by heart, I simply read them through three times and could recite them. It didn't take me much time and I was able to spend the rest of my time reading novels, classic and modern, both Chinese and foreign, such as *Outlaws of the Marsh*, *Romance of the Three Kingdoms*, *The Scholars* by Wu Jingzi, *Tales of the Sui and Tang* by Zhu Renhu, *Jinghua Yuan* by Li Ruzhen, *Qixia Wuyi* and *Xiao Wuyi* (Judge Bao stories), *The Cases of Judge Peng* by Tanmeng Daoren, *The Cases of Judge Shi*, *Sherlock Holmes* and *Robinson Crusoe*. Many of the foreign novels had been translated into Chinese by Lin Shu (1852–1924). I also read new writers such as Hu Shi, Lu Xun, Mao Dun, Ba Jin, Lao She, Cao Yu, Bing Xin, Ding Ling, etc., etc. I also read the *Shanghai Weekly* edited by Zou Taofen (1895–1944) and read many books published by the Kaiming bookstore and Beixin bookstore. Every term I bought a large shelf of books.

St. Ignatius College had been established by French missionaries and the language of instruction was French. In the upper school, apart from classical Chinese, all classes including maths, physics and chemistry were taught in French. The native Chinese teachers taught in French. Even geography was taught by a Frenchman in French, using French textbooks. This method of teaching is unimaginable today and can be described as a typically colonial form of education. Whichever way you look at it, I learnt French and could read French novels in their original language by the time I graduated from high school.

In the summer of 1932 I needed to consider the pressing question of what I would do next in my life.

Part II

Seminary Life

8
Seminary of the Sacred Heart of Jesus (1932–35)

In 1932 I graduated from St. Ignatius College in Xujiahui and took the entrance examination for Aurora University, matriculating the same year. The school arranged a retreat to practise the spiritual exercises of St. Ignatius before our graduation. Part of this involved a subject for meditation called 'two opposing flags' in which the forces of Lord Jesus battle those of the Devil. The former force desires to establish peace and save humankind, whereas the latter spreads hatred and chaos. Jesus needs our support to complete his plan for humankind. My spirit was moved and I decided to follow Jesus and become his soldier.

When I was very small I had looked forward to mass and played at being a priest after we got home, cutting up newspapers to make vestments and teaching my younger brother how to serve. My mother encouraged me and often said that she would raise me to be a priest. She even took such steps as only taking my younger brother to attend the weddings of relatives. She left me behind, saying that I should strive with all my strength to become a priest. When I grew up I realised that the intention to join the priesthood had stayed with me.

On 3 September 1932 I entered the Sacred Heart Seminary. This decision had a lot to do with the teaching I had received as a child. There were 22 other students who entered the seminary at the same time. It was said that there had never been so many young men wanting to study for the priesthood. Out of the twenty-two, ten became priests, six remained laymen and six died early of illness.

The Sacred Heart Seminary was in fact a juvenate college. Apart from theology the main course was Latin, with two classes in the morning and two in the afternoon. We also studied Chinese classical literature, Church history, Church liturgy, Church music, etc. First year Latin was taught by Mr. Huang Jiang—he taught the introductory course and was a pedant. The second year teacher, a Frenchman named Rev. A. Durand, was concurrently rector of the seminary. We focused on the works of Cicero and Julius Caesar. In the third year we were taught by Rev. Gandon who stressed the works of Tacitus the historian and Virgil's *Georgics*. Gandon was the famous head of the foreign section of the Xuhui Library. He frequently introduced us to books recently published in Europe, especially France, and even bought them for us.

Rev. Durand, as the rector, was responsible for both our studies and our well-being. He was a generous, kind and thoughtful person. His hobby was music, which he also taught us. He was especially kind to me, but I let him down, since, as my singing voice was sonorous, he thought that I was good material for music studies, but it turned out that although I had a good voice I did not have a good ear and could not distinguish the five tones—so he had to abandon his attempts to teach me. During music lessons he would tell me to stand in the very back row, not letting me open my mouth and thereby preventing me from causing any disruption.

The seminary had a very large garden and an exercise area. Next to the Sacred Heart Seminary was the Hu Shi Elementary School. Durand chose about twenty students from among the elementary school kids and organised a choral class. Every day after school he would invite them over to the seminary to learn hymns and sacred music. Since elementary school kids in those days had no homework to do, they were happy to come and play at the seminary. He also organised an association of young Catholics, inviting youths from the Tushanwan arts and crafts workshop as well as young men from a couple of other small factories nearby to come and play football and chess on Sunday after attending mass. He also offered them small snacks. Rev. Durand was a very generous person. He asked me to look after these young Catholics. Before his birthday we would select a few songs to practise and perform them to celebrate the day. When we were practising he heard our weak points from his office and came downstairs saying: "I'd better teach you myself." He thus conducted us and on his birthday smiled with satisfaction at our performance.

Every Sunday evening Rev. Durand would teach us religious studies; he emphasised that we should acquire the three S's. These were *sanctitas, scientia* and *sanitas*. He said that of these we should stress *sanctitas* because we had joined the seminary in order to develop *sanctitas* and to become saints—that would be our lifelong quest. Health and learning should support each other since only a healthy body can support an active mind: *mens sana in corpore sano*. He often repeated that the three S's should be engraved on our hearts.

Rev. Durand was a truly sincere and kind elder, but he had no real power, being totally subject to the orders of Rev. Yves Henry S.J. Rev. Henry was the rector of St. Ignatius College for the duration of my schoolboy years, and then became the rector of my seminary, later on becoming father superior of the Jesuits and auxiliary bishop of the Shanghai diocese for nine years and finally capitular vicar of Shanghai for two years. Thus he spent many years in senior positions in the Shanghai diocese.

On 9 September 1934 my elder sister Mary became sick. She had been teaching at the Congregation of the Helpers of the Holy Souls Qian De Elementary School. She had a high fever. I rushed to see her and called a taxi to take her to Sacred Heart Hospital. I stayed half a day talking to her before returning to the seminary. The next day the hospital called me in the morning to tell me that my sister had already died. In a bizarre manner she died on her birthday, the eve of her saint's day. It must have been the Virgin Mary who called her to heaven on her 21st birthday. When my sister died I was not even able to send her off. Her death was crushingly sad to me. How could such a clever and beautiful woman die so suddenly? I felt that the things of this earth were both empty and meaningless. There was nothing worth pursuing and nothing worth yearning for.

I was left with my younger brother Dayi, who had been clever and handsome from birth. After our parents died there was no one to look after him; he chose unsuitable friends and pursued leisure activities, becoming an habitué of the pleasure quarters. He didn't follow the rules of St. Ignatius College so the headmaster Rev. Aloysius Tsang called me over to tell me that he was expelling my brother. I then arranged for him to board at the middle school of Aurora University, but after a few months the headmaster sought me out to tell me that my brother was being disruptive and would be expelled.

I then helped him find work, but after a few days he resigned and didn't go back to work. He didn't come to see me. I enquired everywhere, but could not discover what had become of him. It was as if he had disappeared in a puff of smoke. I had thus suffered the loss of a father, a mother and a sister, and my brother was lost without trace. One after another they were taken away—my fate was truly bitter.

I thus became an orphan without any close relatives. Uncles, aunts and grandparents had all taken advantage of us. Our great-uncle Jin Fushan had extended a helping hand to us, but shortly afterwards had a stroke and died. I was at this time as poor as dirt, totally alone in the world. Thus, when the time came for the seminary to break up for the summer vacation, where in the whole wide world would I find a place to rest? All I could do was to seek a bed for a couple of days, first with this friendly roommate and then with that one. When my family had been prosperous many relatives flocked around, but now they displayed a different demeanour. Those cousins who had come regularly would now pretend not to see me when they met me in the street. This fact made a huge impact on me, giving me the impression that the world was a cold place. As the saying goes: 'If you are rich in the mountains, people will come from afar; but if you are poor in the city, no one will ask after you.' Later on the fictional narrative that gave me most pleasure was the part in the novel *The Scholars* about Fan Jin.[1]

When I look back on my life, I realise that on every occasion when people wrote me off, at that time the Lord sent well-intentioned people to assist me, allowing me to be saved in the nick of time. I firmly believe that all the poverty of my childhood, the challenges of my youth and many troubles such as our lack of money were blessings from the Lord. They made it easier for me to empathise with the poor and inspired me to do something for the disadvantaged and make friends among the poor. Even if life brings many hurtful experiences, these can also help one to see things more clearly.

My parents' coffins were buried in the Jin Family Village in Pudong, while my sister was buried in a public graveyard set up by Catholics in Qibao, west of Shanghai. In 1951, when I came back from Europe, I moved my parents' and sister's bodies to the Catholic graveyard at Xiyan, to a plot purchased by my friend Rong Dexian. When I was arrested, the Public Security Bureau confiscated all my possessions including the photographs of my parents and my sister. In 1982 I returned to Shanghai and planned to visit the tomb, but people told me that the Xiyan cemetery had been turned into a wild-animal park. My family's tombs had disappeared; even their bodies were not to be found. When I applied to the Public Security Bureau for the return of my belongings, they explained that during the so-called 'Cultural Revolution', the Bureau had been taken over by Red Guards and its records had been dispersed—thus my belongings could not be located. In this way the people I loved most truly disappeared and I became the most bereft person in the world. By my side I have only one photograph of my sister (the one that was printed on her ID card) that

---

1. A fictional character universally despised by his fellows until his unexpected success in the Imperial Examinations, whereupon he became the cynosure of all and sundry.

I had sent to friends overseas before I was arrested and that was returned to me after I was released from prison.

At the time when my sister was dying, apart from Lu Naying, Rong Dexian also came to see me and said: "I'll be your elder sister and look after you the way your sister did." She stood by her words and at great risk to herself helped me out at the time of my greatest difficulties. When my family had deserted me, these two friends were faithful. As long as I live I'll never forget Lu Naying and Rong Dexian—as well as one German family that I met later on.

9
Seminary of the Sacred Heart of Mary (1935–37)

In August 1935 I entered the Seminary of the Sacred Heart of Mary. At this time the various seminaries had become independent of the administration of Rev. Henry and had obtained their own rector, Rev. Felix Maumus. He was more kindly than Rev. Henry, as well as gifted in many areas. As soon as he graduated from the seminary he was invited by the committee to teach theology there. He was also the chief accountant for the diocese, looking after the finances. Later on he was posted to be pastor of St. Joseph's parish in Sichuan South Road for 24 years. He was very abstemious and greatly loved by the faithful. He was appointed to supervise construction of the Datong Road church dedicated to St. Thérèse of Lisieux and the associated elementary and middle schools for girls and boys. He supervised every aspect of the design and construction and thought that he would become parish priest; but when the church was finished the bishop transferred diocesan priests to run the parish and Rev. Maumus was sent back to the seminary to become rector and to teach philosophy. He spent much of his spare time on the construction of an organ. He was a musician, able to both compose and design instruments. Organs are very difficult to build. He was a theologian, an economist, an architect and a musician. Had he not spread his talents but focused on one activity he would surely have had even greater success.

The Sacred Heart of Mary Seminary was also known as the major seminary. The seminarians first studied philosophy for two years, then did practical work known as regency in a parish for one year, then studied four years of theology. Theology was taught by Rev. Payen, a moralist and a specialist in matrimony; also by Rev. de la Serviere, who was also a specialist in history and had written a history of the Jiangnan missions. Both men were French. At various times there were also two Spaniards, Rev. Nieto and Rev. Valcacel, who taught psychology and theology. Philosophy was taught by Rev. Andre and by Rector Maumus, also by Rev. Henry and by two other Chinese priests: Rev. Thaddeus Tsang taught sociology and Rev. Berchmans Tsang (Zhang Weipin) taught Catholic history.

In 1931 Mgr. Haouisée succeeded Mgr. Prosper Paris S.J. as bishop of the Shanghai diocese, while Rev. Peter Lefebvre succeeded Rev. Eugene Beauce as the father superior of the Shanghai Society of Jesus and as auxiliary bishop of Shanghai. The two men worked well together, committing themselves to raise proselytisation in the Shanghai diocese to a new level. They felt that it was most important to train human resources. Thus apart from Rev. Wu Yingfeng and Rev. Wang Changzhi, who were already studying in France, they sent the Jesuits Zhang Boda (aka Rev. Beda Chang) and Chen Yuntang to Britain to study philosophy, then arranged for them to continue their studies at the Sorbonne, the former in literature, the latter in mathematics. Lefebvre and Haouisée also sent the diocesan priests Thaddeus Tsang and Berchmans Tsang to Rome and Paris respectively, one to study sociology, the other Church history. Furthermore they sent Qian Baosen as a seminarian to Rome to attend the University of the Congregation for the Propagation of the Faith. They said that these men would set up a Catholic publishing house on their return to China. Lefebvre decided to turn the Xuhui Book Repository into a modern-style research library. Their basic aim was to bring about a cultural renaissance. Haouisée and Lefebvre both wanted to change the original policy concerning proselytisation, which had only Chinese priests working in the suburbs and the city reserved for Jesuits, especially French Jesuits. In 1933 Haouisée and Lefebvre decided to turn the cathedral of the Shanghai diocese, Dongjiadu Road church, which was an important centre of Church activities, over to the Chinese priests, naming Rev. Zhang Boze as rector. The Society of Jesus withdrew and the school adjacent to the church, Fangde Girls Middle School, was given to the Chinese sisters of the Congregation of the Presentation of Our Lady to the Temple to manage. They also handed over the newly-built Saint Thérèse of Lisieux church in the city centre to Chinese priests, thus bringing about a dynamic new atmosphere in the Shanghai diocese.

But then after only a short time the prospects changed. Lefebvre's six-year term was up and he was transferred to Yangzhou as vicar general, and the previously described Henry took over as father superior of the Society of Jesus in Shanghai. At this time the Japanese invaded our country and Shanghai fell into enemy hands. Henry brought to a halt the publication of national Catholic magazines; moved Wu Yongfeng, who had returned from his studies in the

United States, to work in Subei; moved Thaddeus Tsang from Aurora University to a parish in Zhangjin; moved Berchmans Tsang from the seminary to be principal of the Panshi Elementary School in South Chongqing Road; and prevented Wang Changzhi from teaching theology and made him teach Chinese to the Jesuit juvenate students. The Shanghai diocese took a big step backwards. This view is of course based on my hindsight. Henry was father superior of the Society of Jesus for nine years and then, after Haouisée died, also became capitular vicar of Shanghai. He ran the diocese for a total of eleven years.

During my two years at the seminary, apart from studying philosophy, on Sundays I organised a Catholic youth group for Xujiahui parish. This was supported by Rev. Yang Weishi, principal of Huishi Elementary School, who allowed us to use his unused assembly hall as our gathering place. About 40 young people from different professions came along. Every Sunday I gave them a sermon and organised their participation and various entertainment activities.

One day Rev. Felix Maumus came to talk to me. He had been reading all our letters to outsiders. He was well educated in Chinese and was responsible for authorising our contact with visitors. He said to me that Lu Naying came to see me often and that we had exchanged many letters. He was considering how to deal with this. He also said that if things went on like this it would impact my seminary studies. He asked me to think about it carefully. I explained to Maumus that Lu Naying treated me as her impoverished younger brother, while as her cadet I was grateful to her and respected her. Since her family was so prosperous I had never harboured any other intentions. Maumus told me that according to custom it was time to involve a matchmaker. When he said this I was greatly surprised and thought back over my time at Sacred Heart Seminary and the times when Lu Naying had come to see me. Rev. Durand had warned Lu not to bother me, but Lu had not told me this, so that I only found out from the gatekeeper Old Gu. When I asked Durand and Maumus for their opinion, they said that I should only tell Lu that I now had more homework and could no longer correspond with her. Lu was no fool and came no more to the seminary, but never ceased treating me as if she were my elder sister. So in my heart I have always regarded her with great respect.

10
St. Ignatius College (1937–38)

There were no newspapers to read at the seminary and at that time China had no wireless broadcasts to listen to. All correspondence was inspected by the foreign priests, so we were cut off from the world; our education was entirely circumscribed and our sole sources of information were visiting friends and relatives, and old newspapers and magazines that we read at home during the holidays.

The priest responsible for our Chinese studies was Xu Zongze, while a professor from an external university named Zhu Tingfan was invited to give two classes a week. Our director of studies asked him to provide us with some news of China and abroad before starting our formal coursework. From him we had revealed to us certain significant events from both home and abroad, such as that Chiang Kai-shek was not fighting the Japanese and was thus losing the support of the populace. Professor Zhu was full of negative feelings for Chiang. Zhu wrote good calligraphy so that many shops sought him to write their signboards and several students asked him to correct their calligraphy.

On 18 September 1931 the Japanese aggressors invaded north-east China, but Chiang Kai-shek, in order to concentrate on destroying the Communists, ceded the three north-eastern provinces to them. Then the Japanese declared war against Shanghai on 28 January 1932 and the Nineteenth Route Army resisted the Japanese on behalf of the whole nation. At that time a seminarian named Zhou Junliang raised the national flag in our chapel and prayed for our nation with all the seminarians. Father Durand reported back to the rector Henry. He plotted to prevent this and said that it was forbidden to raise national flags in the chapel. He ordered Zhou to take the flag down. Zhou not only refused to obey the order, but disputed it, saying: "There is a French flag raised in the Sichuan South Road Church." Henry called Zhou's father to appear before him, saying his son had no vocation and that the seminary had decided to expel him. The Zhou family was very wealthy and Zhou's father sought out the Bishop of Haimen, Mgr. Zhu Kaimin, to solve the problem. Thus Zhou senior sent Zhou Junliang to Rome at his own expense to study at the University of the Congregation for the Propagation of the Faith. He graduated at the time of the Anti-Japanese War, could not return home and was accepted as a priest by Bishop Yu Bin of Nanjing, who sent him to Chicago to look after the overseas Chinese Catholics there. He died in the United States. In those days our lives were controlled by foreign priests and our patriotism was considered a sin.

In 1935 I graduated from the Sacred Heart of Jesus Seminary and entered the Sacred Heart of Mary Seminary to study philosophy for two years. In July 1937 I was sent back to St. Ignatius College to do my practical training, teaching French to the second grade and also supervising the religious instruction of Catholic seventh- and eighth-graders.

Five years of seminary life passed peacefully just as I have described above. What caused me most grief was that when the seminary closed for vacation and the seminarians returned to their homes, I was not allowed to reside at the seminary, even though I had no home to return to. After my great-uncle died, his children divided his house, so I was of course not able to go there. I had no choice but to wander about, calling on the kindness of friends for a few days here and a few days there. Once I stayed at Lu Naying's home for ten days from 16 to 25 July 1937. Nowadays the Lu family describes that room as the one that I stayed in to any who come and visit them. There were also two houses owned by relatives that took me in. One was Jin Hesheng; the other Jin Heting. I called them 'uncles'. They treated me with warm hospitality, even giving me pocket money when it was time for me to go. Their descendants even come and see me now. I am very grateful to them. The only one who let me down was my father's elder brother Jin Xinde, who was much richer than either Jin Hesheng or Jin Heting. Even so, every year I went to see him during the vacation. He just stood on his seniority and lectured me without inviting me to sit down. When I visited him at Chinese New Year he never gave me a penny. He was the only genuine elder relative I had—my father's brother, no less.

On 7 July 1937 the Japanese occupied Beijing. Then on 13 August they attacked Shanghai again. The Chinese forces mounted fierce resistance, beginning the so-called Battle of Songhu (Battle of Shanghai) in which the districts of Zhabei, Hongkou, Jiangwan and Baoshan became battlefields. The Japanese ruthlessly bombed the area, forcing a large number of refugees into the foreign concessions. At St. Ignatius College we opened up the school dormitories, but this was not enough, so the playground was covered with simple sheds in order to receive as many refugees as possible. We made great efforts to help them. When the country is divided, only the mountains and rivers remain: the destruction of our homeland was before our eyes.

My year of practical training passed very happily teaching at St. Ignatius College. The college was managed according to the traditional methods of the Jesuits which can be summarised in one word—rigour. The students rose at 5:30 and gathered in the chapel to attend mass, gathered to study, gathered to do sports and gathered again for evening prayers, after which they were not allowed to talk before going to bed at night. The students came from Catholic homes. The fees were fairly expensive, so all the families were well-off and had taught their sons good manners. The students worked hard, paid attention, were friendly and very rarely acted up. Their life was similar to that of today's seminarians and novices. From them I learned the beauty and the innocence of dutiful and active lives. Even though I was their teacher, the boys influenced me and I unconsciously learned much from them. I decided to commit my life more fully to the Lord. I remember some of the boys to this day. Three of them have become priests in the Shanghai diocese, two of them joined the Society of Jesus, yet others became compassionate and charitable doctors.

11
Joining the Society of Jesus

Two Years of Novitiate (1938–40)

On completion of my examination, the rector of the seminary informed me that I would next be going to the Jesuit theological college to study theology. There I would be able to prepare for a master's degree recognised by the Vatican educational authorities. He instructed me to study Greek by myself; but since I had already done my spiritual exercises, after deep consideration I decided to join the Society of Jesus and wrote my letter of application to the Jesuit father superior Rev. Henry. I took leave of my fellow teachers and my personal library and other belongings.

On 20 August 1938 I entered the novitiate of the Society of Jesus. At the same time there were two other entrants, both graduates of Aurora University, one named Yang Laiquan (a graduate of the Medical Department at Aurora) who died suddenly soon after the inception of classes and another named Zhang Xianyou (a graduate of Aurora's Science and Technology Department) who was arrested and sentenced to prison on 8 September 1955 and stayed many years in labour camps in Anhui Province; he was finally released and appointed to teach at Anhui University after the launch of the Open Door Policy; he died there. There were also two graduates from Huishi Middle School, Cai Liangshen and Fan Zhongliang (who is now the Bishop of the Shanghai underground Catholic Church). Another was, like me, a graduate of the major seminary, Lu Dayuan (younger than me by two years, he was later arrested and after his release migrated to Canada, where he died). It was quite unprecedented and never repeated that there were so many new novices at the Shanghai Society of Jesus. The master of novices was a Frenchman named Rev. Eugene Beauce, who had been father superior of the Jesuits in Shanghai and vicar general of the Shanghai diocese. The tutor was Rev. Zhang Shiquan (from Nanzhang in Qibao District)—he was old and very short-sighted. He had written many books, including one entitled *A Ray of Light*.

The novitiate was on the top floor with big rooms, a dormitory and a study, and also a library with 90% French books. In the study each novice had his own desk, chair and *prie-dieu*, all connected together.

The course of study included: (1) one month of retreat and spiritual exercises—this was the core of our training; (2) going on pilgrimage without any money for a month; (3) teaching children catechism for two months; (4) spending two months attending to the sick in hospital. I went to Andang Hospital, set up on Chongqing Road by the Daughters of Charity of St. Vincent de Paul for the poorest of the poor—it took me 50 minutes to walk there; (5) helping the cooks in the kitchen for two months; (6) two months cleaning the building.

Every month there was a charitable activity, meaning that we would help a fellow novice by having him kneel in the middle of the classroom while the other novices pointed out his shortcomings and the number of times he had broken the code. The person being helped listened attentively, was not permitted to make excuses and finally had to thank everyone for their charity. What was termed 'rest' was in fact walking in a group on the veranda. We went to chapel together to read scripture, to attend mass, to take communion, to read the Gospel. Apart from our three meals, we were not permitted to take snacks or carry any food on us, nor carry any money. Apart from the rest period we had to observe strict silence and were not permitted to speak. In summary, this was rigorous group training where, apart from going to the lavatory, everything was exactly as our master Rev. Beauce had experienced in France when he was 20 years old. Since then he had never been back and so did not realise that things had changed in his home country. As it happened, this kind of training prepared me well for my life in prison 17 years later.

The basic premise of spiritual training was to constantly combat the three evils of the flesh, the devil and worldly desires. Of these the temptations of the flesh came first and required us to battle with our bodies, control our physical desires, suppress them and punish the body. On entering the novitiate, every novice was issued a whip in order to flagellate himself. There was also an armband with sharp nails to attach to one's arm (these things have since been abolished). We all slept together in a large dormitory so we all knew exactly who was flagellating himself the hardest.

In those days by a wide margin the majority of Jesuits in Shanghai were French, so we ate Western food. The master of novices taught us how to eat. When eating, especially soup, one could not make any noise; when eating fruit one should use a knife and fork and not just bite at it. However, when eating bread one should not use a knife, but break it with one's hands. Our meals were divided into types for regular, anniversary and feast days. On feast days we got three glasses of wine and on anniversaries, two. The first time I ate cheese, I found it noisome—the cheese they served on feast days was especially rank; but I slowly learned to enjoy eating it. Sometimes at our evening classes the instructor would dine with us, teaching us how to separate a whole chicken into six pieces. Before we slept he would permit us to drink a glass of dry red wine with quinine.

While eating we were not permitted to talk, so someone would read while the others ate: French books at lunchtime and Chinese books at dinner. The novices would take it in turns to take the stage and read aloud. When the reader made a mistake or mispronounced a word the supervisory priest would require him to read it again. The master of novices told us that when we ate we should not concentrate on eating, but rather think about our studies and raise our spiritual level. Looking back over the first half of my life, I have to say that I have listened to many good books during my time at table and indeed learnt many valuable things that added greatly to my knowledge.

While eating, certain Jesuits would make confessions, extending their hands and kneeling in the centre of the refectory, recounting their sins and asking for collective forgiveness. In some cases they would go up to other members of the society, kneel before them and kiss their feet. The first time I experienced this, a priest who was both my teacher and my senior knelt and kissed my feet, which greatly moved me. Yet other priests would kneel in the centre of the refectory, eating from a low table. For myself, I wondered why it was necessary to take matters so seriously when eating should be a time to relax and enjoy the dishes. As I understand it, the Society of Jesus changed this practice after the Second Vatican Council.

Of the six types of training mentioned above, we only did five. The requirement of going on pilgrimage without carrying any money was prevented by the Japanese invasion and the continuous warfare. When I was sweeping the floor of the monastery, my former pupils from St. Ignatius College would see me with my shaven head and old clothes performing the menial task and call out in loud voices: "Brother Jin has gotten into trouble; come and have a look," which I found very embarrassing. When we walked to the hospital to render service, we were unfamiliar with medical knowledge and were sent by a nun named He to wash the feet of the poorest patients (such as coolies, rickshaw drivers and porters) and to smear their sores with disinfectant. We were also sent to work in the hospital kitchen, to clean and peel potatoes, without being allowed to converse with the regular workers.

In the senior class of the novitiate were two students, one named Zhang (whose given names I have forgotten)—a quiet and civilised man—and another named Chen Fengming from Hengsha Island. Chen was very opportunistic; he was made student representative by the master and sought the latter's approval by making regular reports on the other students' infractions. Thus he gained the confidence and affection of the master. Chen was very strict on the rest of us, but most lax when it came to himself, causing the one named Zhang to revolt and quit the novitiate in anger. After Chen, the master nominated another, named Chen Caijun, as student representative and this man was if anything even more eager to report on the novices than Chen Fengming had been. He regarded himself as exceptional and thought that he was the eyes and ears of the master; but he was also neurotic. When the master dismissed him as student representative, he decided that the master no longer trusted him; he sulked silently in a corner and uttered not a word. Sitting there all day he became psychotic and was sent to the Puci Mental Hospital for three months' treatment. When he returned to the school the master looked after him, was overly kind to him and permitted him to continue serving as student representative. For a while he devoted himself to his studies, worked hard and continued to report on his fellows, but after graduation his psychological state remained abnormal. At a meeting in 1952 to discuss whether or not he was able to enter the priesthood, certain of those present objected, whereas I supported his application. He happily became ordained as priest; but I am getting ahead of myself.

The master of novices considered me 'arrogant', relying on my greater age and standing on seniority. He sought every opportunity to challenge my 'arrogance' and I suffered a lot, thinking often of leaving the Society of Jesus and returning to the seminary. On one occasion when I had suffered greatly I opened the New Testament at random and found the passage in Luke 9:62 where Jesus teaches: "No man, having put his hand to the plough, and looking back, is fit for the kingdom of God." At that moment I decided to stay and see it through.

Most Jesuits say that the two years of novitiate were the happiest days of their lives, but I say that my two years were the hardest I had experienced as a seminarian.

However, I made great progress during those two years, building a firm foundation for my spiritual life. I had no one to whom to complain and so relied on regular prayer. We had a library and I read many books that have served me well all my life. Some of these were: *Jésus-Christ: sa personne, son message, ses preuves* by Léonce de Grandmaison (1868–1927); *La Vie et l'enseignement de Jésus Christ Notre Seigneur; Lumen Christi; Tu Solus Sanctus;* and *Le Discours après la Cène* by Jules Lebreton (1873–1956).

These few books I read many times. My spiritual life centred on Jesus Christ. He was the foundation of my faith. I knew that human reason could not fully prove the existence of a Creator. I believed in Jesus, in the Word of the Lord and also deeply believed in the Lord and the Lord's love. Jesus descended from God to this world and became man, but never left the Father. I have similarly spent my life on earth, but in my heart have never left the Lord. I believe in Jesus: He not only teaches us truth, He is himself the path to truth. Only with Jesus is there life. In living, I am living through Jesus. In 1947 I went to France to visit Rev. Lebreton and pay my respects. He greeted me warmly and talked to me for two hours, inspiring me greatly. In 1951 I returned to China and ordered that *Lumen Christi* and *La Vie et l'enseignement de Jésus Christ Notre Seigneur*, vol. *II* be translated into Chinese and published as the Spiritual Library. In 1982 I returned to Shanghai and learned that the Red Guards had burned all our books in French and in Chinese so I wrote to friends in France and asked them to send Lebreton's books, but they wrote back saying: "These books are no longer in print." I was very disappointed. How could such good books become old-fashioned? How could they be out of print? The world was changing too fast and I could not keep up.

Another book I found very useful told the story of Sister Elizabeth of the Trinity. The famous saying of this nun who died at the age of twenty-six was: "I have found heaven on earth, since heaven is God and God is in my soul." I have never forgotten these words. During the many years in which I lost my liberty, I never forgot them and found support in them. Her words comforted me and enabled me to endure hardship even when faced with the greatest difficulties. When I regained my liberty and travelled to France again, I learned that the Pope had already beatified her on 25 November 1984. May the Blessed Elizabeth protect me now and for evermore! Albert Decourtray, Archbishop of Lyon from 1981 to 1994, also venerated Blessed Elizabeth and accompanied me on pilgrimage to her convent. I maintain contact with that convent to this day.

I also read biographies of St. Ignatius Loyola, the founder of our order and of St. Francis Xavier who was the Apostle of the Orient, of the youthful St. Louis Gonzaga, St. John Berchmans, the lay brother St. Alphonsus Rodriguez and of St. Peter Claver of the mission to black slaves, all of which helped me to fully appreciate the main instruction of the Society of Jesus: "Glory through effort". In sum, one must strive to take actions that glorify the Lord, with emphasis on the word 'effort'. Also, the core of the spiritual exercises of the Jesuits is the love of Jesus Christ. The love of Jesus Christ displays itself through the love of others as the love of the Lord. Do not speak empty words; take more action. The two years of novitiate caused me to love the Society of Jesus, to assume my membership of the Society with pride, never to sully the name of Jesuit. I also became accustomed to seeing all Jesuits as my brothers, even though many of my subsequent troubles came from fellow members; but still I love the Society of Jesus. This I can say with all the wisdom of hindsight.

The master ruled that the novices should remain sequestered during their studies, not be permitted to read newspapers and either only very occasionally or not at all see relatives and friends. During those two years there was only one of my former students who thought about me and went to see the master to gain permission to see me. I was very grateful to him. He was a very capable person and became head of the Sijing Chamber of Commerce at an early age, but sadly lived only until 1954. I greatly miss him. His Christian name was Bonaventure.

12
Taking First Vows

Juvenate (1940–41)

Two years passed and on 8 September 1940 I took my vows along with some others. Later on, when I was arrested on 8 September 1955, it was quite a coincidence. Was this a heavenly message? When I took my vows I told no one, so no one came to congratulate me. I immediately transferred to the Juvenate College. There I taught Latin to the second grade class at the Sacred Heart Seminary in Xujiahui. Up to that point the class had always been taught by French priests. There were four lessons a day, two in the morning and two in the afternoon. I taught the speeches of Cicero and the *Gallic War* by Julius Caesar. There were seven students, among them Zhuang Huanyuan, Song Zhijun (they went on to study in Rome and then, because China had been liberated by then, were sent to Taiwan) and Zhuang Guangfu (he has always been in Shanghai and died only recently). There was also one named Zhou, who was expelled for lack of ability.

While I was working at the seminary I was able to attend other classes with the students. At that time the rector of the juvenate college was Rev. Wang Changzhi, a man from Sijing who was raised in a scholarly family and was well-educated in classical Chinese. After graduating from St. Ignatius College, he had joined the Society of Jesus and, after completing the novitiate and juvenate courses, had taught at St. Ignatius College before being sent to Britain to study philosophy for three years. He then studied theology at Lyon for four years. After graduation father superior Beauce ordered him to continue his studies abroad, so he studied philosophy at the Sorbonne, gaining a national level doctorate of philosophy with a thesis on the neo-Confucian philosopher Wang Yangming (1472–1529). He concurrently won a doctorate in theology from the Catholic University of Paris with a thesis on St. Augustine. I remember that I once met Rev. de Lubac at the Jesuit College in Lyon and paid him my respects, but he replied: "The real genius was a youthful fellow student Wang

Changzhi—his achievements in theology have been remarkable." He asked me whether Wang was teaching theology. I replied that he had always taught Chinese literature to juvenate students and had edited a children's magazine entitled *Christian Soldier*. Rev. de Lubac said: "How can this be? This is to hide the light under a bushel." Wang had indeed applied several times to teach theology, but each time Rev. Henry had rejected him out of hand. Thus Wang Changzhi was truly a talent without any outlet.

Wang Changzhi taught us the *Analects* of Confucius, the *Dao De Jing* of Laozi and the works of Zhuangzi. The central tenet of the *Analects* is obviously 仁 (*ren*, benevolence), even if his favourite pupil Zengzi once said: "The way of the sage is loyalty"—as if loyalty could be said to encompass all of Confucius's teaching—and even if other scholars emphasise Confucius's lifelong search for the re-establishment of the rites. The meaning of benevolence is all-encompassing. It is not possible to find a foreign word that can both translate it and be exactly equivalent to it. Also, it is hard to define benevolence precisely; one can only try to describe the concept from different angles. Confucius is a wonderful authority on this life, but he does not describe the far shore; he discusses man, but not heaven. He only discusses the path of man, how to refine one's spirit with honour and commitment, how to establish a family and to rule a kingdom, bringing peace to those under heaven. He does not deal with the relationship between man and heaven.

Laozi writes of the Way (道, *dao*), but when he composed the *Dao De Jing*, in the very first sentence he wrote: "The Way that can be spoken of is not the constant Way"; and later on: "There is a thing confusedly formed, born before Heaven and Earth. Silent and void it stands alone and does not change, goes round and does not weary. It is capable of being the mother of the world. I know not its name so I style it 'the Way'." The Way Laozi is talking of is a very mysterious one. The word *dao* from the start refers to the beginning of things, the origin of all things. Laozi writes: "Dao gives birth to one, one gives birth to two, two gives birth to three, and three gives birth to all things."[1] The *dao* goes along, directing all movement and progress. Thus *dao* also becomes a path, even a road. *Dao* is the prime mover. All things come from *dao*, so humans also come from *dao* and take the *dao* as their path, a path that when taken reaches the *dao*.

---

1. English translation from *Lao Tzu: Tao Te Ching*, translated and with an introduction by T.C. Lau., Penguin Books, 1963.

Zhuangzi's work is a totality, with beautiful words and a superior vision achieved by 气 (*qi*, spirit) and aspiring to beauty. His central thought is to travel with the Creator, to allow humans and heaven to meet. Zhuangzi had a very clear view of this world, this earth, this life. He emphasised the constancy of change which overcomes life and death. Zhuangzi explores the deepest desires of the human spirit, attempting to delineate the existence of true happiness in order to make up for the lacunae of Confucianism. From ancient times on, many Chinese intellectuals have espoused Confucianism in society and Daoism in private; thus on the surface they cling to the path of Confucius and Mencius, while reserving Daoism for their deepest feelings.

13
School of Philosophy (1941–42)

At the end of August 1941, Rev. Henry sent me to Xianxian in Hebei Province to study philosophy for a third year. In Shanghai seminaries the course was only two years, while the Jesuits required three years, so I had to make up a year. According to the dispositions of the Society of Jesus at that time the school of philosophy was in Xianxian and the school of theology in Shanghai, with the examination centre in Wuhu in Anhui Province. I set out by train in early September with Zhu Shude and Chen Tianxiang. We crossed the Yangtze River and then took a second train to Bengbu, where we stayed for two nights and visited the Bengbu diocese. The Italian Jesuits there gave us a warm welcome. Bishop Cassini received us. We visited the boys and girls middle schools, the latter being administered by the Sisters of St. Ursula from Italy. Among the nuns was the fourth daughter of my benefactor Jin Fushan. The Jesuit house was next to the station. At night the rumbling of the trains prevented us from sleeping soundly. Three days later we continued on our journey by train, arriving the following day at Botou in Hebei Province.

Shen Daiqi, a Jesuit who had already been studying at Xianxian, was waiting for us. He arranged for us to take a flat-top wagon pulled by two mules, for there was no bus route between Botou and Xianxian. The wagon had wooden wheels bound with iron which ran into the deep ruts left in the dirt road by the preceding carts. As I sat on this conveyance I was reminded of the Chinese saying: 'You may close your door to build a cart; but when you issue forth the wheels must align with the ruts'. As I sat on the cart, I thought of Confucius long ago travelling from state to state by means of just such a contraption. The means of transport had not made any progress in over 2,000 years. At nightfall we slept at the church in Liuxin township. To cushion us from the violent jolting of the cart, Brother Shen borrowed a quilt to put on the flat-top and told us to lie down, which was indeed a big improvement. The carter cracked his whip regularly, once in the air and once on the ground, causing the mule to think that another mule was being whipped and making it go a little faster. On the second day we continued our journey, arriving half a day later at Yuntai Mountain, about 20 *li* from Xianxian. This place was the agricultural base of Xianxian diocese, with about 200 hectares of good land used for growing cereals, fruit, vegetables and many grape vines. They made their own wine which they sold all over China. In the evening we arrived at the nationally-renowned Zhangjiazhuang church. The church covered a wide area and had an imposing facade. It was surrounded by thick, high walls like those of a city, wide enough to ride a horse along and with crenellations for firing guns. At the time of the Boxer Rebellion in 1900, the Allies sent a troop of French soldiers to defend the church and foreign residents. Xianxian diocese consisted of a male college and a female college; the former included the cathedral, the bishop's palace, the Jesuit house, elementary and middle schools, a seminary, a novitiate, a juvenate college and a school of philosophy, a printing house and publishing company, a very large library and farm. The female college included a foundling hospital, an orphanage, girls elementary and middle schools, the convent of Our Lady of Xianxian, a convent of the Congregation of Helpers of the Holy Souls and a convent of the Sisters of the Holy Spirit from Canada. There was also a fairly large hospital. The church had its own generator, water plant and had central heating for winter. In the courtyard was a large pond where one could skate in winter and row boats in summer. We went to the county town of Xianxian, which had walls of packed earth and very few brick and tile houses inside. (The contemporary TV serial character Ji Xiaolan is from Xianxian.) The standard of living of the missionaries was so far above that of the common people that it was bound to give rise to animosity.

A few days after we arrived, we were suddenly surrounded by Japanese troops. Apparently, a few days before some Japanese devils had been relaxing on Yuntai Mountain and some of them had been killed by bombs thrown at them by the Communist Eighth Route Army. The Japanese seized all of us Chinese and the bishop and incarcerated us in a small building on Yuntai Mountain surrounded by well-armed Japanese guards. We were not permitted to speak. At the school in Zhangjiazhuang the soldiers found a KMT flag in one of the classrooms and took away the headmaster. In the printing house they found some anti-Japanese material on the press, so they arrested the brother in charge and a few of the typesetters and locked them in prison. After a day, a Belgian father named Lichtenberger (known as Li in Chinese) brought us blankets and provisions from Zhangjiazhuang.

The news of the siege of Xianxian and Zhangjiazhuang by Japanese troops and the arrest of Bishop Zhao and all the Jesuits and brothers reached Tianjin where the president of the University of Industry and Commerce, Rev. René Charvet rushed around the French, Canadian, Italian, American and British consulates to ask them to put pressure on the Japanese. One morning the Japanese gathered all of us together in one room and then registered us one by one, separating Hebei residents from those from other provinces. After questioning, they allowed the Belgian father to take us all back to Zhangjiazhuang, so we were only locked up for half a month. The Hebei people were, however, thrown into prison where the Japanese shot a priest named Feng and a lay brother of the same name as well as five of the print-shop workers. After half a year the remaining prisoners were released and we went to Xianxian town to welcome them home.

At this point I would like to tell you more about Rev. Lichtenberger. He was originally a nurse. When the doctors at the Xianxian hospital, in particular the surgeons, saw the Japanese troops, they took fright and returned to Shanghai. Without any physicians at the hospital, what was to be done? Many people came to the hospital every day, including the wounded from the Eighth Route Army actions. There was no point in telling them that the doctors had all gone because there was nowhere else for them to go. So the Belgian priest said that he would undertake the operations. He rolled up his sleeves and put on a white coat, gathered the nurses together and asked them to prepare to operate. He opened chests, amputated arms and legs and went on working until the end of the Anti-Japanese War. He performed at least 1,000 operations without a single casualty. After the defeat of Japan, the Jesuits sent him back to Belgium to study medicine and to qualify as a doctor. In the summer of 1948, when I went to Belgium, I met him at the Jesuit house. He was very happy to see me and gave me a big hug. He complained that the medical faculty required him to learn from the beginning and spend several years earning his degree. He said that he had performed many more operations than the lecturers and knew more about surgery than them, "but they require me to waste my time learning from books."

Zhangjiazhuang in Xianxian was the base of French missionary activity in China. At the school of philosophy, apart from the Chinese students, there was an Italian named Priuli and three Spaniards named Suátrz, Goyoyaga and

Laranaga. There was also a French Jesuit named Pierre Tritz who was sent to the Philippines after Liberation, where he worked with the poor of Manila, setting up several leprosaria, curing several tens of thousands of lepers. He also opened many free schools, educating several thousand children so they could escape illiteracy. He was awarded honours by the Philippine government and also given honorary medals by the French government. He was the most successful Jesuit in our class, still alive today, working hard on behalf of the poor.

The school of philosophy had several professors, the Spaniard Palacios, the Canadian Dallaire as well as priests from Hungary and France. The philosophy taught was mostly traditional scholastic philosophy. The French Jesuits taught mainly the two French philosophers: Bergson's *L'évolution créatrice* and Blondel's *Action*. The former was better known, but the latter, in my opinion, more profound. The Hungarian taught critiques of Kant and Hegel, as well as a shallow critique of Marxism. There were no Chinese teachers and no Chinese philosophy was taught.

When the Japanese army laid siege to Zhangjiazhuang, the Italian Bishop of Bengbu, Cassini, rushed to Xianxian to ask after us and to visit the commanders of the Japanese troops. The Japanese Jesuits sent a German Jesuit who stayed at Zhangjiazhuang during the crisis. When the Japanese troops came he would go out and greet them. Since the Japanese, Germans and Italians were allies, the Japanese troops would pay them more respect. Thus the international nature of the Society of Jesus demonstrated its effectiveness. In front of the west door of the church were hung French, German, Hungarian, Spanish, Italian, American and Canadian flags, inter alia, to demonstrate its international status. Most Japanese troops were brought to a stop by this display.

Our life there was very comfortable. Every day we drank milk and coffee, had two eggs, bacon, butter and jam. In Shanghai I had got used to eating bread and considered it better than *mantou* (wheat flour buns). Thus once when I was visiting the children of the village and asked them: "Is *mantou* good to eat?" I got the reply: "*Mantou*? You mean white flour *mantou*? We only get to eat that at Chinese New Year. Usually we eat *wotou* (cornmeal bread)." At that moment I was overcome with shame and I have never forgotten those children's words. Nowadays all the villagers eat wheat flour; by contrast cornmeal is only served at banquets as a speciality.

On 8 December 1941 the Japanese attacked Pearl Harbour and proclaimed war on the United States and Britain. The US also declared war on Japan and so the Pacific War broke out. Up to this point, while Japan was invading China,

US goods and military materiel had still been exported to Japan. In her speech of 1941 to the Americans, Song Meiling had said: "Up until this moment, the steel used to make the Japanese guns that shoot at the Chinese has been US-made steel and the oil that powers the Japanese planes that bomb our cities has been US oil." Now that they had been attacked themselves, the US formally joined the war. Since there were American and Canadian priests and nuns at Zhangjiazhuang, the Japanese army returned and took them away to the concentration camp in Tianjin.

While the Japanese were besieging Zhangjiazhuang, the original father superior and vicar general Joman fell gravely ill and wrote to the Jesuit Visitor to the China Missions Rev. Georges Marin asking to be allowed to resign. Marin sent a telegram to René Charvet, president of the University of Industry and Commerce in Tianjin, appointing him to the position of head in Xianxian and replacing him with Rev. Aisier. To Charvet this was a hard and profitless appointment, but he said not a word and left immediately for Xianxian, taking an interest in priests and lay people, leaving Bishop Zhao Zhensheng at the county town. After the Japanese surrender, the Eighth Route Army Hebei Unit treated Charvet as a spy and arrested him, threw him into prison and then expelled him from China. In the educational materials of the early Liberation period Charvet was given a whole page to himself and his 'rotten name' was known to all and sundry. He went back to his own country, but everywhere spread word of the Church in China. He came from a distinguished family. In 1949 I saw him in his hometown and he was already aged. Before he died he told people: "You need not make any speeches at my funeral. I'll do it myself." He had prepared and recorded a funeral oration for himself and at his funeral they played the recording he had prepared. Thus he gave his own funeral oration.

While talking of Charvet, I ought not to neglect Bishop Zhao Zhensheng. His story is a tragedy. In the 1930s the French bishop Le Croix of Xianxian became senile and basically lost his memory. Rome then appointed Zhao Zhensheng to be the first Chinese bishop. Zhao was a Jesuit who had studied in France for many years. The former bishop Le Croix's illness had a unique feature—even though he had forgotten everything, he had not forgotten that he was a bishop. Every day Le Croix wore his bishop's robes and the pectoral cross of his office. When Le Croix heard that he had to ordain a bishop to replace him, he made a huge fuss about it, so Zhao was unable to be ordained in Zhangjiazhuang and went to Tianjin to be ordained privately by the Bishop of Tianjin. When Zhao returned to celebrate his first mass he was unable to wear the bishop's mitre or to carry the crosier to bless the faithful. When the photograph was taken, Zhao didn't sit next to Le Croix, but stood behind him. When the photographer pressed the shutter, Zhao quickly took out the cross and hung it round his neck, before hiding it again. Just as Le Croix finally went to meet his maker, the Japanese arrived and restricted Zhao's movements, keeping him under house arrest in Zhangjiazhuang. After the Japanese surrender and the Eighth Route Army takeover, Zhao fled to Tianjin and then to Beijing. When Chiang Kai-shek went to Beijing in December 1945 he met with Zhao, who begged him to send troops to the south of Hebei. When Bishop Tian Gengxing fled abroad he made Zhao his successor in Beijing. When the whole country had been liberated, Zhao went into hiding and travelled in secret. Finally a Catholic in Xianxian, who had been a partisan in the Anti-Japanese War, took Zhao into his home as a fugitive and hid him, providing him with three meals a day. Zhao led a life in which he never saw the daylight. After a year the Communist party finally found him and asked him to come out of the mountains and continue as Bishop of Xianxian, but the man who had hidden him was punished. At the National Catholic Conference in 1957 the government forced Zhao to attend and he was chosen to be the deputy-chairman of the Catholic Patriotic Association (CPA). Along with Bishop Pi Shushi of Shenyang he went on to ordain as bishops priests chosen by the authorities. During the Cultural Revolution the Red Guards seized him and struggled against him mercilessly, beating him and locking him up in prison, where he soon died. His story is truly tragic.

In April 1942 Jesuit father superior Henry visited Xianxian to inspect us Shanghai Jesuits. He called me to his room and said: "The Japanese are winning victories every day. Now Hong Kong and the Philippines have fallen to them. It looks as if they will stay in China for a long time, so we need a man who is fluent in Japanese. I have decided to send you to Tokyo in September to study Japanese at Tokyo University and come back with a degree. I order you to go to the University of Industry and Commerce in Tianjin in June, where someone will teach you Japanese. In late August you will go to Japan." In my heart I thought that this would make me a traitor. In political terms was this not a death sentence? Would not my name be scorned for 10,000 years? What should I do? Foreigners could not appreciate how much we Chinese hated the Japanese. My heart was in turmoil. Should I obey his order or disobey? I resolved on a policy of passive resistance.

School of Philosophy (1941–42)

At the end of May 1942, after a year's study at Xianxian, I left with a passive attitude and travelled with Zhu Shude for a week's vacation in Beijing while wondering what to do next.

In Beijing we stayed at the Jesuits' Chabanel House. By day we went out with a map to explore, but could not go even as far as the Western Hills, for these and other places were in the hands of the Eighth Route Army. We went to pay a visit to the great archaeologist and philosopher Rev. Teilhard de Chardin. He welcomed us with warmth and accompanied us to his exhibition hall, taking out one fossil after another, explaining everything to us with the greatest enthusiasm. After he had been going on for half an hour he realised that we had little interest in the subject and said: "Let's go to the refectory together." He had already prepared several delicacies with which to entertain us and after thanking him we returned to Chabanel House. We had only been to see him because he was a famous person. He was at that time mainly busy assisting in the dating of Peking Man. We were totally ignorant of paleobiology.

After leaving Beijing I went to the University of Industry and Commerce at Machang Road in Tianjin where my friend Liu Nairen gladly welcomed me. I met the Hungarian Jesuit László Ladány, who slipped away to Hong Kong before the Liberation and established a journal entitled *China News Analysis* that was anti-communist. Later on he vehemently attacked me, calling me a traitor who had sold out my fellows in order to be permitted to return to Shanghai; but this all happened much later on.

The president of the University of Industry and Commerce was named Aisier. He told me that he had found a Japanese man to teach me his language for two hours a day. He was not a bad fellow and taught me conscientiously, but I would not learn. After two weeks I had not even learnt *hiragana* or *katakana*. Finally I gave up. My teacher reported to the president that he was not able to teach a student like me. So Aisier wrote a letter to Henry, who ordered me back to Shanghai to study theology. My passivity had gained the desired result.

The president of the University of Industry and Commerce, Aisier, was not well liked. Both Chinese and foreign faculty members wrote a letter to Rev. Marin, the Jesuit Visitor, who sent Rev. Drexel to investigate. Marin was Canadian and thus unable to leave Shanghai, whereas Drexel was Austrian and was thus, after the Anschluss, issued with a German passport. Drexel held discussions with all the Jesuits and discovered that all were in favour of appointing the Chinese Liu Nairen as president. Drexel returned to Shanghai and reported to Marin, who approved his suggestion and transferred Aisier, appointing

Liu as his successor. Liu was the first Chinese man to be appointed president of a Catholic University. He had a gift for leadership and could unite people and was good at social relations. He raised large sums of money and built the University of Industry and Commerce into Jingu University. Liu had been born into a Catholic family, one of four brothers of whom three became priests. I realised that the Frenchmen in Xianxian were much more receptive to the spirit of the Gospel than those in Shanghai and more active in carrying out the directions of the Pope, appointing the first Chinese bishop in 1936 and the first Chinese university president in 1942. In 1950 they appointed a Chinese head of the Society of Jesus and were ahead of Shanghai in sending priests abroad for education.

After the outbreak of the Pacific War the Japanese tightened the policy of enslavement through education. Every school was required to appoint a Japanese deputy head. Liu applied via Rev. Charvet for the assistance of the Japanese Jesuits, who arranged for a lay graduate of Sophia University in Tokyo named Miura to come to Tianjin as deputy head.

On arrival in Tianjin this man worked very closely with Liu Nairen, saying to Liu: "I've come to protect you and not to control you. All I need is for you to give me a small villa, a car and a nice office to entertain visitors from the Japanese High Command and I will pay attention to nothing else." Once he said to Liu: "The Japanese want to arrest such and such a graduate student. Why don't you arrange to have him transferred outside the military zone?" The two men called on the student and then Miura sat next to the driver and Liu sat in the back with the student at his feet covered with a blanket. When they got to the edge of the concession, Miura got out of the car to talk to the guard. The guard let them pass and they drove into the neutral zone. Miura and Liu breathed a sigh of relief and Liu told the student: "You are free." Miura and Liu returned to Tianjin. I heard this story from Liu's own mouth. Miura was very helpful to the Church. The University of Industry and Commerce was not harassed by the Japanese army. The university could continue with classes as before and its reputation increased substantially. After the Japanese surrender, Miura was sent back to Japan and we lost track of him. Liu once wrote to the Jesuits in Tokyo to enquire after him, but the reply was that he was nowhere to be found. Miura proved that there were good people among the Japanese.

When Tianjin was liberated, the Communist leaders immediately went to visit Liu. He considered that their interest in him could not be good news so he made a plan to escape. He took 300 silver dollars and dressed up as a peasant and set off. When he reached the city limits, the guard discovered his money and asked him why he needed to carry so much on him. Liu said that he was returning to his hometown to find a bride, so the Liberation Army let him go. He travelled to Inner Mongolia, then to Xi'an, Shanghai and Hong Kong before ending up in East Timor, where he died.

14
Studying Theology (1942–46)

In late August I left Tianjin to return to Shanghai. At that time the Japanese army was guarding the main railway line and the trains from Beijing to Shanghai were not getting through. We got off at Pukou to cross the Yangtze, spent a night at Zhendan Middle School in Nanjing and then caught the Shanghai train. Upon my return to Shanghai I reported to the theology college in Xujiahui. In those days the college of theology was located where the Oriental Department Store and adjacent buildings are today. The rector Rev. Peter Lefebvre gave me a warm welcome.

The study of theology took four years and there were 103 students and 14 faculty members from China, Canada, the United States, Mexico, Columbia, Uruguay, Chile, France, Ireland, Italy, Spain, Hungary, Switzerland, Holland, Austria, Germany, Portugal, Belgium and Indonesia. Among them were the citizens of several warring countries, but the students got on very well together and lived like brothers. This fact should be credited to our rector, the above-mentioned Rev. Lefebvre. His leadership had direction. Whatever our culture, politics or background, he taught us to go beyond nationality, asking us never to forget that we belonged to the big family of the Society of Jesus of the Roman Catholic Church. Lefebvre had been president of Aurora University, father superior of the Jesuits in the Shanghai diocese and vicar general of Shanghai. He treated us in every way as a benevolent father would. He was very good to me. In my second year at the theology school, I was made student representative. The role of the student representative was to report the mood and conditions of the students; on one hand to represent the scholars and reflect their thoughts to the rector, on the other hand to represent the rector and convey his directions. Every day at 8 a.m. I was required to go to Lefebvre's room to make my report. He talked to me about how to be a good Jesuit, pointed out how to conduct oneself in society, how to be an effective shepherd of souls. He often talked of his own experience, how to behave in society, how to lead people towards an objective, how to be cautious in handling matters. Sometimes he would talk to me of matters he was still studying or what he had gained from study. These talks have benefitted me all my life. Even now I consider him to be my benefactor and will never forget his noble influence.

The Xuhui School of Theology was recognised by the Vatican Congregation for Catholic Education and was permitted to issue MA degrees. The theology course lasted four years and included the following subjects: systematic theology, moral theology, bible study, Catholic canon law, history, liturgy, spirituality and so on. All subjects were studied in Latin. In order to study the Bible in the original we had to learn Hebrew and Greek: our days were very full.

In those days the course of study at Xuhui School of Theology was very traditional. All the theology was as per the Council of Trent and the First Vatican Council. The professors only taught scholastic theology. In particular, one American professor named McCarthy insisted on teaching creationism and not evolution, saying that God had directly created the universe, exactly as is described in the Old Testament; that God had created Adam and Eve, our ancestors. Unsurprisingly, when these professors first heard Teilhard de Chardin's speeches in 1946 they all shook their heads in disbelief. In 1947 I went to Paris and saw Rev. Teilhard. After talking with me for an hour he sent me off with a pat on the shoulder, saying: "My brother, you are at least 40 years out of date."

Previously I have explained how I made a good friend named Tritz while studying philosophy and how he subsequently became a famous philanthropist in the Philippines, taking loving care of the poorest of the poor. While studying theology I also had a good friend named Luis Ruiz Suárez, a Spaniard, known in Chinese as Lu Yi. He was three years older than me and was at that time deputy student representative. We studied and worked very closely together and became priests on the same day, although in separate churches. After graduation he was sent to Anqing in Anhui Province to work as a missionary. In the early 1950s he was expelled from China and worked in Macau. In our country he has established over the years several leprosaria and treated countless lost and neglected poor. Of my theological college contemporaries, most have now gone on to the next life, but Tritz and Suárez are still with us. As Confucius said: "To the benevolent is granted longevity."

The traditional way of teaching systematic theology was not very demanding. The contents of the course were: the existence of God, the Trinity, creation, redemption, the sacraments, the life to come, christology, mariology, ecclesiology, angels, etc.—each subject only had a few topics. In every class we would review the topic under discussion, talk about its importance, talk of various opposing views through the ages. Then we would open various summaries: (1) what the Bible says, various useful passages; (2) what the Fathers of the Church have said, various useful passages; (3) what the Church says, various passages from general councils of the Church or papal letters. Summaries from the Fathers of the Church and of Church doctrine could always be brought to class. When made use of, we had only to read a few passages without bothering to open or read the original text. Preferably we would use short passages to elucidate meaning. For example, in the case of modern Jesus studies, the priority was to prove the existence of the historical Jesus and then examine why the historical Jesus was recognised as the Messiah and thus became the Son of God whom we believe in; then discuss how in history we overcame the opinions of non-believers to build our faith.

Among the professors, the most enlightened was a Spaniard who taught moral and canon law and was named Rev. Eliseus Escanciano. He had gained a doctorate in canon law at the Gregorian University in Rome before coming to teach in Shanghai and act as the legal advisor to the Shanghai diocese. In the beginning he had been very strict and had applied the letter of the law to any small infraction that called out for the bishop's understanding. Rector Lefebvre felt that his knowledge was all book learning and that he lacked human experience. Lefebvre arranged for him to do parish duties on the weekend at the parishes of Sijing in Songjiang and Xiaodongxu in Qingpu. Once he had come in contact with the masses, particularly with the working people, his attitude changed. He sympathised with the faithful and began to think altruistically when considering problems. From then on, whenever he was faced with requests he would reply: "According to such and such a legal requirement your request is denied; but according to other decrees it is allowed." He no longer strictly blocked things and sought to find a way out, proving the importance of parish work. People who sit in offices with their noses in books have no knowledge of the suffering of the working class, nor of how to see their point of view.

When the Pacific War broke out, the Japanese detained foreign nationals in concentration camps, allowing them no freedom and subjecting them to terrible conditions. The chief accountant of the Shanghai diocese, Rev. Verdier, had a discussion with the Japanese High Command and arranged for the Jesuits of foreign nationality to be gathered in the Jesuit house in Xujiahui. Thus those who were studying theology were able to continue their studies. Verdier also persuaded the Japanese to permit the transfer of a Canadian missionary from Xuzhou to Xujiahui Seminary. Thus a few foreign nationals managed to secure better treatment. They were free to move around at will within the confines of Xujiahui. The Japanese appointed a junior officer to go daily to the Jesuit headquarters and the seminary to take the roll-call. Anyone who wanted to visit the urban area of Shanghai had to obtain his permission. The officer they sent was a Catholic who behaved impeccably and granted every request that was made.

The Jesuits had been granted a special favour by His Holiness the Pope. After only three years of theological studies, Jesuits could be ordained priests, before going on to complete the fourth year.

On 19 May 1945 I was ordained a priest at Dongjiadu church (at that time the cathedral) by Mgr. Haouisée of the Shanghai diocese. In my class there were a total of 33 students. At that time Haouisée was already over 67 and pleaded his age, saying that he had not sufficient energy to ordain 33 people. He ordained me and Zhu Shude who were both Shanghainese. The remainder were ordained by Mgr. Coté, Bishop of Xuzhou at the Xujiahui church. The very next day I celebrated mass for the first time at Chongqing South Road church. That afternoon I officiated at the marriage of my good friends Li Junyi and Yao Dezhi. My uncles Jin Hesheng and Jin Heting helped me to arrange things. My mother's younger brother Zhang Zongpei owned a coffee shop and sent over several hundred pastries on the day of my first celebration of mass. Jin Hesheng and his wife also arranged for me to say mass at my place of birth and also at Jin Family Village church in order to give thanks to the Lord. My father's eldest brother did nothing at all.

Having become a priest and taken a holiday, I was sent by Rev. Henry to Jinshan, Tinglin and Hongqiao to be acting pastor for two months (as the parish priest was on vacation in Shanghai). On 15 August it was the Feast of the Assumption. There was suddenly an outbreak of firecrackers and people were running about passing on the news that the Japanese army had surrendered. The Anti-Japanese War was won. The day we had waited for for eight years had arrived. Thanks be to God!

15
Subei (1946–47)

In June 1946 I graduated and the following day Henry called me to him and said: "You have graduated. During the vacation I am sending you to Dongtai in Subei to relieve Rev. Klement. You will be acting parish priest. Return here at the end of August to go to Wuhu in Anhui Province." I was aware that fighting had broken out between the Nationalists and the Communists. Chiang Kai-shek had broken the ceasefire and Dongtai had fallen into the hands of the New Fourth Army. Dongtai was a key objective of the KMT army. As the KMT advanced on Dongtai the battle was already raging. Since the life of Americans was greatly valued, it was important to withdraw them from the area of fighting and get them out of harm's way. I was sent to die in their place. The very next day I took the train to Zhenjiang and then took the ferry across the Yangtze River to Yangzhou. Thence I took a bus to Taizhou, where I was warmly received by the parish priest, Rev. Zhou. The next day I took a small boat, the passengers of which exchanged not a word. After a while, the boat left Taizhou and two hours later reached the area controlled by the New Fourth Army. On the bank were child soldiers bearing rifles on patrol. The master of the vessel said that the child soldiers were very strict and would not permit anyone without a pass to proceed. It was very difficult to cope with their questions. The boat sailed for ten hours so that passengers who could hold it in for no longer had to go to the back of the boat to urinate into the water. I could not do that and so suffered as best I could, which was very uncomfortable. In the evening we arrived at our destination, the town of Dongtai, which had been known as 'Little Shanghai' before the Liberation. I knocked at the church door and the parish priest Rev. Klement issued forth in a state of great joy. He had known in advance that I was to replace him so that he could escape danger. He left the very next day for Shanghai in high spirits.

At the Dongtai church were three nuns from the Congregation of the Presentation of Our Lady to the Temple. Their leader was Sister Shen, aged 50. The oldest was Sister Huang, aged 70, from Haimen County. The youngest, named Rong was from Shuyang in Subei and was aged 30. When I arrived this last was busy teaching the children how to sing and dance. Rev. Klement had left no money. The daily expenses were raised by Sister Huang seeing medical patients. She was good at acupuncture and skilled in paediatrics. Rev. Klement also had some medical training and had left some medicines. Since I had no training we sent the medicines to Director Wei of the People's Hospital. He was delighted, because with the KMT embargo he had none and the New Fourth Army was very short.

In Dongtai town there were only a few Catholics. Most days when I said mass only the three nuns and an old doorkeeper named Jie made up the congregation. Jie had a long beard down to his chest and a long brown visage. Some people said that he was descended from Jews, but he said that his ancestors were from Kaifeng (indeed there were Jews recorded at Kaifeng in the Song dynasty, but most of them had adopted Chinese customs). On Sunday about twenty or so Catholics who worked in the fields in the suburbs of Dongtai came to mass. Most of the time, I had nothing to do. It was as if I had been sent there to be a mere caretaker. A few days later, Rev. Rouxin, a Frenchman, pastor of Anfeng parish, sent some people to tell me that he was sick. I hurried over. He had dysentery. He was happy to see me and we talked for many hours. After I had given him the last rites I went back to Dongtai. Two days later some of the faithful came over to tell me that Rouxin had died. I went back to take care of the funeral. Rouxin's predecessor had been Rev. Xu Piwen. On returning to Shanghai, Xu had left behind a large case of books, so I selected a few volumes to take back to Dongtai with me.

At that time the KMT was advancing partly from Taizhou and partly from Yangzhou. The Nationalist army commanded by Zhang Lingfu (1903–47) was heading south from Xuzhou, encircling the Communist New Fourth Army. The KMT air force passed over Dongtai repeatedly, so that we felt at the very centre of the action. The streets were full of troops of the New Fourth Army rushing about. Very few pedestrians were to be seen and the town looked deserted. Who would have thought that so soon after the end of the eight years of the Anti-Japanese War, our people would be fighting again?

A few days later, a priest who had been a missionary at Yancheng for many years named Rev. de Prunelle came to see me. He said that he was familiar with the county chief of Dongtai, Dong Xibai. When de Prunelle had been a teacher at St. Ignatius College, Dong had been his student. Later on Dong had studied in France and joined the Communist party. De Prunelle said that he would take me to meet Dong. So we went and found the county government in a big temple. When we had announced ourselves, Dong came out in person at once and invited us to sit in his office and drink tea. Dong told us that when in his youth he had entered St. Ignatius College, he had been rather skinny and had been bullied by the other students. De Prunelle had taken special care of him. He was grateful to de Prunelle. Dong and his subordinates all wore grey tunics in the style of Sun Yat-sen. When we left, Dong politely saw us off at the temple gate and told me to come and find him if I met with any difficulties. When I returned to China in 1951 I learned that Dong was working as the head of the Department of International Treaties at the Ministry of Foreign Affairs. On this occasion it was my very first time to enter a liberated zone and I was quite trepidatious. After meeting with Dong I got the measure of the situation and calmed down, even staying on in the liberated zone to visit the church.

Rev. Klement realised that I had faced danger by replacing him in the battle zone, enabling him to return to safety. Later on he was transferred to missionary work in the Philippines. He remained grateful to me. When in 1982 I was released from prison and permitted to return to Shanghai, he heard that I was setting up a seminary and was badly in need of funds. He was kind enough to send me US$3,000 a year to help me, for a total of twelve years until he died.

During my two months at Dongtai, I ran into no difficulties and had very little parochial work to do. On Sunday only about twenty people attended mass. They were mostly peasants from Qidong who grew cotton on the wastelands and lived very simply. I had two opportunities to go and visit them. They lived in very basic reed huts with only one room, a single bed and a small table with two or three small stools and a wok in the middle. These peasants farmed the saline land, which needed to be flushed with fresh water several times before it could be used for growing crops. The peasants grew mainly cotton to sell to the textile factories in Nantong. The fields of the Qidong people could at a glance be distinguished from those of the local Dongtai people—the Qidong people's crops grew vigorously and there were no weeds. While Rev. Xiang Zongze had been at Dongtai, he had given money to the Qidong parishioners who came to mass, but I gave them nothing during the two months I was there. After I returned to Shanghai, one among them named Zhang, who had some education, wrote to me and kept me up-to-date with their news.

The days in Dongtai passed peacefully; there were no newspapers to read, no radio to listen to the news on and because it was vacation time there were no students in the school. So there was plenty of time to pray. Next door there lived a Chinese herbal medicine doctor named Xu, who often came to chat with me. I told him about Catholic teaching and he expressed an interest in joining the Faith.

During those two months there was one dangerous interlude: one afternoon an army group arrived with about 200 men and many horses, saying that they were requisitioning the church and that we should hand over the property immediately. All this time the horses were neighing and the hubbub was overwhelming. I sent the gatekeeper Old Jie to deal with them and went into the church to pray to St. Joseph to protect us as he had protected the Holy Family. After praying I felt calmer and walked out of the church only to see the soldiers leading their horses away. I returned to the church and thanked St. Joseph for his intervention.

When, finally, the end of August came, I went to Dong to obtain a leave of passage. In the liberated zone there were patrols of child soldiers everywhere: they guarded the limits with zeal and would let no unauthorised person pass.

The boat returned to Taizhou and entered the KMT zone. The young KMT officer who boarded the boat to make an inspection suspected me of being a member of the New Fourth Army being sent to work underground in Shanghai. He detained me and questioned me for several hours. At first he threatened to arrest me, but later on let me go.

On my return to Shanghai, Rev. Henry told me: "You are not going to Wuhu; instead you will go to Huaiyin in Subei." A priest named Fu Shenglan who had originally been instructed to take up residence at Huaiyin and Lianshui parishes had heard about the fierce fighting there and had refused to go. Thus, at the last minute I was chosen to replace him and face death once again for a period of one year. At that time the KMT had ordered General Zhang Lingfu to advance on Huaiyin and Lianshui. The KMT fought with vigour, while the New Fourth Army met them with courage. It was a bitter fight and a very dangerous place to go. At Lianshui one nun of the Congregation of the Presentation of Our Lady to the Temple, on seeing Chiang Kai-shek's planes fly over on a bombing raid, had tried to save herself by climbing on the roof to hoist the Vatican flag, only to get shot by the New Fourth Army. Two French priests named Revs. Homo and Robert had travelled with the two priests Zhang Xiaosong and Zhang Jingchao from Haizhou in the KMT zone to the parish church of Shuyang in the liberated zone, where Rev. Zhang Dengyang was pastor, to celebrate a parish festival. When Zhang Lingfu's force took Lianshui they fiercely attacked Shuyang County. The New Fourth Army arrested the five priests and had them dig a big pit before shooting them. Rev. Fu had then been ordered to take up the vacant position, but had stayed in Shanghai and refused to go, which in the circumstances was certainly pardonable. I followed instructions and returned to Yangzhou, where I planned to take a boat to Huaiyin. While I was in Yangzhou waiting for the boat I learned that the Communists had retreated and that the KMT had opened up the Grand Canal.

Before the opening of the Tianjin–Pukou Railway, the Grand Canal had been the main north–south artery in China. North China and Beijing in particular had depended on the rice and salt that was transported from the south along the canal. The canal is very strange, standing as it does some four metres above the surrounding countryside, somewhat like a belt in mid-air. Due to the silting of the canal and the lack of dredging, the bottom of the canal has always kept rising and so the dykes have had to be raised higher and higher, so that now one can stand on the dyke and look down on the houses and the passers-by on the roads. On occasion the dyke has burst and then the water floods a thousand square kilometres, turning large areas of fertile land into a muddy waste and rendering thousands homeless and without land to farm. All these people could ever do was to become refugees and move south of the Yangtze in search of work as day-labourers. As I sat on the boat from Yangzhou we passed through Shaobo, Gaoyou, Baoying and Huainan, and finally reached Huaiyin, covering some 400 *li* in a day and a night. Huaiyin is an ancient city. It is famous as the place where the Han dynasty General Han Xin crawled between the legs of a local thug rather than take him on in combat. The Huaiyin Catholic church lies outside the city walls and had an elementary school. The priest's house was well known and very liveable.

Huaiyin is a big centre for the Protestants, with a very large hospital, a big church and splendid pastor's residence. The famous author Pearl Buck was born there. She went on to write 50 novels set in China and to win the Nobel Prize for Literature in 1938.

Huaiyin is also known as Qingjiangpu and is a thriving inland port.

The Catholic church was outside the city walls. There were only a few dozen parishioners because of the preponderance of Protestants. The elementary school, however, had over 300 students. After I got there, I invited many graduates of normal colleges to join us as teachers, thus raising the standard of education and attracting more students. Every day at 4 p.m. the students would gather in the playground and I would address them before they went home, which I enjoyed very much, so much so that I missed the students on Sundays. While I was at Huaiyin I added to the teaching materials and sports facilities, later on building three new classrooms. I have special place in my heart for Huaiyin and for Subei. Before then I had shared the prejudice of all Shanghainese and looked down on Subei people; but my experiences in Dongtai and Huaiyin caused me to like Subei people and to feel at home when I heard their dialect.

Not long after my arrival, the Huaiyin representative of the United Nations Relief and Rehabilitation Administration (UNRRA), Mr. Zhang, came to visit me and asked me to become his advisor. I happily accepted. On one occasion I travelled with him to Lianshui and in passing visited the Catholic church there. Of all the places I had visited up to that point Lianshui was the poorest: there were no two-storey buildings, just single-storey dwellings and reed huts. The impoverished inhabitants had few pieces of furniture in their homes. They wore old clothes covered in patches. The county chief took us around. We were filled with pity. Our job was to register each family and to report to our superiors. Within a few days Zhang and I returned with several trucks of flour, which we distributed. Zhang said that we should not rely on the government or the police to do this for us, but should distribute directly into the hands of the people. We proceeded according to the list of registered households and, ticking them off, gave out one bag after another to the people. Each household got two bags of white flour. On the return trip Zhang told me happily: "See how glad the people were!" Who could have known that we rejoiced too soon. Later on we learnt that after we had left, the local authorities had gone from home to home saying: "If we do not register you, you don't get any flour. So if you want to get any next time, you'd better share half with us now." So the unhappy people had no choice but to deliver up a half-share. The KMT were so corrupt, it is hard to exaggerate.

After I had been there for several months I learnt that the New Fourth Army was only sparing the cities. The KMT could only control the main highways and the suburban roads as well as some towns and villages along the Grand Canal, while most of the countryside was in Communist hands. One of the most shocking phenomena of that time was the emergence of the landlord militias. The Communist party would implement land reform, taking fields from the landowners and distributing them to the peasants. The landowners would then flee to the cities and form militias. When the KMT army was around, the militias would follow along, intending to settle scores. Armed with weapons the militias would take back land and property from the peasants with great brutality. These actions helped the KMT to lose the support of the people and led to their inexorable defeat.

On behalf of the elementary school I applied to Zhang for several hundred bags of flour and soya beans, which I used to build the new schoolrooms and to enlarge the school. When we were ready to inaugurate the new buildings we invited Zhang to come along and cut the ribbon. In his speech he said: "I have distributed great quantities of food aid; but it seems that only the Catholic Church has made good use of it." (Zhang had been principal of a middle school in Yangzhou and was very honest. He didn't allow his family to take any food aid, nor even an inch of cloth. When I visited his home in Yangzhou, I didn't see any grand furnishings. I greatly respected him.)

At the Huaiyin Church there were also three nuns. Their leader was an older woman named Chen. The other two were younger women and mainly involved in teaching the children. One of them was named Miao and was a graduate of Yangzhou Aurora Middle School; the other was named Rong and came from Shuyang. She had been transferred from Dongtai. The food they prepared for me was delicious—four dishes at every meal. On one occasion I visited their quarters (which I rarely did since it meant leaving the main gate of my lodging and entering in by the main gate of the female area) and found that the three of them were sharing just two dishes. I said to them: "You must eat the same food as I do," to which they nodded their heads in assent. A few days later I went again and they still had only two dishes. I lost my temper and said: "If you can only feign compliance with my orders, I will stop eating myself." The next time I went they had changed. Outside the city walls of Huaiyin there was no electricity so that we used oil lamps; but the nuns would save money by using cooking oil with a grass wick and do their homework by its meagre light. I again lost my temper and ordered them to use paraffin lamps. These nuns were really good: abstemious, dutiful and totally committed to serving the parish, worthy of my praise. If only today's nuns were like them! May God grant our prayer.

In the first half of my life, before I was arrested, I collaborated with the nuns of the Congregation of the Presentation of Our Lady to the Temple at Dongtai and at Huaiyin. That these nuns were instructed by foreign superiors is something I can never forget. In my estimation the sisters of the Congregation of the

Presentation of Our Lady to the Temple have a very elevated position. In those days the foreign nuns living in China all worked in the cities and lived in good conditions with Western food and accommodation. The vast countryside was looked after by the Chinese sisters. They endured tough conditions and worked hard. They followed my work with total commitment, asking for no reward, doing everything for the Church. They were truly admirable. May the nuns we train today exceed in devotion the ones once trained by foreigners!

In March 1947 I was visited by a Frenchman who subsequently played a significant role in my life. His name was Rev. Marcel Bith (1883–1963). He was the provincial superior of Paris of the Society of Jesus, to which Shanghai reported. Every six years the provincial head was required to inspect his territories. On this occasion Bith specifically requested to see me and so I travelled to Yangzhou to meet him and Rev. Fernand Lacretelle (1902–89). Bith and I talked for an hour. The next day Bith said that he would like to go to Huaiyin, so we took the long-distance bus, which was in those days very uncomfortable with wooden seats and a low roof, whereas Bith was rather tall. The bus took six hours, a most exhausting ride. Both men stayed in Huaiyin for a day, noting the life of the Subei missionaries. I suggested to Zhang of UNRRA that Bith and Lacretelle might get a ride back to Yangzhou in the UN jeep. Before Bith left China, he called a conference at which he stated his intention of taking me back to France with him, after which he intended that I should go to Rome to study for a doctorate of theology and one day return to China as a teacher of theology. Some of the French attendees at the conference opposed this idea. In particular Rev. Joseph Verdier struck the table with his fist and told Bith that Chinese who went to Europe did not follow orders and on return no longer respected the French missionaries. He also said that Chinese were not qualified to teach theology. The French missionaries had been in Shanghai for 100 years and in that time Chinese had never been permitted to teach at Aurora University, at the Observatory or at the College of Theology. Bith could do nothing; just report to the superior general and let him decide.

I had lived with the Jesuits in Shanghai for ten years and had spent one year at Xianxian. Shanghai came under the Paris province and Xianxian under that of Champagne. Of the two, the Champagne province paid more attention to the encyclical of Benedict XV entitled *Maximum Illud*, which required the indigenisation of human resources and the early transmission of dioceses to local candidates. The Champagne province was more open and more far-sighted in this regard.

In the 1930s the Society of Jesus of Xianxian in Hebei Province suggested to Rome the appointment of Zhao Zhensheng as bishop; in the 1940s the Chinese Zhang Silian became father superior; they also sent many Chinese abroad to further their studies. By contrast, when the Bishop of Shanghai Haouisée fell sick and the Paris province had to name a successor, their choice fell on another Frenchman named C. Dumas, whom they transferred from the Observatory and appointed as the dean of Sheshan District. Dumas told his friends that the only reason his superiors would not let him do astronomy was because they wished to prepare him to be bishop. However, Dumas couldn't speak Chinese and when he took over at Sheshan, he was unable to communicate with the local priests, who for this reason did not welcome him. Accordingly, Bishop Haouisée and Jesuit father superior Henry realised that their plan to cultivate Dumas had failed and so they moved him to Aurora University as president. Evidently, as late as the 1940s the Frenchmen were still unwilling to transfer power, not even when the whole country had been liberated, leading to them finally being ejected beyond China's borders.

While I was living in Subei, Rev. Henry came to see me. He travelled from Taizhou to Dongtai and then on to Yancheng. On entering the liberated zone at Funing he was immediately arrested. Henry had a long beard that fell to his chest and looked somewhat like a Daoist immortal, so the New Fourth Army just put him under house arrest and limited his movements. For nearly three months Shanghai had no news of him and the diocese and Society of Jesus considered that he must have already been killed. They arranged a large memorial mass in the cathedral, the whole church billowing with black streamers. Later on the Liberation Army had made a strategic retreat and Henry had been freed to return to Shanghai. He appeared in the church in the middle of the memorial mass and told everyone: "I am still very much alive." The whole congregation burst into applause and the memorial mass turned into a thanksgiving mass.

Part III

Life as an Overseas Student

16
Travel to Europe

In mid-June 1947 I received a letter from Rev. Lacretelle telling me that Bith had petitioned the superior general and that the latter had authorised me to travel to Europe. The letter instructed me to go to Shanghai to prepare to leave for my studies in France. My immediate superior, the supervisor of Yangzhou district, Rev. Lauzon wrote to Lacretelle saying that he was aware that the superior general had authorised me to go to Europe, but that he could not spare me before the end of August. Lauzon set out for Huaiyin in order to detain me, but only arrived three hours after I had already left on the long-distance bus to Shanghai. In those days there were no mobile telephones, so he had no means of calling me back.

Upon arrival in Shanghai I learned that Rev. Zhang Boda (1905–51) had strongly recommended that Zhu Shude go to France, while Rev. G. Germain had suggested that his subordinate Wang Rensheng should visit France. I also learned that Germain had bought Wang a second-class ticket, while Zhu Shude and I myself had to make do with third class. In the second half of June we boarded the *S.S. Andre Lebrun* and left Shanghai. This ship had originally been German, but in 1918 after WWI the French had seized it in reparation. When Deng Xiaoping travelled to France for work and study he sailed on this very ship, which was remarkably old. The first port of call was Hong Kong, where we stopped for two days to board passengers and cargo. In those days Hong Kong only had about 400,000 inhabitants and was far smaller than Shanghai. We went on shore to visit the cathedral and the Jesuit-run Huanan Seminary and Huaren Library.

The second port of call was Saigon (today's Ho Chi Minh City) where we stopped for three days during which we were warmly entertained by the priests of the Paris Overseas Missionary Society. We visited many churches and the

Chinatown of Cholon outside Saigon, which had a population of some 200,000 at that time. Cholon was reminiscent of Canton.

The third stop was Colombo where we visited churches, Church schools and hospitals. In the evening the Marist Brothers invited us to dine in their garden by the seashore. The sun went down in the west, the myriad stars shone, the scenery was beautiful. At this moment all fell silent and as I relaxed in my chair my worries fell away: "Oh Sea, praise the Lord." This hymn came into my mind and I realised that Ceylon was an earthly paradise with tall coconut trees everywhere and coconuts hanging high up in their foliage. A young man carrying a wooden stick climbed up to the top of a tree and picked several coconuts, cut them open and drank off the milk—a most satisfying and therapeutic taste. We ate supper in the garden. The first course was a plate of noodles, with an accompanying dish of yellow sauce. I saw our host pick up the dish and empty its contents over his noodles, mix it together and eat. I did as the Romans do and poured the entire contents of my dish over my noodles, only to realise at the first mouthful that it was incredibly spicy and hot. This was my first taste of curry. Out of courtesy to my hosts I had no choice but to finish my plate, drinking copious quantities of water after every mouthful. On finishing I could only imagine my stomach burning up, as if I had been plunged headlong from heaven into the fiery pit, all the while smiling and conversing with my host. I will never forget that embarrassing occasion.

The steamer sailed from Colombo into the Indian Ocean. It was already the time of the summer monsoon and huge waves continuously lifted the ship right up and then crashed it down, so that the hull rolled back and forth. Most of the passengers were violently sick and lay in their bunks, causing the usually busy saloon to be empty of diners, so that I took my meals completely alone.

After more than ten days at sea in the Indian Ocean, life became tedious and nothing appeared on the horizon. There were two interludes to break the monotony. On one occasion a French woman, after quarrelling with her husband, jumped in a fit of rage over the side of the ship into the ocean. When the other passengers saw this they rushed up on deck and raised the alarm. All they could see was that the woman had not sunk and that her two arms and head were intermittently visible swimming towards the ship. The ship moved rather fast and the woman was obviously unable to catch up. The passengers saw her slowly receding into the distance and became frantic, so the captain ordered an about-turn and a group of sailors were lowered in a lifeboat by others operating the ropes. On reaching the woman they pulled her into the boat and the sailors on deck raised the boat up again. The dripping woman was returned to her husband and the little family drama, like an opera, drew to a close with everyone heaving a sigh of relief and leaving the deck.

Another episode saw an elderly passenger suddenly die of a heart attack. It was the height of summer and very hot. In those days there was no air-conditioning and no cold store that could be used to preserve the body from rotting for a few days, so the family agreed to a burial at sea. The old man was carried to the deck, his national flag was raised and the ship came to a stop. To the sound of the band they tipped his body into the ocean and gathered in the ropes. As he slipped beneath the waves the ship resumed its passage westwards. The old man was a Frenchman who had spent many years in Vietnam and had planned to spend his last years peacefully in his hometown, but instead had found a watery grave. In comparison, the woman preferred to take her own life, but when faced with death, changed her mind and her life was saved.

The steamer made its way slowly across the Indian Ocean. The monsoon blew constantly and the waves roared without cease, while rain poured down. It was truly a case of being exposed to the elements. Most of the passengers could not stand up and spent every day lying on their beds in the hold. It was very boring. There were no birds in the sky and no fish to be seen in the sea. Apart from looking at faces one was already familiar with, there was no other life to be seen.

In order to avoid the worst of the monsoon, the captain made a change of direction, making the journey longer and causing a shortage of water that forced him to order an unscheduled call at Aden to refill the tanks.

The steamer slowed down and left the path of the monsoon; the wind fell and the waves subsided while the sun emerged from the clouds. We could at last see the shore and the passengers on deck all spontaneously cheered the sight. People cannot live without land, nor can they go without the society of others.

Aden is located at the point where the Indian Ocean and the Red Sea meet. It is a place through which the maritime trade between Asia and Europe must pass; this was especially true before the passage of the Suez Canal. It was occupied by Britain, originally as a protectorate, later on as a colony and finally became an important naval base (in November 1967 the Republic of Yemen was established, with Aden as its capital). When I went on shore I discovered that Aden is built on rock and that the whole city is a dusty grey, without any greenery. Because there is no soil, it is a place where nothing can grow apart from a few trees, planted in imported soil that had subsequently been blown away causing the trees to die. The city had no agriculture, no horticulture and no animal husbandry. All fruit, vegetables and meat were imported. There was, however, some industry in the shape of a very large petroleum refinery (supplied with oil from the Arabian Peninsula). Aden had soldiers, workers and civil servants, but no farmers. We visited a wonderful middle school organised by the Marist Brothers, where we were warmly welcomed.

The ship now entered the Red Sea, bringing to my mind the Old Testament story of how Moses led the Israelites out of captivity in Egypt by crossing the Red Sea and how Pharaoh's army pursued them and came to grief beneath its waves. I soon discovered by looking at it that the Red Sea is far from being red. The surface of the sea also seemed very vast. In order for the sea to part and for a large group of Israelite refugees carrying heavy burdens to cross, for one half of the sea to stand up like a liquid wall reaching to the clouds and for this situation to continue for several days and nights, until, when Pharaoh's army advanced onto the seabed of the Red Sea, the wall collapsed and caused the soldiers to drown, would require an earth-shattering event so rarely seen that one can only wonder why it left no historical evidence. I could not help pondering this question.

The ship entered the Suez Canal. The Red Sea and the Mediterranean are only 200 km apart, separated by a strip of land that at the same time connects the two continents of Africa and Asia. From ancient times, all ships that wished to sail to Asia from places such as Italy, Spain or France, had to sail first not east, but west into the Atlantic Ocean and then travel south some 8,000 km to reach the Cape of Good Hope, circumnavigate the cape and then follow the east coast of Africa for some 6,000 km before finally turning east for Asia. This huge detour added more than 10,000 miles to every voyage. Then in the 19th century a French engineer named Ferdinand de Lesseps (1805–94) decided that it was necessary to build a canal at this intersection between the two continents of Africa and Asia, but he had little time and no money. He travelled everywhere at great speed, doing site investigation, making designs and raising money. He met with a thousand obstacles and spent more than ten years to realise his dream. The Suez Canal was 190 km long, 20 m deep and 67 m wide (it was later deepened and widened). De Lesseps' work has enriched humankind and his renown will last for a thousand years. The same man also designed and built the Panama Canal that joins the Atlantic and Pacific Oceans.

Our ship stopped for half a day at Suez and again at Port Said, then entered the Mediterranean and headed for Marseilles in France.

In those days the Mediterranean had not been polluted; the waters were azure blue and the surface was mirror-still. During the several days that we steamed across its waters, the weather was perfect and at dusk the falling sun reflected off the water with a thousand rays, while the sky filled with stars, causing me to recite ceaselessly: "Oh Sea, praise the Lord."

After only a few days we reached Marseilles, viewing from far off the steeple of the great church on the hill with its bronze statue of the Virgin Mother. Marseilles is an ancient city and has been a port from time immemorial. The inhabitants are either fishermen or sailors, who pray fervently to the Holy Mother to protect them and to bring them safely home. While they are battling the waves they continue to pray to the Virgin, while their families on shore pray for their safe return. From boarding the ship in Shanghai to disembarking in Marseilles had taken 32 days—a journey I now make by airplane in some 12 hours.

17
Tertianship in France (1947–48)

At Marseilles an old Jesuit brother met us off the ship and assisted us with immigration procedures, collecting luggage and transport to the Jesuit house.

In the summer of 1947 it was only two years since the end of WWII and one could still see many sunken ships in the harbour, with only masts or funnels poking above the surface. No one had had time to salvage them. Walking through the streets one could see ruined walls and wreckage, creating a desolate effect and reminding one of the horrors of war and of humankind's need for peace.

We stayed two days in Marseilles. On the third day we took the express train to Paris, leaving at 8 a.m. and arriving at 10 p.m.—covering some 800 km in 14 hours (a journey that today takes just 3 hours). A few young Jesuits waited for us at the station and brought us to the Jesuit house at 42 Rue de Grenelle. The next day the three of us went to meet Provincial Bith, who expressed joy at our arrival. He suggested that we first explore Paris, then attend the inter-provincial congress he had proposed be organised to explore the issue of how the Society of Jesus could contribute to the objective of world peace.

There was a constant flow of Jesuits coming to Paris—on business, for tourism, as immigrants. The father minister looked after all of them and was extremely busy. He told me that he had accommodated over 2,000 Jesuits in 1946. According to the daily number of visitors, he needed to arrange for them all to say mass once a day. He collected no extra fees, but according to the Jesuit rule of *Ubi Missa, ibi Mensa*, each visitor expected an altar at which to say mass and a table at which to dine.

I had lived with French Jesuits for over ten years and was used to their food and drink, but there was an embarrassing moment when, after lunch, a small dish of fruit appeared, including a bunch of grapes. I started to eat them according to the Chinese custom, spitting out the skin and the pips, only to see all around me swallowing them whole. I could not spit, but was also unable to swallow, so could only retain more and more skins and pips in my mouth, such that I could no longer talk to the people next to me and just smiled, waiting with difficulty until the superior rang the bell and read the post-prandial prayer. Then, while the rest of the group proceeded to the chapel for the Adoration, I slipped into the lavatory and was finally able to spit out the contents of my mouth.

On arrival in Paris the father minister took Zhu Shude and me to the police station to register, so that we could obtain bread ration coupons. In those days bread was rationed, with each person getting 500 g of black bread (made with maize flour), which was later reduced to 250 g, apart from which we ate potatoes. I thought the cooked food worse than in Shanghai. The United States had launched the Marshall Plan to send agricultural products and other commodities to relieve the famine as well as lend capital and make grants to help with the reconstruction of Europe's industrial capacity. France considered that accepting charitable donations of food was a national disgrace and initially refused to subscribe to this plan. Meanwhile other countries joined the Marshall Plan and quickly improved their peoples' living standards, causing their economies to rapidly pick up. When France saw this and realised how long it would take to recover without foreign assistance, she realised her mistake and joined up. The people immediately got white bread and plenty of meat products and France caught up with the other Western European countries.

Paris had once been the cultural capital of France and of all Europe, counting among the most beautiful cities in the world. When the Nazis took Paris in WWII, the French army surrendered and the French government announced that it would not defend Paris and retreated so that the German air force would not bomb the city. Thus Paris escaped the destruction that would have ensued had it been subjected to attacks. Similarly, when, later on during China's civil war, Chiang Kai-shek ordered Beijing to fight to the death, to the potential destruction of all, General Fu Zuoyi (1895–1974) made a plan to surrender the city peacefully to the Liberation Army and thus save it from destruction.

We explored Paris in the company of two young French Jesuits, starting at Notre Dame de Paris and the Sacré Coeur. The latter is an awesome basilica on a hilltop in the suburbs, at the foot of which is a convent which is the original location where St. Ignatius and his followers initiated and established the Society of Jesus. I said mass there and prayed to God that I might all my life be a dutiful Jesuit.

Apart from visiting churches, we also went to museums, the Arc de Triomphe and the Étoile at which nine streets meet—an extraordinary sight. We also strolled along the Champs Élysées and the banks of the River Seine. I was very interested to see all the second-hand book stalls along the banks of the river. We also visited the Eiffel Tower, but since we had no money to buy tickets, we could only admire it from below. After this I visited the tower many times, but each time the price had gone up and we always found it too expensive. In recent years I have visited Paris many times, but was always too busy to take time off and so I have never yet ascended the Eiffel Tower.

The architecture of Paris is distinguished by the fact that the government does not permit the construction of tall buildings, so that from every rooftop one can look out on the whole city without any impeding sky-scrapers (which may only be built in the suburbs). This is very different from the notions governing the development of large cities in China. For example Beijing's city wall has been destroyed and there are not many traditional courtyard houses left.

We also visited various middle schools and charitable institutes managed by the Jesuits. I visited the offices of the monthly *Études*, paying a visit to the object of my admiration, Rev. Jules Lebreton. He was a famous theologian and an expert in Bible studies. I had read many of his books and he gave me a warm welcome.

I also paid a visit to Rev. Teilhard de Chardin, the world-famous palaeontologist and philosopher (whom I have already mentioned). He and I had a long conversation. As he accompanied me to the door, he slapped me on the shoulder and kindly said: "You are at least 40 years out of date." Because of his advanced thinking and expositions, critical letters flew to Rome like flakes of snow. He went to Rome to explain himself. At that time the superior general of the Jesuits was Jean-Baptiste Janssens (1889–1964), a scholar of Catholic canon law. The people he trusted, such as the Belgian theologian Edouard Dhanis (1902–78), all opposed modernism and were unable to understand Teilhard's work and made no attempt to speak in his defence. A number of theologians led by the Dominican Reginald Marie Garrigou-Lagrange (1877–1964) and other Roman theologians all strongly criticised him. At one meeting Teilhard pointed at Garrigou and said: "That man wants to burn me at the stake." Later on Teilhard could do nothing but leave Europe and seek refuge in the more liberal atmosphere of New York and hide out at the Jesuit house there. On leaving Paris, Teilhard planned to give his most important manuscripts to the *Études* publishing house; but the director and chief editor René d'Ouince

(1896–1973) told him: "If you leave your books here they definitely will not be published, since they will have to be investigated and authorised by the Church authorities and progressive books are bound to be suppressed. Perhaps you'd better give them to a trusted friend and ask him to look after them and find a way to publish them." Teilhard took d'Ouince's advice and gave his works to a close friend who published them after his death; they have never been out of print since and have been translated into many languages. Teilhard lived a very quiet life with the Jesuits in America. He died on Easter Sunday, 1955 and some ten people attended his interment.

The Jesuit Inter-Provincial Peace Conference took place at Versailles, near the former palace that Louis XIV built to entertain himself and his courtiers and mistresses. After WWI the Paris Peace Conference had taken place in 1919 in the famous Hall of Mirrors. That conference was organised to distribute the spoils to the victors and was neither fair to the weak, such as China, nor anything but extremely cruel to the defeated nations, Germany and Austria. On the day of the signing of the treaty, the presiding French prime-minister Georges Clemenceau (1841–1929) used a most dismissive cry to "bring on the Germans" and sought to punish the Germans, thus laying the seeds for WWII. The same conference awarded Germany's treaty possessions in China to Japan, which was treated as a national disgrace by both the Germans and the Chinese.

The Jesuits had a famous school named the College of St. Genevieve at Versailles. The students were all high school graduates and came there to spend two years preparing to enter the *grands écoles*. The school grounds were very large.

Apart from the provincials of the four Jesuit provinces of France, attendees came from several US provinces and universities, filling the hall. The conference was opened by Rev. Bith. He said that when he had been in Rome for the election of the new superior general, he had talked to many fellow provincials and had found that they mostly shared his view that it was vital to educate a new generation dedicated to peace and filled with the spirit of love and the desire for peace. Because of the lack of communication and cooperation in the Society of Jesus he felt the need to call such a meeting.

Several famous experts were called to give papers at the conference including: the Marxist thinker Rev. Gaston Fessard (1897–1978); René d'Ouince, the publisher of *Études;* the theologian Henri-Marie de Lubac (1896–1991), who shortly after was dismissed and then later appointed cardinal; Teilhard de Chardin and his assistant Pierre Leroy. During his speech one US provincial said: "We are discussing the most vital problem. It is among youth that we should plant the seeds of peace. Yet I notice that in this very school there are many photographs of WWI and WWII, which can only lead French youth to hate Germans. I suggest that the French Jesuits change these photographs in this and other schools." His speech was greeted with long applause. Once when I was talking to a French youth in a hotel about being friendly to Germans, he firmly said: "No way." I said: "In the future we will all go to heaven and spend eternity together." He replied: "If there are Germans in heaven, then I have no desire to go there." This story demonstrates the bitter hatred between the French and Germans. Fortunately after WWII the French, German and Italian nations produced three great politicians—Conrad Adenauer in Germany, Alcide de Gasperi in Italy and Robert Schumann in France. They insisted that France and Germany should bury the hatchet and build a mutual friendship. They first organised the European Coal and Steel Community and shared their resources, thus overcoming a basic cause for war. They believed that war was in fact a creation of capitalists competing for resources and trying to control markets. For this reason they signed the Treaty of Rome in 1957, the first step towards today's European Union. Now there is no hatred between citizens of Europe. The French and Germans get on well together and war cannot take place.

After the conference Rev. de la Largère, head of the missionary department of the Paris province of the Society of Jesus, who had been a missionary in Shanghai, came to see me. He told me that he had recently bought a motor car and needed to run it in. Would I like to join him on a road trip? I of course accepted and travelled with him to Evreux, Rouen, Tours, Le Mans, Laval, Poitiers and other towns. We visited many churches and Jesuit schools. At Laval there was a Jesuit noviciate where I saw two old acquaintances: one named Rev. Alliaume, who was recovering from an illness. He had been parish priest of Hengsha Island in Shanghai for many years, then deputy parish priest of the Xujiahui Church. He had left his heart in China and hoped to return to Shanghai after his recovery. The other was a young man named de Margerie, a graduate of the Law Department of Aurora University. His father had been consul general of France for the French Concession in Shanghai in the days when that was a truly powerful position. The father was reputed to be a lapsed Catholic, even though the mother was very pious, so one would not have guessed that the young man would become a Jesuit. Both men greeted me with enthusiasm. Later on the younger man went to the Soviet Union as a missionary and died in Paris in 2003.

After driving around northern France we returned to Paris and I went back to Versailles again where eight young men were studying Chinese with a view to taking up missionary work in China. They were being taught by two Oratorian brothers: one named Wu from Suzhou in Jiangsu, the other named Huang from Anhui. Both men enjoyed singing Peking Opera and playing the *huqin*—every evening they would entertain us with a few tunes. They had both originally been members of the Communist party, holding senior positions. When Chiang Kai-shek arrested thousands of communists in April 1927 their influential families were able to save their lives by sending them to Paris. They had first studied at Lyon University; then they met the Jesuits and, abandoning Marxism-Leninism, had followed Christ and been baptised. They had asked Rev. de Lubac to be their father master. They decided to abandon their families, take holy orders and commit their lives to spreading the word of God. They originally had wanted to join the Society of Jesus, but de Lubac had considered their characters more suited to the Congregation of Oratorians. Thus they joined the Oratory and later on became priests. Rev. Huang had translated *Laozi* into French, a rendition that I consider to be the most faithful to the original. Another good friend of mine, Rev. R.P. Golliet was also an Oratorian and much later gave me a large sum of money when I set up the Guangqi Training Centre in Shanghai. He didn't want his name recorded, but asked that the gift be used to preserve the memory of the two Chinese Oratorians Wu and Huang. When I was about to return to China in 1951 I ran into them again. They said that they had known Liu Shaoqi and Zhou Enlai and would come to no harm in China. Now I realise that, had they returned home, they would have been arrested as traitors and spies, shut up in prison and tortured to death.

On 6 October Rev. Zhu Shude and I left Paris and travelled to a small town near Lyon called Paray-le-Monial where we reported to the Jesuit house and began our tertianship. Just as the name implies, the tertianship is the very last practical test and examination, unique to the Jesuits. To become a Jesuit, one can take one's first vow after the novitiate, which lasts two years. There follows the study of literature, philosophy, theology and so on. Then one begins the tertianship, after which one is called to final vows within the Society of Jesus.

Paray-le-Monial is a small town, famous for the appearance of the Sacred Heart to Saint Margaret Mary Alacoque of the Congregation of the Visitation of the Holy Mary. As a result of the visitation many orders had built convents there and the place attracted large numbers of pilgrims to pray at the Chapel of the Visitation.

Tertianship in France (1947–48)

Some thirty or more people had already registered for tertianship, including two Americans, one Lebanese, one Egyptian, one Brazilian, one Argentinian and we two from China. The others were all French. When I returned to France in 2003 I learned that they had all gone to see their creator and that I was the only one still on this earth. The instructor and teacher was an old priest named Rev. Verny, who was already 70 years old. He had lost an arm in WWI and had spent most of his life in Beirut in Lebanon where he had been Chancellor of St. Joseph University for many years. He loved Lebanon and would often talk of the country's beauty and the kindness of the people. How sad it is to think that Lebanon has since become a war zone.

The main topic of the course was spirituality. Every second day the instructor would teach us spirituality and expound the rule of the Jesuits: to strengthen our spiritual skills, pray and read the Bible. Most important was to do the spiritual exercises of St. Ignatius for a month and also go to the parishes to preach for 40 days. During those 40 days there was no one at the house so Zhu Shude used the time to go to Paris University and listen to lectures and work on his doctoral thesis. I went to stay at the Jesuit theological college in Lyon.

This theological college is situated at the top of a small hill named Fourvière outside Lyon, not far from the great basilica and the archbishop's palace. In those days the theological college was full of creative energy, bringing together many famous theologians such as Henri-Marie de Lubac, Joseph Bonsirven, Pierre Ganne, Alexandre Durand and Henri Rondet. They emphasised the return of theology to the origins of the Church, the Early Fathers and the Bible. They used contemporary language to transmit the wisdom recorded by the Jews and the Greeks. Fourvière had a great influence on the study of theology, bringing alarm into the lives of traditional theologians and exciting hostile reports that were constantly sent to Rome. Given any group, there will always be tale-tellers whose reports give pleasure to the leaders: it has always been thus, from ancient times until today, both in China and abroad, without any exception. The superior general of the Jesuits sent his trusted follower, the Belgian Rev. Dhanis to be inquisitor and to inspect the two French schools of philosophy and two schools of theology, in particular the theological college at Fourvière. In consequence the Pope published the encyclical *Humani Generis* in 1950, as a result of which the teaching staff at Fourvière was fundamentally changed; the original lecturers were removed and replaced with ones from the conservative wing of the Church.

While I was at the college of theology the authorities arranged for me to stay in the room next to that of Rev. de Lubac, giving me the opportunity to have long conversations with him from which I reaped no small benefit. He taught religion at Lyon University. He led a group of young men who became the leading priests of their generation. He and Rev. Jean Daniélou (1905–74) collaborated in the publication of the great works of the Early Fathers, known as the *Sources Chretiennes* series, which were widely disseminated. Daniélou later became rector of the Institut Catholique de Paris and was made a cardinal by Pope Paul VI.

During WWI, since young Frenchmen were all called up to serve in the army, the factories were short of labour and the Beiyang government sent many young Chinese to fill their places, thus enabling production to continue. Under the Boxer Indemnity agreement, the French government returned a sum of money, which the Chinese side used to build a Chinese–French University at Lyon. For this reason there were many overseas Chinese in Lyon and the Jesuits had set up a small organisation to help them. On Sundays I would go there to lend a hand. I greatly respected one young labourer who came from Qingtian in Wenzhou. His family had been very poor and his education level was low, but he had decided to explore the world, with only a basket of Qingtian stone and not a word of any foreign language. From Wenzhou he had made his way to north-east China, then to Siberia, Ukraine, Poland and Germany before he arrived at Lyon. Several years later he married a lovely French girl and opened a fairly large store, selling leather goods. Wenzhou people are really impressive.

People had told me that not far from our house was the famous Trappist monastery Abbaye des Sept Fons. The Trappist rule is very strict. The monks are not permitted to leave the monastery after entering, and are required to devote their lives to prayer and labour, singing the daily office, rising in the middle of the night to pray together, strictly maintaining silence, talking only to God. Before the Liberation there were Trappist monasteries at Yangjiaping and Zhengding in Hebei. Two of my school-fellows went there to praise the Lord, one named Zhu Sipei from Caijiawan in Qingpu and the other You Zhongjie from the parish of St. Joseph in Shanghai. I have great respect for the Trappists.

One day I requested a day's leave from our instructor and went to the Trappist monastery to pray. The brother who received me told me very happily that they had a young Chinese monk in the monastery and called him to accompany me. Soon there arrived a very handsome young man who spoke precise Parisian French, but could not speak Chinese. He introduced himself saying that his name was Wang Chuan and saying that he could only write two characters: the four strokes of Wang (王) and the three strokes of Chuan (川). His father was a KMT diplomat, his mother a daughter of Li Zhike, manager of the Commercial Press in Shanghai. His father had originally worked at the Chinese embassy in Paris, but had left his son in the care of a French family when he had been transferred to South America. Thus Wang could only speak French and knew no Chinese. After the war his parents had come to see him, but his father could only communicate with him through his bilingual mother. While at his foster parents' home Wang had read the moving story of St. Thérèse of Lisieux and had been inspired to become a Catholic. After graduation he had, after long thought and prayer, decided to become a monk and had chosen the strictest order, the Trappists, so that he could devote his whole life to praying and working for the whole human race. He had travelled at great risk across the German occupied zone to Vichy to seek admittance to this monastery. We had a very enjoyable conversation. After returning to China I remained in correspondence with him up until the day I was arrested and imprisoned. When I recalled that Dr. Wu Jingxiong (1900–86), second representative of the Republic of China at the Vatican, also became a Catholic after reading *The Story of a Soul*, the autobiography of St. Thérèse of Lisieux, I came to realise that she is one of the greatest proselytisers of the Church.

While I was doing my tertianship, the instructor invited many theologians and social activists to come to Lyon to talk. Many of these talks I have forgotten, but one Jesuit worker-priest's speech really inspired me and has remained with me. This priest was about 40 years old and of about medium height with a square face. He wore workman's clothes and told us very directly about his vocation. He said:

> In the past France was an agricultural country and the Church rooted itself among the farmers. At the centre of every village there was a church, with a Church school next to it and a cemetery on the other side. The faithful went out at dawn and returned at dusk, then went to church to read the Bible. Everyone was registered at birth with their christening in the church, spent their school days in the Church school, was married in the church and after death was buried in the cemetery. The Church was the centre of the farmers' lives. When people had a problem they went to the parish priest to sort it out and even arbitrate disputes. For over 1,000 years it has been so.

> When the Industrial Revolution started factories were built and the surplus rural population moved to the towns, losing their lands and gaining no property, instead living in cheap workmen's cottages built for them by the capitalists. They also became estranged from the Church and the parish priest. The capitalists exploited their labour ruthlessly and no one protected them or spoke up for them. The urban poor came to feel abandoned and to be filled with hatred. The children were uncared for and uneducated: after two or three generations the workers had lost their homes, their religious faith and had become a working class, falling to the lowest level of proletariat. The number of peasant farmers slowly decreased and that of workers rapidly increased. Faced with the aristocracy, the capitalists and the Church, the workers resorted to class warfare and social stability was affected.

The priest said that in the past all the bishops and abbots were members of the nobility and thus had always served the wealthy more than the poor. Over the last 200 years the number of faithful had declined, the ranks of non-believers had swelled and no Church served the proletariat. The Church needed to proselytise the proletariat, not preach the Gospel to everyone but the workers. Also, we should join the workers, use our bodies as witness, spread the Gospel anew and give rise to a worker-priest movement. The priests should not ape the manners of the bourgeoisie, but should become workers, work alongside workers, share the lives of workers so as to be accepted by them, gain their attention, their trust and bring them back into the Christian fold. He said that the life of the worker-priest was very hard, living in a tiny room, without proper furniture. Were the priests to live well, the workers would pay no attention to them. Worker-priests should not eat more than a worker's salary could buy and should wear the factory-issued clothing or buy the cheapest clothes in the market. When the other workers returned home after the eight-hour shift, the worker-priests' work had just begun. They visited workers, helped them, avoiding elegant words and a dignified bearing and instead adopting the workers' straightforward language and coarse character so as to be accepted and not treated as an outsider.

He said that on one occasion a certain worker had found a dead rabbit in a rubbish bin and had cooked it and invited him to eat. The priest was obliged to share in the worker's pleasure at this special meal. After a time the worker-priests and the workers came to share the same language, the same scale of values and share the same benefits. The worker-priests also joined the labour unions and the fight against the capitalists. They struggled together, demonstrated together, even got arrested by the police together with the workers. In the 1940s the leader of the worker-priest movement, Jacques Loew (1908–99), was well received by the workers, but was resented by the capitalists and by the upper class. The latter felt that the worker-priests were neglecting their proper duties, stirring up trouble and losing the respect due to the priesthood. Critical letters were sent to Rome. Pope Pius XII issued an apostolic exhortation. The Archbishop of Paris, Mgr. Maurice Feltin (1883–1975) travelled to Rome to see the Pope and plead the case of the worker-priests, but the Pope would not listen to him and issued an order instructing priests not to become workers. This brought a thriving movement to a premature close. There were a few worker-priests who did not want to leave the workers and continued as before, but they were not many. People felt that it was a great shame that there were no successors to the worker-priest movement. In my heart I retain great respect for those worker-priests.

After Easter I returned to Paray-le-Monial to complete my tertianship. On one occasion I was invited to a girls' middle school to give a speech on the Church in China. Afterwards a woman brought her daughter to visit my spiritual advisor, saying that her daughter had been inspired by my talk and wished to donate all her savings of about US$1,000 to the Church in China. I was deeply moved. The girl was named Teresa. Later I was invited to visit parishes in Macon, Creuzot (the town where Deng Xiaoping had worked during his stay in France) and Autun to give talks about China. At the parish of Sainte Foy, a child named Raphael Cannard wrote to me saying that he had always been a naughty child and a poor student, but had changed his attitude after listening to me. I continued to correspond with these two children, but lost contact with them when I was arrested. I miss them to this day. While at Paray-le-Monial I was often sent to the parish church to say mass and hear confessions, so I learned a great deal about the ordinary French people.

18
Learning English

After the tertianship was over, I went to Provincial Bith and applied to go to Ireland to learn English. He gave his permission. I intended to travel first to the Enghien College of Theology in Belgium. A Jesuit who had learned that I planned to go to Belgium approached me and told me that his aunt was returning to Belgium the following afternoon. Would I like a lift in her car? Naturally I accepted. The next day the aunt and her husband came to the Jesuit house to pick me up, thus saving me a lot of money. They were very friendly. They lived at Courtray, not far from Lille. It was a four-hour drive to their home, which was a very large house with an expansive garden. Later on they took me to the station and bought me a ticket, after which it took me about an hour to reach my objective. There I attended the ordination and celebration of my old friend Pierre Tritz.

After leaving Enghien, I went to Bruges where I stayed at the Benedictine Monastery of Saint-André. Lu Zhengxiang (aka Lou Tseng-Tsiang 1871–1949) was there and I wanted to pay him a visit. Lu was a Shanghai native, who had originally been a Protestant. During the late Qing dynasty he had matriculated at the School of Foreign Languages in Shanghai and later joined the foreign ministry. He was sent to work at the Chinese embassy in Russia, where he married the niece of the Belgian ambassador and converted to Catholicism. He was clever and hard working, so the ambassador Xu Jingcheng promoted him in his career. Later on Xu was transferred back to Beijing where he got mixed up in the Boxer Rebellion, when an uprising with the slogan 'Support the Qing and Destroy the Foreigners' was combined with superstitious rumours of invincibility to swords and bullets that at first convinced the Empress Dowager Cixi that it could rid China of the foreigners. Xu recognised that the Boxers were talking rubbish and that they were a motley rabble only able to bring chaos to China. He wrote a memorandum to the court, but, in order to win favour with the Boxers, Cixi ordered him to be thrown out of the Meridian Gate of the Palace and beheaded. Lu Zhengxiang was promoted to be minister in Russia and after the 1911 Revolution was recalled to Beijing by Yuan Shikai to be minister for foreign affairs and also, for a short time, prime minister. Yuan Shikai's ambition was to make himself emperor and so, when the Japanese militarists issued the 'Twenty-One Demands', hoping in vain to dominate China, Yuan gave in and ordered Lu to sign the treaty, which Lu regarded as the biggest mistake of his life.

After WWI, Lu represented China at the victors' conference at Versailles. The British, French and Americans gave the German treaty possessions in China to Japan, giving rise to fervent opposition in China and the outbreak of the May Fourth Movement. Lu and his fellow delegate V.K. Wellington Koo (1887–1985) refused to sign the treaty and returned to Shanghai by ship, where they were given a hero's welcome. At this point Lu's wife fell ill and wanted to return to Belgium, so Lu resigned his position as foreign minister. His wife went back to Belgium and the Beiyang government appointed him to be minister in Switzerland. Lu's wife was gravely ill and constantly cried out in pain. Lu told her that if she were to return to the Lord, then he would enter a monastery. After hearing this, his wife calmed down and bore the agony without further complaint. They had no children of their own, just an adopted daughter, so after his wife had died and the funeral was dealt with, Lu set about keeping his promise. After careful thought he chose the Belgian Order of Benedictines, where he was welcomed by the abbot. On the appointed day his close friends accompanied him to Bruges, along with 14 trunks of baggage. The abbot protested at the sight of so many trunks, but Lu answered that 14 trunks was the minimum he took to each diplomatic posting. Lu took his vows and in 1935 was ordained priest by Archbishop Costantini. Wellington Koo attended the ceremony. On that occasion Lu asked the abbot if, instead of a separate dinner, his guests could dine in the refectory among the regular monks.

In 1937 when the Japanese launched all-out war on China, Lu Zhengxiang could no longer stand the quiet life of the monastery. He travelled about making speeches, broadcasting the crimes of the Japanese. Because of his special status, he drew large crowds. He also published many articles calling for national autonomy. In the second half of his life he truly became a model of patriotic educational fervour. During WWII the Roman curia appointed him an abbot without portfolio, granting him the status without the responsibilities.

While I was at Bruges his secretary Rev. Neut looked after me. Neut greatly loved China, loved Lu and regarded him as a father figure. Neut was also a sinologist and knew a lot about the history of Chinese thought. He devoted his life to looking after Abbot Lu, washing his feet every night and even helping him to defecate from time to time. Thus he acted more like a son than a secretary. Lu was very lucky to have such an acolyte to look after him in his old age. The secretary told me that Lu had stipulated in his will that his corpse should be returned to China after his death.

Rev. Neut told me: "Abbot Lu is not in good health. He is unable to raise the host himself. He is looking forward to your mass. After mass he will see you for a few minutes, but don't talk for too long." I saw Lu enter the chapel wearing the common habit of a Benedictine monk. He was about five feet tall with a very pale complexion and very thin. After mass I went to his bedroom: a bed, a table, two chairs, a bookcase, a wardrobe. On the wall were two characters in his calligraphy 慎獨 'Vigilance in Solitude'. With reserve, he invited me to sit down and whispered to me in the manner of an elderly person. It was soon over. Then I told him that I was carrying the fond regards of Lu Yingeng, Lu Naying and the whole Lu family, at the same time explaining my own relationship with them. He immediately brightened up and said: "I have lost contact with Lu Bohong. Bohong is a great benefactor of the Church. I have the greatest respect for him." And so on—in this manner I managed to extend my visit for an extra ten minutes.

I went to the reception room and there saw the many paintings and calligraphies that Lu had brought to the abbey. On the tables were many antiques which, although I am no expert in this field, I could nonetheless see were valuable. After Lu died the abbot cleared all these things into a storeroom. Later on his successor decided to clean it out and asked a Chinese priest from Paris named Wei Qingxin to come and appraise the collection, with a view to keeping the best and selling the rest. Rev. Wei used this opportunity to tell the storekeeper that most of the antiques were no good, at the same time putting the things he liked on one side and saying: "This has no value; let me have it" to which the brother said: "Take them away then." I have no idea what became of these things after Wei's death.

I inspected an excellent middle school set up by the Benedictines and also a rather large printing shop. The brothers had published *Le livre du Chretien* which was very useful and had sold several million copies.

In January 1949 Lu died, but it was not possible to meet his request that his body be repatriated at that time, so he was buried in the abbey. When I returned to Bruges in 1990 I prayed for our country at his tomb. I realised then that had his stated wish been honoured and his body returned to China, it would have been desecrated by the Red Guards during the Cultural Revolution, like the tombs of the many bishops whose bones were dug up and strewn in the streets. At that time all the tombs of priests and monks as well as the public cemeteries in Shanghai, the Church of the Holy Sepulchre and the tomb of the Ming poet and painter Wu Li (1632–1718) were without exception reduced to rubble.

After leaving Enghien, I went to Ostend to catch the boat for Dover in England. When I was going through customs on the British shore, the customs officer asked me how much money I was carrying. I answered: "Twenty pounds." He was shocked and said: "So little." I replied: "I am a Jesuit. Wherever there is a Jesuit house, there I have a home." After going through customs, I caught a train. In those days the trains were pulled by steam locomotives, burning coal, and could only go about 60 km per hour. It was necessary to shut the window when going through tunnels in order to prevent masses of soot from entering the carriage. After leaving the train I went to the main Jesuit house in Mount Street, close by the house at No. 221 Baker Street where Sir Arthur Conan Doyle had described Sherlock Holmes as living. There were many tourists, mostly American, having a look; I went over and briefly joined them.

Every morning, after saying mass and having breakfast, I took a map and a tourist guide and went to visit London on my own. I went to churches, museums, galleries, Buckingham Palace, the Thames, Hyde Park and so on. Inside Westminster Abbey are the tombs of many famous people, including that of Charles Dickens. During WWII the Nazis had bombed London and there were signs of destruction everywhere. Many places were just piled with fallen masonry and roof tiles. Even though the war had been over for three years, not everything had been cleaned up and it appeared very gloomy.

One day, after supper, I had a long talk with the father minister. He started by saying that I was different from a Chinese priest named Wang Zhe who had previously visited them. Wang had spent every day shut up in his room and never went out, whereas I spent most of each day away from the house. I said that staying in one's room obviated the necessity of leaving home at all. He then asked me what I thought of London. I said that I had known about London from my childhood and had always dreamed of seeing it. Now I was able to realise my ambition. Sadly London was terribly damaged. War was terrible and peace invaluable. He told me a phrase in Latin: *Si vis pacem, para bellum*, that is, 'If you desire peace, prepare for war.' After WWI the Allies had considered that their enemies had been thoroughly defeated and that they could lay down their weapons, sit back and enjoy life, without a thought for the future. Instead the Nazis had seized power and invested all their energy into putting Germany on a war footing, building fighter planes and tanks. Britain tried to avoid war, giving in to Hitler's demands one after another, using the strategy of making agreements and hoping to thus preserve peace. The French premier Daladier and the British prime minister Chamberlain had flown to Munich to meet Hitler and obsequiously signed the Munich Agreement on 28 September 1938, giving Hitler permission to annex the Sudetenland, a large part of Czechoslovakia. Chamberlain had flown back to Britain and told the crowds that greeted him: "We have guaranteed you twenty years of peace." The British people cheered with happiness at the prospect of peace; but within less than a year Hitler and Stalin had joined forces to invade Poland and started WWII. Since France had not prepared for war, the German general von Rundstedt was able to sweep across France and capture some 1.5 million French troops. France could only surrender. The British priest told me that countries that do not defend themselves will be defeated, the enemy will invade and the words of the Latin phrase proved prescient yet again.

While in London three people made a particular impression on me. On one occasion I got lost while in the City of London and so set out in search of a policeman on duty. He told me in great detail how to get to my destination and which buses to take. He was very patient. When I thanked him and said how much we Chinese could learn from the English, he immediately became serious and said: "I am not English." I asked: "Are you Irish?" He said not, so I asked again: "What nationality are you then?" He puffed up his chest and said: "I am Scottish." Later on I learnt that in Ireland there are many things they do not like about the English. On one occasion an Irishman picked up two coins to show me, an English one with the king's head on it, and one minted after the establishment of the Irish Republic. He said: "Look, on this one there is no English king, just the head of a pig."

On another occasion I was walking on the streets of London when I saw a man wearing a Chinese gown on the opposite side of the street. On closer examination, I realised that he was the Austrian, Rev. Gaechter, who had taught us the New Testament at the School of Theology. So I crossed the street to greet him. He was delighted to see me and gave me a big hug. During WWII he had opposed the Nazis, so his supervisors had sent him to China to escape danger. When the war was over he had returned to Austria. He spoke enthusiastically about China, saying how much he had liked my country and that he wore a Chinese gown to prove his point. I don't remember much of what he taught us, with the exception of one sentence. At that time we had a hymn with the opening line: "Society of Jesus, our mother." He said: "We already have the Virgin and the Church as our mothers, which is quite enough. We should sing 'Society of Jesus, our home.'"

After dinner one Saturday, a young man who worked in the refectory came to see me and said: "Father, tomorrow is my day off. I want to show you around for a day. Would you like that?" I replied: "Of course." So the next morning he got up early, put on formal clothes and came to fetch me. He took me to visit many places, including the zoo, where he insisted on buying the tickets. He also bought me lunch and accompanied me back to the house in the evening. I grasped his hand tightly to thank him. He said: "No need to thank me. All I want is for you to take a good impression of British people back to China." I was very touched. His actions demonstrated his genuine patriotism. He voluntarily took on the role of ambassador. I wondered whether I could manage the same. Could our people give foreigners a good impression both in China and abroad?

On leaving London I went to Oxford which, along with Cambridge, is the most famous university in Britain. I chose Oxford since it had a Jesuit house, where I found 20 young Jesuits. They were studying for various degrees at the university and living at Campion Hall. This name is a memorial to the English martyr Edmund Campion (1540–81) who was a Jesuit. At the house there was a superior, a father minister, a priest and a coadjutor brother. They had different jobs, but a common objective—to serve the students.

One Jesuit took me to visit the university. It is the oldest in Britain, having been established a bit earlier than Cambridge. The organisation is a bit different from that of most state universities. Oxford has some 30 colleges, where undergraduates must be registered. The colleges are independent, with chapels, halls, libraries, classrooms, dormitories and gardens, all full of ancient charm. The students pursue their studies in the colleges. There are also six graduate colleges. The university has a chancellor who is not resident and a vice-chancellor who runs the administration. Beneath the vice-chancellor are the wardens of the colleges who meet a bit like a cabinet. There is also the senate, of which all the professors are members and which operates from a building in the centre of the university. The centre also has a library with several million volumes, among which are many rare books, which is open to all students. From time immemorial Oxford has been a university. Hospitals, shops, etc. all serve the university. Today there is also a new zone with motor car factories and other industries.

The British love to drink tea. In those days, all factories and offices took a break at 4 p.m. for 20 minutes so that the workers and staff could drink tea. At Campion Hall, the superior told me, all members had to gather together to drink tea. In those days food was still rationed, but the tea always came with fruit, cakes, candies, etc.

After leaving Campion Hall, I took a train to Liverpool where I stayed at the Jesuit house and visited the port. In the evening of the next day I took the ferry to Ireland. My berth was close to the engine and I was unable to sleep due to the incessant rumbling. In the morning we arrived in Dublin, the capital of Ireland. Ireland is an island in the far west of Europe on the Atlantic coast. The next stop is the United States. Ireland is about 70,000 square kilometres in size (smaller than Zhejiang Province in China), with a population of some 3 million.

The Irish are devoted followers of Roman Catholicism, so that when Henry VIII established the new Church of England, he and his many followers ruthlessly suppressed and persecuted the Irish. The Irish rose in rebellion many times, but, being hopelessly outnumbered, were always defeated and subjected to greater oppression. After several centuries of trying, Ireland finally became fully independent in the 1930s, but the history of repression stayed with them. During WWII Ireland did not support Britain and remained neutral, thus avoiding the damages of war. As soon as I arrived in Ireland I could sense the contented nature of the Irish people. In those days Ireland was the most committed Catholic country in Europe. One hundred percent of the population was baptised and ninety percent went to mass on Sunday. Every time a bus passed a church, the driver would make the sign of the cross. In recent years the country has modernised and the people have become more materialistic, so that the numbers attending mass have dropped. Ireland used to be an agricultural country and rather poor, so many farmers migrated to the United States. The population never grew and remained about 3 million for a long time. More recently, since Ireland joined the European Union, the economy has taken off and the people's quality of life has improved.

I left Dublin and travelled to the Jesuit novitiate house at Emo Court in County Laois. There I found a father master, a father minister, several old priests and about twenty novices. The house has expansive lawns and a lake. It is a lovely place. Every afternoon I went for a walk to meditate and praise the Lord's creation.

The presiding priest appointed a novice to teach me English. I worked hard. Every time I said "OK", he stopped me saying: "That's slang and cannot be used in polite society. Educated people all say 'all right.'" After a few years the whole world, including China, learned to say 'OK'. Indeed 'OK' became the most common phrase on the planet.

The novitiate house had five meals a day. Breakfast was after mass, elevenses at 11:30, lunch at 3 p.m., tea at 5:30 and dinner at 8 p.m. Every day a lot of time was spent eating. After sharing the restricted diet of the French, I could really appreciate the sweet benefits of peace.

After a month at the novitiate I returned to the juvenate college in Dublin where a brother named Derek Reid taught me English with great devotion. Later on he became a priest and went to be a missionary in Hong Kong. He spent many years as the principal of Wah Yan College. After retirement he stayed on at the school doing odd jobs. One morning the cleaners found his dead body in the rubbish bins. His death is a mystery; I miss him greatly.

19
Gregorian University

After the holidays I returned to Paris, then took the train to Rome and reported to the Gregorian University of the Vatican. This university used to be called the Roman College and was founded by St. Ignatius. It is already some 400 years old. It is directed jointly by the Society of Jesus and the Vatican and is located at the centre of Rome at No. 4 Pilota Square, next to the Pontifical Biblical Institute, which is also managed by the Society of Jesus. In those days the teachers were all Jesuits, from all over the world.

The head was Paolo Dezza (1901–99), an Italian. The Frenchman Charles Boyer was head of theology. The School of Philosophy was headed by another Frenchman named Arnou. The School of Missionary Work was headed by an Italian named d'Elia, who previously had worked in Shanghai, translated Sun Yat-sen's *Three Principles of the People* into English and devoted much effort to the study of Matteo Ricci. He had published the complete works of Matteo Ricci single-handedly. There was also the Law School and the School of History. I asked Rev. Boyer to be my instructor and he gladly accepted me. He pointed out to me that the core teaching of the Gospel of St. John is the unity of God the Father with God the Son and of God the Son with us. Jesus' last wish was that we be united. We should look to the commentaries and conclusions of the Fathers of the Church for evidence of this. Apart from spending a lot of time reading, I also took some courses.

The three main schools of the Society of Jesus are the Gregorian University, the Pontifical Biblical Institute and the Pontifical Oriental Institute. All three come under the superior general who appoints his representative to direct them. In those days the representative was a Frenchman named de Boynes, who had been provincial of Paris. He paid a lot of attention to the religious affairs of Shanghai and was very kind to me. Many leaders of the Shanghai diocese had been his pupils.

The Gregorian University is situated in the centre of Rome. Although it is not situated within the Vatican, it is still part of the Vatican according to the terms of the Lateran Concordat of 1929. Thus all the comestibles used at the university were sourced from the Vatican, including meat, vegetables, fruit—even wines and spirits. Because of there being no excise tax in the Vatican, the prices were very cheap. The daily provisions for each of us were much better than they had been in Paris, but the cost was only about US$1 per day. For example a packet of cigarettes was only about a quarter of the market price in Rome.

The Gregorian University had over 2,000 students, in those days all male, but later on this policy was changed to accept lay people and women, including many nuns. The Gregorian is the cradle of the world's bishops: according to a census held in 2001, about 700 of the world's 3,000 or so bishops had studied at the university.

In those days the Gregorian had about 60 teachers on campus, all Jesuits. There were also visiting scholars from Italy, Germany, Spain, France, Belgium, Holland, England, Peru, Columbia, and so on. There were no Asians or Africans. Many professors were advisors to the various departments of the Roman Curia. Some had great influence. For example Paolo Dezza was the confessor to Pope Pius XII. The German Lenerz was the Pope's theological advisor. Yet another, of short stature, who always went about with bowed head, hugging the walls and not talking to anyone, was, I was told, a German named Leib who acted as the Pope's personal secretary. The Pope's advisors in theology and canon law were also German Jesuits.

In truth the Gregorian University is just a large building in the city centre, without any garden. On entry there is a large, square hall which is used as a reception room for large meetings. In every direction from the bottom to the top floors are classrooms and lecture theatres. On the second floor are the offices of the principal, the head of religious affairs, the head librarian and the heads of various other departments. On the extreme right of the building are the library and the records office where are kept details of students, as well as masters and doctoral dissertations going back hundreds of years that could be accessed at any time. On the fourth floor and above were the teachers' living quarters, including the common room, large and small dining rooms, large and small chapels and sitting rooms. According to the rule of the Jesuits, apart from the superior, each Jesuit could only have one room. On the roof it was flat, so on each side there were pots of flowers grown by the teachers. In those days there were some 100 Jesuit doctoral students living among the teachers, so they could seek advice from their advisors at any time. I was the last to report, so there was no room left for me. The father minister cleared out a small storeroom for me, without windows, so that the electric light had to be on all day. Two weeks later a priest named Zhang Jisuo from Xianxian arrived. He had been the head of the seminary there. The father minister ordered a coadjutor brother to vacate his room to make space for him.

All the students were day-students (apart from those who were Jesuit doctoral candidates). They lodged at the various colleges and convents where they had chapels, refectories, libraries, study rooms, dormitories, etc. The largest of these was the German College which mostly welcomed German-speaking students, including those from Germany, Hungary, Switzerland and Austria. This college had also been established by St. Ignatius about 400 years ago. In those days the German youth were very direct, full of courage and ready to dispute, even engaging in street brawls, so the saint required them to wear red *soutanes* only, which helped people to see them coming and to watch out. The German College students wore this uniform until the 1960s.

The German College was in the busiest part of the city. On the street front there were several floors rented out as shops and offices at a very high rent, yielding a lot of income. Not a few of the graduates went on to become cardinals and bishops. These did not forget their alma mater and would make grants of money, causing the college to have many assets. In the suburbs it had a garden with sports grounds. On holidays the students would go there to relax and to exercise. About 100 km from Rome they also had a villa, whither the entire student body would go at Easter and on other big holidays to restore themselves in the vegetable and flower gardens, sports grounds and swimming pools. I also went there for vacation. The German College had also bought many fields over the years which they rented out to farmers.

20
Two Eminent Persons

After settling into the university I made haste to pay visits to the people I most respected, one being Archbishop Celso Costantini (1876–1958) and the other Wu Jingxiong J.D. (aka John Ching Hsiung Wu 1900–86).

Above I have talked of how the Pope appointed Mgr. Costantini as his first apostolic delegate to China in 1922. He lived in China for ten years during which time he worked so hard that he got ill and had to return to Europe for recuperation. When he left Shanghai the faithful gave him a ceremonial umbrella in recognition of his meritorious deeds. After he had recovered his health the Pope appointed him to be secretary of the Congregation for the Propagation of the Faith and he committed himself wholeheartedly to this work. This congregation oversees the College of the Propagation of the Faith, which saw a big improvement in educational standards under his direction. It had previously only been an undergraduate college, but since Costantini felt that the missions needed better-trained recruits, he established the Pontifical College of the Apostle Peter, dedicated to accepting master's degree students from the provinces of the propagation of the faith as well as doctoral students. He instructed priests from the Missionaries of the Divine Word to manage the school. Both Rev. Lin Dezong from Suzhou and Rev. Shi Antang from Haimen received their doctoral degrees here. Later on both went to Taiwan where they made significant contributions to the Church. Mgr. Costantini loved art and was an artist himself. Some of his sculptures have survived to this day. While in China he emphasised that the Chinese Catholic Church as well as its religious art should take on Chinese characteristics. At the schools he initiated in China—Furen University, Yuanhua Seminary and Huanan Seminary in Hong Kong—there is a common Chinese element.

Costantini was delighted to see me and told me many things about himself. For example (and there is no written evidence for this) he told me that in

1945, in the final year of WWII, when China became a victor nation and the KMT emissary to the Vatican, Xie Shoukang, had petitioned Pope Pius XII to appoint a Chinese cardinal, the Pope refused, saying that all candidates had already been chosen and there were no vacancies. Since Costantini had already been chosen as a candidate for cardinal, he went to see the Pope and asked to have his name withdrawn and replaced with that of a Chinese bishop. When Xie Shoukang heard about this he asked the Pope to consider Yu Bin or Lu Zhengxiang (see above), but the Pope did not like to take suggestions and appointed the German Divine Word member Tian Gengxing (aka Thomas Tien Ken-sin, 1890–1967). When Pius next appointed cardinals in 1953, Costantini was elevated and so left the Congregation for the Propagation of the Faith. Costantini had designed his own tomb under an altar at the College of the Apostle Peter, but when he died on 17 October 1958 he was buried in his hometown at the request of family and friends.

Wu Jingxiong was a genius from Ningbo in Zhejiang Province. He had originally been converted to Christianity by the Protestants and had studied in the United States, where he earned a doctorate in jurisprudence. Later on he went to Germany to pursue advanced studies before returning to Shanghai to work as a lawyer. After reading *The Story of a Soul* by St. Thérèse of Lisieux, he became a Roman Catholic and wrote *The Science of Love*. Later on he went to Chongqing and acted as a legal advisor to Sun Ke, then president of the Legislative Yuan. Sun asked Wu to draft a constitution and to lodge at his home. While at Chongqing Wu first of all used the style of Qu Yuan's poem *Li Sao* to render the Psalms into Chinese and then translated the New Testament into classical Chinese. Both translations were first given to Chiang Kai-shek to read. Chiang read both works several times and suggested several alterations, all of which Wu accepted. Wu once showed me the original text with Chiang's annotations. In 1946 the KMT appointed Wu as its minister to the Vatican.

When I arrived in Rome I went to visit Wu. He invited me to a meal so I met his wife and thirteen children. His attaché Luo Guang (aka Stanislaus Lo Kuang 1911–2004, later Archbishop of Taipei and president of Furen University for many years) was also present. One of Wu's sons later took holy orders, joined the Maryknoll Congregation and did missionary work in Taiwan. Ambassador Wu used his many moral essays to win respect for himself and for China. Pius XII liked him a lot and allowed himself to be photographed with Wu's entire family. When the other ambassadors asked to be accorded the same honour the

Pope answered: "I will permit any of you with thirteen children to be photographed with me."

Wu told me that the Pope had given him one special mission, which was to translate the mass into Chinese. The Pope had said that although Latin was beautiful, it was too difficult for Chinese Catholics to learn. His plan was to grant the Chinese Church special permission to say the mass in Chinese. This plan of his was later realised by his successor Pope John XXIII when he opened the Second Vatican Council and his successor Pope Paul VI launched the reform of the liturgy, permitting the Churches in every nation to say holy office in their native languages. In Wu I saw the qualities of a Confucian scholar in combination with the considerable virtue of a follower of Christ. Wu himself taught a course at the Gregorian University entitled 'From Confucianism to Christianity'.

After north-east China had been liberated by the communists in 1948, Sun Ke became president of the Executive Yuan and sent a telegram asking Wu to return home. When Wu returned to China and saw the way things stood with the country he said to Sun: "The state of affairs is already beyond recovery. I urge you to resign as president of the Executive Yuan and I will no longer be ambassador. We will find another way." Wu returned to Rome and accepted an invitation to teach at the University of Hawaii, later on going to be professor of law at Seton Hall University, where he helped establish the Asian Studies Department. He died in Taiwan.

21
A Few of My College Friends

I had thought that I needed to be able to read and comprehend German in order to do my research, so someone suggested that I go and study at the German College. I wrote a letter to the rector of that college, setting out my objective and after a few days he came to the university to tell me that I was welcome to go there during the Christmas vacation. This man had been an assistant to the previous superior general of the order, with responsibility for the German-speaking Jesuits. After WWII the Germans kept a low profile and he was sent to the German College to be rector. At that time there was a father spiritual named Rev. Klein at the college, who had been the provincial of the western part of Germany (he died in 2003 at the age of 104). In addition there was a father minister and three tutor priests (also known as repeater teachers because they made up for the fact that some courses at the university were so oversubscribed that there were too many students to supervise, so this need was met by the colleges). The teachers and students gave me a warm welcome and I spent a total of three vacations with them.

I was deeply impressed by Rev. Klein. He was full of humour. His name means 'small' in German and he really was small in stature. Since he knew that I wanted to learn German he taught me two words: *dummkopf*, which means idiot and *donnerwetter*, which means blast. These are the first two words of German I learnt and I have never forgotten them.

I got on really well with the young seminarians. They enthusiastically taught me German. They were the sharpest minds in each diocese, both clever and lively. One of them was an amateur photographer. He put his camera in his briefcase and made a small hole in it and took photographs of the professors during lectures. Every photograph was from a funny angle. He would develop them and show them to us. All the students wanted to buy them and he made quite a bit of money. When the professors saw them some laughed at them and others were offended, but it mattered not to him. I also bought a set, but later sadly lost them.

When I returned to Germany in 1986 I looked up those German College fellow students of forty years earlier. Some of them had gone to meet their maker. I was able to make contact with the vicar general of Hildesheim, Rev. Ackermann. He already had cancer and was being looked after by his sister. He invited me to a meal, but had already died before my next trip. On another visit to Germany the head of the China Centre of the Divine Word Missionaries at Sankt Augustin, Rev. Malek, told me that an important visitor was expected that afternoon. It was the papal nuncio in Germany, the Hungarian Archbishop Kádár. We had a very long conversation. He was very open-minded. Most people in Germany welcomed him, but a minority was not happy with him. The Pope transferred him to be nuncio in Spain, so when I went to Madrid he invited me to tea. He said that when he left Germany he had had an audience with Pope John-Paul II and had said that he liked Germany and got on well with the bishops who welcomed him, but the Pope had said: "Some people object to you." In truth a very small minority of conservatives had complained about him in front of the Pope and asked for his transfer. Their intention had been to deny him a cardinal's hat, which usually went to the German nuncio. Later he returned to Hungary and died of cancer.

Another person was the famous theologian and prolific author Hans Küng. He had no recent publication, but gave me a signed copy of an existing one. Küng had, along with Joseph Ratzinger, been an expert theological advisor to the Second Vatican Council. He later fell afoul of Professor Ratzinger and they ceased to cooperate. Ratzinger went on to become Archbishop of Munich, a cardinal and the present Pope Benedict XVI. Küng has always been treated as a dissident and an outsider. He once wrote a book entitled *Infallible?: An Inquiry* (1971). This upset the previous Pope and the Vatican banned him from teaching in religious schools, but despite this Tübingen University kept him on their faculty until he retired. When he came to China I invited him to give a short talk to our seminarians. Someone reported this to the former Pope who said: "Bishop Jin has really gone too far in inviting Hans Küng to talk." In fact I had only invited him to sit down and chat with the seminarians, but as a result of this incident I learnt that those around me make secret reports to the Vatican and even exaggerate matters.

After Vatican II a number of theologians published a theological review entitled *Concilium*. To celebrate the 25th anniversary of the council this publication organised a conference in Belgium and Hans Küng suggested that I be invited. Theologians from all over the world came to the meeting. At the opening ceremony I was put on the top table with Hans Küng, Leonardo Boff and Edward Schillebeeckx. When Cardinal Danneels arrived, it was obvious that the dissidents were being treated as honoured guests and which direction the conference was likely to take. On that occasion I didn't make a speech. Knowing the views of those close to Rome I decided that there was valour in discretion and that silence was golden.

On another occasion I attended a conference at Rice University in the United States at the suggestion of Hans Küng. I introduced the Church in China. I have lasting respect for Küng. He was always diligent. He took the truths inherent in the means of expression available to people 2,000 years ago and used words comprehensible and accessible to people today to expound those ideas without loss. He was very dedicated and I greatly admire him. When the current Pope Benedict XVI was elected, Hans Küng wrote to him and the new Pope immediately replied and received him at Castel Gandolfo, where they talked for several hours and shared dinner. This helped to restore Küng's reputation and gave rise to an excellent response in the wider Church. Everyone said that making a Pope out of a professor had changed the man; but others said: "Let's wait and see."

Another person who went on to have great influence was the Cardinal Archbishop of Munich Friedrich Wetter (b. 1928). Munich is the capital of the German state of Bavaria, which used to be an independent kingdom, then a republic, before being the last of the states to join the German federation. Pope Pius XII had been papal nuncio to Bavaria in his younger days, later moving on to Berlin. The archbishopric of Munich is the second largest in Germany with over two million Catholics. When I was at the German College, Wetter was already a second-year theology student. Once he had earned his doctorate he returned to the diocese of Munich to work. At the age of forty the Pope made him Bishop of Speyer. He became Archbishop of Munich in 1982 and in the same year Pope John-Paul II promoted him to cardinal. After reaching the age of 75 he applied to retire several times, but the Pope always refused him. In late 2006, when he was nearly 80 years old, Pope Benedict XVI accepted his resignation, but made him apostolic administrator, with continuing responsibility for the archdiocese of Munich. In evidence of the Vatican's high regard for him, the Pope only appointed his successor in 2008.

On every trip to Munich I visited him and was always accorded a warm welcome. My visits were usually arranged by the China Centre. On one occasion I went to Munich and the centre did not arrange a meeting for me. Upon my return to Bonn, Wetter suddenly telephoned the China Centre and said: "Why has Bishop Jin been to Munich without seeing me?" The next day the centre arranged a car to drive me the 500 km to Munich and back to call on him. He has generously supported the work of the Shanghai diocese, meeting all our requests for help. I am very grateful to him.

Another fellow student I met when studying in Rome was Albert Decourtray. At that time he was a recently-ordained priest from the Lille diocese and had come to Rome to obtain his doctorate of theology. After classes he and I would converse very agreeably and he invited me to visit his home during the vacation. His home was close to Lille, in a small village called Seclin. He said that during the German invasion at the start of WWII his father had taken the whole family away to escape danger. After the French surrender they returned home to find the house destroyed. They built a new, smaller house from which, after their father had died, his sister Paulette ran a small wine shop. She was unmarried. At the time of my visit their grandfather was still alive and 80 years old. After supper the family gathered around the fire for warmth and to chat. I was told: "Grandpa has no watch, but he always gets up from his chair and goes to bed at precisely 8 p.m." In truth during the days I was there he rose every evening at exactly 8 p.m. It seems that people do have some kind of internal clock.

After Decourtray had obtained his doctoral degree, his bishop, Cardinal Achille Liénart, sent him to do his biblical studies. On my return to China I lost touch with him. He first taught at a seminary, and then became principal and then Auxiliary Bishop of Dijon. He at that point developed mouth cancer and lost the power of speech. The Pope had planned to make him Archbishop of Paris, but appointed Jean-Marie Lustiger instead. While at Dijon he got to know Sister Elizabeth of the Trinity, who was a very holy person. He sought her help, was cured and recovered his speech. The Pope made him Archbishop of Lyon and later on a cardinal. He also became a member of the French Academy of Sciences. In 1985 I was invited to go to the Philippines by Cardinal Sin of Manila and saw there an announcement that Decourtray had been made Cardinal-Archbishop of Lyon. I therefore wrote him a letter asking whether or not it was he who had been my fellow student and he replied at once: "It is me. I have always thought about you. You are still alive! I invite you to visit France."

On my return to Rome I reported to the Jesuit house just across the road from the Vatican and St. Peter's Church. Shanghai came under the French province, so I visited the assistant of France, Rev. Gorrostazu. He had been the provincial of Toulouse and was famously open-minded. Because of this he had been chosen as an advisor to the superior general to oversee the French Society of Jesus (in those days divided into the four provinces of Paris, Lyon, Toulouse and Champagne) with a total of some 3,000 Jesuits. Who would have thought that after arriving at the Rome house, his thinking took a 180 degree turn and he became an extremely traditional Jesuit? Some of his colleagues couldn't believe their eyes, while others said that it was hardly surprising: the eternal city of Rome could weaken anyone's resolve.

I also went to visit the chief accountant of the order, a Canadian named Rev. Durocher, who was famous in the Italian world of finance. Before WWII the Italian government had paid large sums to the Vatican as compensation under the Lateran Concordats, so the Vatican had large deposits in Italian banks. When WWII broke out Durocher felt that the combatant countries would definitely experience inflation and so he advised the Vatican to move their deposits to US or Swiss banks. The Vatican took his advice. Later on the Italian lira was debased and prices took off, but the Vatican felt nothing.

The head of the propaganda department was a Canadian Jesuit who came frequently to talk to me. He had been a missionary at Xuzhou in Jiangsu Province. He described to me in detail the problems that had been faced by Archbishop Costantini while he had been in China. When the latter had arrived in Beijing, which was the seat of government at that time, the bishop was a Frenchman who would not allow him to take up residence there. Shanghai also extended no welcome, so he went to live in Hankow (modern Wuhan) because the bishop there was also Italian. Later on the Chinese Catholics gave him some money to buy a house at Naizhitou in Beijing, where he then moved.

On another occasion, when Costantini had just arrived in Xuzhou, he learned that he had been invited to attend the consecration of a new auxiliary bishop in Shanghai. He thought that he must have been invited to officiate as the papal nuncio in China, but realised only after he had arrived in Nanjing (where the ferry across the Yangtze River was in those days) that the French Bishop of Xianxian was to officiate and that his assistants were also to be French. The Shanghai diocese had only invited him as a courtesy. He had no choice but to return to Beijing, stopping in Xuzhou on the way. The Canadian told me: "Costantini had a tough time. It was incredibly difficult to break the stranglehold of the foreigners on the Chinese Church."

For Europe, 1948 proved to be a very momentous year. WWII had just ended. The loyalists from those countries that had been conquered by

Germany—Poland, Czechoslovakia and Hungary—had gathered in London to form governments in exile. When the Nazis unconditionally surrendered, these people all made their way home to resume power. However, in 1948 Communist parties seized power in those countries and started to implement socialism. In Italy and France the workers' and Communist parties grew in power and won the votes of many citizens. The political and Church leaders of France and Italy were extremely alarmed. The Communists also felt that power was within their grasp through the ballot box. The Vatican was also worried and many cardinals and bishops, heads of departments and heads of religious societies made preparations for both eventualities. Many departments sorted through their important files and prepared to send them to the United States for fear that they might fall into the hands of the communists. The Pope said that even if the Communist party were to take power in Italy, he would remain at the Vatican; but he permitted other important departments to move to Switzerland or other safe havens.

On the eve of the election the Pope broke his commitment to stay out of politics and gave a speech to the Italian people, urging them to vote for the Christian Democrats and not for the Communist party. On the day of the election, all the monks and nuns of the secluded orders went out to cast their votes, with the result that the CDP won and the leaders of the Catholic Church heaved a big sigh of relief. The new prime-minister, de Gasperi, stayed in power and set in motion reforms that calmed the situation. In all he served as prime-minister seven times. He stressed the importance of western European integration and won his place as a great leader alongside Adenauer of Germany and de Gaulle in France.

The whole city of Rome is a museum, a treasure house of world civilisation. Cultural remains from the Roman Empire, the Middle Ages and the Renaissance are preserved in the city and are greatly valued; whichever party was in power would have to preserve them. No political entity in Italy had ever damaged them; they all understood that these things are a precious inheritance left by their ancestors and should not be broken. Whoever damaged them would be condemned as a criminal for a thousand years. Every Saturday afternoon the French Jesuits in Rome would invite a researcher of history to be our guide. I also joined these tours and gained a lot of knowledge. This was an added benefit of studying in Rome.

22
Archbishop Paul Yu Bin

On 8 December 1948 when I was still at the Gregorian University in Rome, my fellow students Wang Zhe and Gao Yupu told me that Archbishop Yu Bin had arrived in Rome and was staying at the KMT's embassy to the Vatican. So we hurried over to Wu Jingxiong's residence and Yu Bin came out to receive us. At the same time the chargé d'affaires and the head of educational affairs at the University of the Congregation for the Propagation of the Faith, Rev. Du, had also arrived. Bishop Yu briefly outlined to us the state of affairs in China. At the end of his talk he described talking to the head of the Ministry of Defence just before leaving Beijing. He had been briefed on the state of military activity (at that time the battle for north-east China was over and those for Tianjin and Beijing as well as the Battle of Huaihai for Shanghai had not yet begun). He told us that the KMT was preparing to retreat to Taiwan. He also said that on the eve of departure he had told the priests of the Nanjing diocese: "I am not coming back. You are free to flee if you can." He also arranged for the Nanjing seminarians to be sent to Spain to complete their studies. He said to me: "Father Jin, you shouldn't go back to China. I know all about the Communist party. The state of Eastern Europe today will be that of China tomorrow."

At this point let me tell you a few things about Yu Bin. He was born into a non-Christian family in the County of Hailun in Heilongjiang Province and converted to Catholicism as a young man. The French Bishop of Jilin sent him to Shanghai to test for St. Ignatius College. The priest looked at his examination results and said: "On the basis of your French, I can only admit you to the first grade; but on the basis of your Chinese I can appoint you to be a Chinese teacher at the school. In my opinion you had better go to the Special Education Department at Aurora University, then after a year you'll be able to enter the first year of undergraduate studies." Yu went to take the test at Aurora, but later on his bishop changed his mind and sent him to the University of the Propagation of the Faith in Rome to study. After graduation he stayed on to teach Chinese to the Chinese students. In his spare time he passed the examinations for two doctorates, including one in jurisprudence. In 1933 he returned to China and passed through Shanghai where he paid a visit to the Sacred Heart Seminary where I was then studying, so I got my first look at him then. He was very tall, about 1.9 m and had a deep and sonorous voice and spoke with great fluency. In 1936 he was appointed Bishop of Nanjing diocese by the Vatican. At his ordination ceremony in Beijing he invited no important guests, except the former warlord Wu Peifu. During the Anti-Japanese War he went to Chongqing and travelled frequently to Europe and the United States to condemn the Japanese militarists and to raise assistance for China. Wherever he went he was enthusiastically received.

On this occasion he had received a cool reception in Rome, which made him think back to 1945 when China had been one of the five victors of WWII and he had been met at Rome airport by several cardinals and bishops. In the Church it is best to come from a powerful country if you want to be treated with respect.

When Yu went to see Pope Pius XII, the Pope expressed dissatisfaction with his overly intimate relationship with Chiang Kai-shek and gave him clear instructions not to go to Taiwan but to return to his diocese in Nanjing. But Yu Bin knew that he could not return to the Mainland and asked leave to go to the United States. Pius strictly told him that after arriving in the United States he should follow the instructions of the papal nuncio in the USA and not leave the country without the nuncio's permission. Archbishop Yu Bin stayed in the United States for ten years. In 1958, after the death of Pius XII, he went to Rome for his funeral. All the bishops who attended the funeral mass had been allocated seats; but not Yu Bin, who was forced to stand to one side. When he realised that Cardinal Roncalli had been elected Pope as John XXIII he was very happy as he knew Roncalli well.

He at once wrote the new Pope a letter and asked to be allowed to go to Taiwan to establish a new university. After a few days the new Pope met him and gave him permission to go to Taiwan and a grant of US$100,000. After Yu Bin went to Taiwan he moved quickly to establish Furen University and invited the diocesan priests, the Divine Word Missionaries and the Jesuits to join the project. He also asked Song Meiling (aka Mme. Chiang Kai-shek, 1898–2003) to chair the supervisory board. At the Second Vatican Council he made a speech saying that after a few generations of work, China would emerge on the world stage and play an important role. Paul VI made him a cardinal. When Yu Bin went to Rome for the funeral of John-Paul I and prepared to attend the secret conclave to elect his successor, he died of a heart attack on the eve of the election of the new Pope. He was 79 years old.

23
Necessary Measures in the Society of Jesus

Visitor Burckhardt

The Society of Jesus was about to take necessary measures. The superior general Janssens urgently called Rev. Burckhardt, the head of the Jesuit mission in Jing County, Hebei Province, back to Rome for consultations.

At that time the Society had 880 Jesuits in China, spread over three Chinese provinces as well as Hong Kong and Macau. They belonged to eleven separate Jesuit provinces. Jesuits in China were required to report all important matters back to their respective provinces. The Shanghai diocese came under the province of Paris; that of Yangzhou came under the California province; Xuzhou under the Canadian province; Wuhu under Castile and Anqing under Leon, both Spanish provinces; Bengbu under Rome; Xianxian in Hebei under Champagne; Jing County under the Austrian province; Daming under Hungary; Hong Kong under Ireland and Macau under Portugal. Superior General Janssens appointed Burckhardt as Visitor in China with the power of the superior general to oversee the whole. Macau and Hong Kong were given special treatment, with the appointment of the American Jesuit Rev. O'Brien as deputy visitor.

At that time (late 1948) the Vatican already knew that the Liberation Army would shortly conquer all of the Mainland, but it made the following miscalculations: (1) that the United States and Chiang Kai-shek would soon return to the Mainland; (2) that, even if they did not return, the Chinese Communist party would follow the Yugoslavian model. Thus the Vatican instructed its nuncio at Nanjing, Archbishop Riberi, to stay there and all the missionaries to strive to stay in the Mainland. In case they were driven out, they should not return to their mother countries, but stay in the region and wait for the KMT to return. The superior general further ordered that all young Jesuits and seminarians should leave China to continue their formation and only return after their studies had been completed. Over a thousand left and not one of them ever returned.

Burckhardt was a sinologist who had come to Jing County in Hebei as a young man. He had been a parish priest, the rector of a seminary and provincial of the Austrian Jesuits. During the Anti-Japanese War, Jing County had fallen into the hands of the Eighth Route Army along with Xianxian, Daming County, etc. (Bishop Zhao Zhensheng's efforts to enlist Chiang Kai-shek's support having been fruitless). As a result of this experience Burckhardt fully understood the policies and strategies of the Communist party.

While Burckhardt was Jesuit father superior of the Jing County diocese he had already moved the seminary to Wang Fu Ma *hutong* in Beijing. When Burckhardt had been in Rome he had called Wang Zhe, Gao Yupu and me to have a talk with him. He said that he was not optimistic about the future of the Church in China, but that everything was in the hands of the Lord. He urged us to study hard and not to worry too much about the internal politics of China. He only spent a few days in Rome before returning to Switzerland to visit his elderly mother and then flew back to China. His first act on returning to China was to charter two airplanes to carry all the seminarians to Manila in the Philippines. He also ordered the Shanghai diocese to direct Cai Zhongxian to lead the Shanghai seminarians to the Huanan Regional Seminary in Hong Kong. Rev. Zhang Jiashu and Rev. Liu Guobang led the seminarians of the Mother of God Congregation in Shanghai to a new home in Macau. The Jesuit novitiate and the juvenate were also moved to Manila (at that time, the Philippine government was extremely afraid of infiltration by the communists and would permit no Chinese to immigrate so Burckhardt applied via Cardinal Spellman in New York to the United States government to obtain a quota for 400 visas from the Philippines to allow the Chinese seminarians to migrate there). The young Jesuits and brothers were sent to the theological college in Lyon, France. Burckhardt himself remained for several years at the Xuzhou diocese's Shanghai office in what is now West Jianguo Road. His secretary was an Italian Jesuit named Rev. Li in Chinese.

Rev. Liu Nairen, who had been president of Jingu University in Tianjin, also came to Rome to report and the superior general permitted him to travel to the United States to investigate Catholic universities. He told me that the Communists would definitely envelope the whole of China and would control it for a long time. His objective was really to hide abroad, as far away from the

Communists as possible. Later on he went to East Timor in Indonesia and died there.

After this, one missionary after another fled China and came to Rome to report, bringing depressing news for both the Roman Curia and for the Society of Jesus. Only Bishop Berlinger of Jing County remained optimistic, saying that the Lord would certainly protect the Church in China. In that year the Pope beatified the martyrs of the Boxer Rebellion of 1900. The Pope asked Bishop Berlinger to officiate at a beatification mass in St. Peter's Church. Later on Berlinger would say that this had been the greatest honour of his life. On the occasion of this ceremony the Chinese government made no official response.

As for myself, I devoted all my efforts to the writing of my doctoral thesis.

24
Vacation in Switzerland, Austria and West Germany

Another year had passed and once again it was vacation time. European universities have a particularly long summer vacation—about three and a half months. In order to pursue my German studies I obtained permission from the new provincial of Paris, Rev. Goussault, to travel first to Switzerland and then to Austria and Germany on vacation.

I first travelled to Florence, Venice, Brescia and Castiglione, the former home of St. Luis de Gonzaga; then to Milan and on to Dormodosola on the Italian–Swiss border. In order to reach the Swiss border post at Brig we had to cross the Simplon Pass at an elevation of 2000 m. While I was waiting for the long-distance bus I got chatting with the customs officials and happily passed the time. After a little while, a privately-chartered Swedish tourist coach drove up. The customs official said to them: "How about giving the priest a lift?" When he saw that they were reluctant he said: "If you don't want to take him, I will have to give your luggage a very careful inspection." He got up to carry out his threat, so the driver of the bus quickly answered: "Okay, okay," and invited me on board. Once I was on the bus the customs official waved us through. The scenery along the route was wonderful. As we drove along among the many peaks, the sky was exceptionally blue, something I had never seen before. Not a cloud was in the sky; the air was bright and fresh and totally invigorating. On the way we stopped to rest and drink tea. It was summer and yet the snow on the surrounding peaks had not melted and the silence was awesome, so that one felt closer to God and to heaven.

In the evening we arrived at Brig where I got off and thanked the Swedes, waving until their coach disappeared from view. I then followed the instructions given to me to find an Ursuline middle school that I had been introduced to, where two Jesuits were working as teachers. Switzerland is the most civilised and liberal country on earth, but curiously its constitution stated that the Jesuits were banned. Naturally there were ways to get around this rule: the Jesuits simply scattered and found work in various legal entities two or three at a time. The two Jesuits at this middle school greeted me enthusiastically and the nuns invited me to give a talk about China to the whole school of some 500 students. I spoke in French and answered their questions. In Switzerland about 70% of the population speaks German, about 25% French and the rest Italian or Romansh. All four are official languages. An elderly Jesuit named Richter showed me around and I truly felt the warmth of the Society of Jesus, which, like a large family, treats all Jesuits as if they were brothers.

From Brig I travelled to Lucerne, a famous tourist spot with a lake surrounded by mountains (the highest peak some 2,500 m). Lucerne is similar to Hangzhou, but the lake is larger and the mountains much higher. In Lucerne I spent the night at a seminary with Jesuit teachers. There were over eighty seminarians and about ten teachers all eating together in the refectory.

I went to visit an old people's home. In Europe many of these places used to have Shanghainese nuns. At this place I asked whether there might be any and in fact they called out a nun from Caijiawan in Qingpu County, Shanghai. Her job was to manage the kitchen. She was very reserved and timid, giving only monosyllabic answers to my questions. Then the director appeared—a young and beautiful American nun. Nuns go all over the world to work in old people's homes. They are modest, reserved, ardent and gentle. The Qingpu nun retired as soon as she saw the director. The latter was from a very well-off family and had been well educated. That she was willing to leave her family and travel far from home to serve the elderly filled me with admiration. I only chatted with the Qingpu nun for ten minutes; but talked to the director for two hours. The director guided me around the home. The elderly were in the sitting room, relaxing on the sofas, reading, playing chess, listening to music. Everything was clean and well ordered, far above the standard in China. The home had a large garden where the residents could take the sun and enjoy themselves. I thought that given the opportunity I would like to establish a similar old people's home in China. Today I have set up two of them, but neither reaches the Swiss standard. We still have far to go.

When the time came to leave Lucerne I went to the director of the seminary to pay for my board and lodging, which he accepted. The resident Jesuits were unhappy about this and went to the director to explain that since I was their brother, he should not have me treated this way. The director promptly returned my money and apologised several times.

My next stop was the famous Basilica of Mary at Einsiedeln. This basilica is managed by the Benedictines, the abbot also serving as the bishop of the diocese. The Benedictines had also set up a boarding school where I stayed the night. The headmaster was most hospitable. As the school was closed for the holidays, there was no one else in the dormitory and I was only able to see the library and the laboratory.

In 1949 Switzerland had no unemployment. The banking and tourism industries were well developed. The watch industry was famous so I bought an Omega watch which I used until my arrest. Switzerland has no oil and no resources, so their high standard of living is entirely due to their invention and industry. According to statistics their per-capita income is the highest in the world—higher even than that of the United States or of the oil-producing nations. As soon as China was liberated, Switzerland recognised the People's Republic, at least ten years before France.

The railway system in Switzerland is very advanced. The stations have no surrounding walls, nor ticket inspections. One can get on and off as one wishes. The ticket inspector is on the train. On getting off one can switch trains, which is most convenient. While I was waiting for a train I needed to go to the lavatory and so asked someone to watch my bags. He said: "Don't worry. There are no thieves here" (I had just come from Italy where the thieves are world-famous and professional). I noticed that none of the suitcases in Switzerland had locks. Today matters have changed and even the Swiss admit that there are now thieves in their country.

I travelled east to the Austrian border where the atmosphere changed. Austria had been partitioned by the victors of WWII and I was going to the French sector. After passing immigration the train travelled east to Innsbruck where I got off. Leaving the station I went to the Jesuit school of theology to stay the night and was warmly received by the father minister as the rector was not present. Apart from the school of theology, the Jesuits also managed the famous Canisianum, which took German-speaking students from Germany, Austria and Switzerland. There were about 300 seminarians there. I was invited to give a talk, which a seminarian helped me render into German. Many of the Jesuits were teachers at the National University of Innsbruck, where the president was also a Jesuit named Rev. Hugo Rahner, a renowned historian whose younger brother Karl became a theologian.

Innsbruck is located in the Alps, with a glorious situation. The town is old and remarkable with many historic buildings. I quickly became a friend of Karl Rahner's and we went for a walk together every afternoon, discussing theological problems, the challenges of the Church and many other topics. Afterwards we would go to a coffee shop and eat cakes. Rahner was an ordinary Jesuit and had no money so, since I had a travel allowance, I picked up the bill.

When I got out of jail I asked after Karl Rahner, only to learn that he had become famous, his works well known and widely disseminated. I wrote to him, explaining my situation. He agreed that I should come out and work and encouraged me. At the age of 80 he got tired at his birthday party and after a few days suffered a heart attack and suddenly departed this life. Apparently it is not such a good idea to celebrate old age too heartily. After his death he was mourned with honour. Some people compared Karl with St. Augustine, while others felt that he had not been given his due estimation in life. When he was young he wanted to pass his doctorate of philosophy, but his supervisor had rejected his thesis. As a result he unexpectedly failed the examination. Today, while no one remembers the name of his supervisor, Karl's name will be remembered for a hundred generations.

Quite a few Austrians told me how Austria had been part of the Austro–Hungarian Empire and had been a Catholic country covering a vast territory. After WWI Austria was one of the defeated nations. The two Protestant nations, the United States and Britain, had been particularly hard on Austria, giving Hungary its independence and alienating a large part of Austria's territory to other countries, in particular Italy. Italy had entered WWI on the side of Germany and Austria, but seeing the way the war was going had switched sides and joined France and Britain against Germany, thus allying with the victors, for which it was rewarded. On the eve of WWII Hitler had annexed Austria and swallowed it up, making it one of the victims. Italy first joined Germany and Japan in the Axis, but in the late stage of the war surrendered to Britain and the USA, again joining the winning side, whereas Austria was treated as a defeated power. The United States, France, Britain and the USSR had jointly occupied Austria, causing great distress to the Austrian people. When I visited Austria in 1949 the country had no government and was divided into four sectors administered by the four occupying powers. The capital Vienna was also divided into four, but since the Russian sector surrounded the whole city, it was necessary to pass through it to reach the other sectors.

The headquarters of the French sector were at Innsbruck and the French administered the sector. In order to improve relations with the French authorities, the Austrian provincial asked the French Society of Jesus to send a young seminarian who had been an officer in the army to Innsbruck to study, while at the same time going in and out of the French headquarters and solving many problems. In contrast to this successful outcome, Hungary was in the hands of the communists and the Church was in trouble. The superior general ordered all young Jesuits to leave Hungary, but as they were very closely monitored, they could not apply to leave as a group. The Hungarian authorities refused to issue them with passports. All 200 or so Jesuits in training went to the railway station in small groups and boarded a train. The train driver was a pious Catholic who sympathised with their plight and decided to assist their flight. When they reached the Austrian border and were waiting for the passport inspection, the train suddenly set off and crossed into Austrian territory. The border guards didn't realise their mistake until it was too late and the birds had already flown. They could only stand and watch them go. Thus the young Jesuits were able to change trains in Austria and move into the French sector. After a few days' rest the young Jesuit I have mentioned arranged papers with the French authorities that permitted them to proceed to Italy where they continued their studies at a Jesuit house about 20 km outside Rome.

Not far from Innsbruck is a small village named Alpbach, which has become famous for its beautiful scenery. In September a group of European university students and teachers including Rev. Rahner and Rev. Daniélou from France were all invited. Daniélou was studying God the Father and taught at the Catholic University of Paris. Later on he was elected rector of that university. Pope Paul VI made him a cardinal. Rev. Rahner arranged for me to join the group and for me to lodge with the parish priest of Alpbach, who was very hospitable. The priest told me that the village had originally been very quiet. The villagers had worked in the fields and had been very simple; but since the place had become a tourist destination the number of visitors had grown and the place had lost much of its charm, the air was now polluted and the residents had learned bad habits. He was most upset about this.

The National Radio of Austria visited me and asked me to make a special address to the Austrian people, but I couldn't make up my mind to do it as my German was not up to scratch. At this time a young German female student named Donate Seeger came to see me. She volunteered her services, saying that she wanted to help me. She said: "You can speak in Latin, French or Italian and I will translate into German for you." I talked with her and found that she spoke French like a native, was fluent in Latin and very competent in Italian. So I decided to speak in French. The next day she handed me the text of my speech clearly written out. When the radio reporters came to see me I read out her text and according to the audience response the results were fine. I now regarded Donate with increased respect—how could such a young person of only twenty have such a command of languages?

After the conference I went for a walk with her and discovered that her knowledge was quite profound. She told me that she was interested in China and that in her home there were many Chinese books translated into German, such as *Dream of the Red Chamber*, *Outlaws of the Marsh*, the *Analects* of Confucius and Laozi's *Book of Tao*. She had read quite a few of them. Her home also had the game of mahjong and chopsticks for eating. Her mother was a psychoanalyst who was also a professor at Köln University. She knew that I was about to go to Germany and so she gave me her home address and telephone number and insisted that I contact her mother. Donate later went on to study in Italy and France, where she earned a doctorate of arts with a thesis on the French writer Georges Bernanos. Later on she changed paths and studied psychology. She thought that the German debt to the Jews was too great. She decided to marry a Jew and make amends for her whole people. Later on she died of cancer at the age of 39. She was the most intelligent woman I have ever met. I will refer to her again later on in this story. After the conference was over I returned to the Jesuit College at Innsbruck.

The father minister saw that I had ringworm of the nails and sent me to the university hospital to have it looked at. I went to see the head of the Dermatology Department. This man was also a professor and as soon as he saw my condition, that both my feet and my left hand had ringworm, he immediately called over more than ten students and, pointing at my feet, said: "I have spoken to you of this disease which is recorded in the textbooks; but here is an actual case for you to examine." He then went on to explain to the students how this disease is common in humid climates where people eat rice. It is very hard to cure, but can be treated with radiation and other methods. So, in accordance with his instructions, I went to the hospital for radiation treatment and in the beginning saw some improvement, but because my visa was about to expire, I couldn't finish the treatment. In Shanghai many people have this disease. I did nothing more about it and to this day have ringworm in my toenails.

After the four powers had withdrawn from Austria the People's Party and the Socialist Party quickly formed a coalition government and established a republic. The four powers retained ultimate power and all laws had to be authorised by them. Initially Britain, France and the US were supportive, but the USSR opposed. In 1955 the interim president travelled to Moscow and won agreement from the USSR that all four powers would completely withdraw and pass power to the Austrian government. Austria announced that it would be a neutral country and joined the United Nations.

I travelled first to the capital of music, Salzburg, and then via Passau entered Germany, which was at that time also divided into four sectors. In the beginning the four powers ran the country and did not permit Germany to unify. Each sector had a plenipotentiary responsible for all administrative and legal matters in that sector. In 1948 the British and American sectors merged. Shortly after, France joined them and thus formed what became West Germany. Finally these three powers agreed to form the Republic of Germany with its capital at Bonn (which had up until this point been a cultural centre with a small population and no industry). In September 1949 they called a congress and elected a president and a chancellor (who held the executive power). On 15 September 1949 I reached Bonn and, after learning what was going on, went to the congress (which was held in the assembly hall of a school). Initially I was not allowed to enter, but I said that I was the only Chinese in Bonn and thus had representative status. The guards consulted their superiors and then allowed me to enter the press gallery and watch the ceremony. I saw the whole process of the election. Conrad Adenauer was the winner and the Socialist party leader Kurt Schumacher had to concede. It was said that Adenauer had voted for himself; but facts subsequently demonstrated that Adenauer was the right choice for Germany.

Conrad Adenauer was born in 1876 and became a lawyer before becoming a politician. From 1917 to 1933 he had been mayor of Köln, which he had built into a modern city, before being removed from office by the Nazi party. After WWII he became mayor of Köln again and established the Christian Democratic party. When he was elected chancellor of Germany he was already 73. He served for 14 years and gave birth to West Germany. A few years ago a survey in Germany asked the question: who was the greatest man in German history? Adenauer came first, followed by Martin Luther and Karl Marx in third place. In 1949 under Adenauer's guidance Germany took the path of peace, prosperity and autonomy. The country recovered very quickly. The Germans revere him.

When I went to Germany in 1949 I could sense the misery of people's lives. Many wore old, threadbare clothes and some children went to school barefoot. There was insufficient grain to go around. It was hard to maintain even the lowest standard of living. Germany's gold reserves had been completely confiscated by the Allies. The vital machineries of factories in West Germany had been taken by the United States, Britain and France as war booty, while in the east everything was shipped to the Soviet Union. What remained in the German factories was insufficient to restart operations and so the unemployment rate was high. People told me that a whole set of encyclopaedias could be exchanged for only a few loaves of bread. Occasionally the car drove past a place where there were no houses or pedestrians, but still there were tram rails set in the road—I was told that it had once been a town. At the end of WWII the United States and Britain had sent thousands of bombers to carpet-bomb German cities. After the planes had passed over, the city below had simply disappeared from the map. The Nazi planes flew low and were slow; they were unable to intercept the Allied planes, so that those who suffered the most were the ordinary citizens. People told me that the industrialised Rührgebiet had not suffered such heavy bombing as half the shares of the factories were in the hands of United States capitalists and the US did not wish to damage them. Soldiers in battle fought to the death, while the big capitalists toasted each other in neutral Switzerland.

When he came to power Adenauer insisted that in order to abolish war it was first necessary to end the centuries of enmity between Germany and France. He stressed common ownership of resources and joint development. War always took place because strong nations always cornered the market in resources. If the capitalists of two opposing countries had common interests, then the incidence of war could be reduced. He suggested setting up the European Community to which Schumann of France enthusiastically responded. Their work can never be destroyed.

I first went to the Jesuit college at Pullach, then to the regional seminary of the order at Frankfurt and finally to Köln to see the famous cathedral, which had taken seven centuries to complete—an extraordinary achievement. I asked a Jesuit to call the mother of my friend Donate and she invited me to her home at No. 1 Paulistrasse. Donate's parents and another friend were awaiting me.

They said that Donate had telephoned twice to ensure that they would take good care of me.

Meeting Donate was a great gift of the Lord's. Through her I met her mother Edeltrud and her stepfather Georg Meistermann (1911–90), who later became famous as an impressionist painter and designer of stained glass for many cathedrals. Her brother Claus worked hard to become the chairman and general manager of the Hanover Reinsurance Company. Their whole family has given me so much help—I will refer to them again later on. I greatly admired Donate's mother Edeltrud Meistermann-Seeger (1906–99). She had married an army officer at 18, after graduating from high school and had four children, two boys and two girls. The officer had a bad temper and was mercurial so after talking it through, they divorced. She took nothing apart from the four children. She studied philosophy at university and at the same time made money, enabling all the children to have a good education. As WWII came to its close the Nazis ran out of options and had to recruit children to serve in the army. She took her children to hide in a village and thus both her sons escaped military service. After the war she joined Köln University as an assistant lecturer, lecturer, junior professor and professor, opened a psychiatric clinic, wrote books, won renown and became a member of the British Royal Society of Medicine.

When I left Rome a student from the University of the Propagation of the Faith named Gu Yunrui asked me to buy him a Leica camera, saying that the price in Italy was too high, whereas in Germany it was only US$200. I bought it, but when I left Germany the customs officials did not permit me to leave with it and confiscated it. I left them with the name of a German Jesuit and, when I reached Belgium, asked him to go and collect it for me. He mailed it to the Gregorian University. I handed the camera over to Gu, who immediately sold it on the Roman market, making a good profit: he certainly had a good head for business. After graduating from the University of the Propagation of the Faith he went to France and stayed there after graduating from Lille University to teach *taichi* to the French—which he does to this day.

The holiday would soon be over so I left Germany and, passing though Belgium, stayed a few days with the family of Rev. Decourtray. When the Belgian Stervelynck family heard about this, they drove over to pick me up and give me lunch at their home, before sending me back to France. Then I returned to Rome to continue my studies.

25
My Second Year in Rome

At the end of 1949 the new Jesuit house in Rome for Jesuit doctoral candidates was completed and named St. Charles Borromeo College. This was close to the Gregorian University and next door to the Church of St. Ignatius. The building was large, with three floors and three elevators. My room was on the second floor with large windows and was very comfortable. Each set of three rooms shared a bathroom. We all thought it too luxurious. Should the priests and nuns of the Shanghai diocese today move in there they would not be satisfied, because it had no en-suite bathrooms, no telephones or television, not to mention computers. The Jesuit in charge of construction was named Delattre. He was a very generous person. Any Jesuit organisation in the world that intended to undertake a large building project had to obtain his approval first. He told me that on one occasion he had received the plans for a Jesuit theological college: after one look he had drawn a red line through the projected refectory and sent the plans back. The submitter couldn't accept his decision and sent a letter asking the reason why a refectory was not permitted. He replied that there was no provision for lavatories in the plan, so naturally there could be no call for a refectory. He asked how could anyone be so careless?

I finished writing my thesis in French and gave it first to my good friend Decourtray to correct, as French was not my mother tongue. Much later, when Decourtray answered the questions of the press, he still mentioned this fact. I handed the thesis in to my supervisor Rev. Charles de Boyer. He read it and was satisfied. Next was the *viva voce*. Since my Latin was very fluent, I tested well. Finally there was a simulated classroom test. My supervisor exited the door and asked three Spanish fathers to test me. I made a big mistake. When quoting the references I failed to mention the Spanish Jesuit theologian Francisco Suárez, which made them very unhappy. The main examiner immediately pointed out the mistake to me and explained that I was disrespecting the Spanish thinker. They only gave me a pass mark.

My studies were now completed. The two other students from Shanghai Rev. Song Zijun and Rev. Zhuang Huaiyuan invited me to join them for a trip to Naples, a famous tourist destination of which the Italians say: "*Vedere Napoli puoi mori*." The city abuts the Mediterranean Sea in the west and is surrounded by hills on the other sides. With water and mountains it is a truly lovely spot. Recent reports say that near Naples rubbish has been piled into huge mountains, quite out of control, causing great concern to the city and the country. In the past Naples was world famous for its natural beauty, whereas now it is infamous for its unmanageable rubbish.

Close to Naples is a small island named Capri, which is considered a world famous tourist spot. There were daily flights from Paris and London. We took a ferry to get there, but when we arrived just saw crowds of tourists, packed together so that one could hardly move. We had seen enough and returned to Naples. On the next day we went to Vesuvius, the volcano. The guide led us to the edge of the crater. The closer one got the hotter it was. Even though the volcano was dormant it still generated plenty of heat. Vesuvius is one of the most famous volcanoes in the world. Its first recorded eruption was in about 6000 BC. Its most powerful eruption was on 24 August AD 79 when the entire town of Pompeii was covered in lava and ash. When we approached the crater we saw that it was about 4 km across and 312 m deep, but unlike Heaven Lake in Jilin Province in China, it has no lake, only a big pond. Vesuvius remains active and last erupted in 1944.

After coming off the mountain we went to visit Pompeii, a town about 23 km from Naples which had been a resort town for the Roman aristocracy. There the high-class villas all had swimming pools, sports arenas and reading rooms. The swimming pools were divided into high heat, low heat and room temperature. In those days paper had not yet been invented so books were all inscribed by hand onto parchment and placed one roll at a time on the table top. The aristocracy was largely formed of military men who, after waging war in distant lands, would bring a few captives home to serve as slaves and enable them to lead a luxurious life. They greatly enjoyed good food and after eating their fill would take herbs to make them regurgitate before resuming their meal. On 24 August AD 79 the volcano erupted just after lunch. Most people were taking an afternoon nap. Suddenly several million tons of ash fell from the sky, covering the whole town. The ash fell into every crevice and was very dense so that all residents, whether rich or poor, all the treasures and all the domestic animals were lost forever. The layer of lava was 3 m deep with a further 3 m layer of ash on top. Pompeii had completely disappeared. Only in the 16th century did people think of excavating, but they did a lot of damage. In the 19th century the Italian government made planned excavations and the town of Pompeii emerged from its deep sleep into the light of day. Because there was no water in the buried town and no air could enter, everything was well preserved. Pompeii gradually became a big museum, providing an important resource for historians and archaeologists.

Facing the ruins I couldn't help thinking: could it have been because there was not one single righteous person there, that the Lord sent down fire and brimstone to destroy it, just as He had destroyed the town of Sodom, as recounted in the Old Testament? I also pondered how history records a place where, when the tide rose, the whole island of Atlantis disappeared and a nation sank beneath the waves. How could an all-loving God permit this to happen? Why did God not protect them? I also remembered a line from Laozi: "When heaven and earth are not benevolent, all things are treated like straw dogs" (*Book of Tao*, Section Five). I thought about this for a long time, finally considering in my own case that the Lord in His wisdom had arranged things marvellously, proving that the Lord had great love for me and had preserved me in the face of many dangers. I thought that the Lord had created the universe and the myriad creatures according to His immutable laws, that He supervises their operation, but also interferes with the course of human progress. He had sent His own son to participate in human history, demonstrating His grace and leading many people to be saved by His kindness. The Lord works in mysterious ways, beyond our comprehension. I could only give thanks, thanking the Lord for having chosen me from amongst humanity and pray that His Father in heaven will in His beneficence save even more people.

Part IV

Returning Home

Part IV

Returning Home

26
Acting on Orders

In May 1950 I received a letter from the Shanghai Jesuit father superior Lacretelle, requiring me to return to China after finishing my PhD. While those in China in fear of danger were being ordered to escape, I was being called from safety abroad to face danger at home, being yet again placed in a hopeless situation. After thinking it over I wrote back accepting Lacretelle's order.

First of all, I reckoned that I had no problems in my personal history, nothing to give rise to fear on the part of the Communist party. Secondly, when I was young, there had been many 'White Russians' in Shanghai, most of whom were aristocrats of great rank and wealth who fled there after the October Revolution in 1917. While in exile, these people had dreamed of the collapse of the communist regime and of returning to Russia, but in fact the Russian revolution had succeeded. The Russian Communists retained power while the exiles saw their fortunes dwindle away in idleness. Their lives became desperate and their situation precarious. I thought that the Chinese Communists would also succeed and rule China for a long time. Were I to remain abroad and not return home, would I not become a 'White Chinese'? Thirdly, those who fled abroad were either foreign missionaries or those looked upon kindly by them. They were a tiny minority. Most of the Catholics in my country were peasants, some workers, and a tiny number of intellectuals. They could not emigrate. If the foreign missionaries and the young seminarians left, our Catholic congregations would be as flocks without shepherds. I was Chinese, a Chinese believer. I ought to be a good pastor and return to care for them. On the basis of these reasons, I wrote to Rev. Lacretelle accepting his instructions and determined to return to China.

I went to the Congregation for the Propagation of the Faith to pay my respects to the then secretary Archbishop Costantini. He fervently loved China and the Church in China and had served as the first papal delegate to China

(I refer to him above and will not repeat myself here). I greatly respected him. He listened to my plan to return and immediately opposed it. He said that he knew that the Chinese Communist regime had already begun to persecute the Church. To return was to take a great risk. He also said that he could send me to work in Latin America, where there was a shortage of professors. He asked me what the leaders of the Society of Jesus thought of my plan. I replied that it was the Shanghai father superior who had written and asked me to return to China. Archbishop Costantini thought for a while and said: "Go then. I give you my blessing."

In June 1950 I left Rome. At the time of my writing this, it is 2008. Even though I have been back to Europe more than ten times, I have never returned to Rome. This is a great pity and I do not know when I may be allowed to return there.

After graduation, the provincial of Paris gave me three months' vacation. I was allowed to go to two places and could spend the time either in the United States or in Europe. I didn't know much about America. While I was studying in Rome I had many American fellow students who formed a closed group, so that I had more interaction with the priests and seminarians from France and Germany (including the future academician of the French Academy of Sciences and Archbishop Albert Decourtray of Lyon, the future Archbishop of Munich Friedrich Cardinal Wetter and the famous theologian Hans Küng). So I went first to Germany, where I knew the family of my friend Donate (see above): her stepfather Georg Meistermann and her mother Edeltrud, the famous psychologist and member of the Royal Society.

Edeltrud was very good to me and wouldn't allow me to call her Frau Meistermann. She insisted I call her mother, so I used the name 'Mami' which satisfied her. She became my adopted mother. Donate's elder brother Claus later became chairman of a Hanover insurance company. At that time he spared an hour every day to teach me German.

After spending a month in Germany, I went to Belgium and visited a wonderful family that I have already described. Charles Stevelynck was a major entrepreneur with factories in Belgium and Argentina. His wife was the charitable Suzanne. At that time I had an idea that since the persecution of the Church in China had begun, the Church would have to go underground and so I'd better learn a trade to support myself since theology would be of no use. I naïvely thought that I could become a taxi driver on my return and thus both support myself and be able to visit my parishioners. Stevelynck's home was in the town of Courtray, very close to France. I stayed at the Jesuit house and went in the morning to the nearby convent of Franciscan nuns to hear mass. Then I would go to the Stevelynck factory. In the morning I learned how to drive a car, in the afternoon how to fix it. The factory directed a man to look after me and I studied hard, going in the evenings to the Stevelynck home to enjoy their hospitality before returning to the Jesuit house. I obtained an international driving license that Mr. Stevelynck got for me without my having to take the test. I also learnt how to repair cars so I could at least manage simple problems should my taxi break down on the road.

On the eve of my departure, I paid a call on the mother superior of the Franciscan convent to take my leave, saying that I was about to return to China in order to spread the Gospel under the control of the Chinese Communist party and would the sisters please pray for me. She immediately summoned a young nun, about the same age as me, and told her that from now on, she should pray for me as her main task. This nun was named Marie; bowing, she accepted this mission. When I returned to Belgium in 1987, Father Heyndriks told me that the same nun was still praying for me. So I went to Rolaire (where the Courtray community had moved) in order to thank her. On my arrival, the mother superior summoned all the nuns and pointed out Sister Marie. I rose and bowed in thanks to her, then said that my survival to that date, after 27 years in jail, all the while maintaining my faith, was not an easy thing and that her prayers had played a big role. She covered her head and said not a word. From 1950 when we first met to 1987 when we met again, 37 years had passed. We had both aged. On my return to China, I wrote letters to her, but when I travelled again to Belgium, I learned that she had died and gone to heaven, where her prayers for the Church in China would be even more effective. I might add that in the 57 years I have been in China, I have never once driven a car.

While I was in Belgium I learned that the head of the missionary department of the province of Paris of the Society of Jesus had already booked my steamship tickets on the packet-boat *Champolion*, bound for Hong Kong on 8 December. So I went to the French consulate in Courtray to apply for a French visa. The consular office told me to fill out the form and come back in 3 months to pick up my visa. I got anxious and told them that I had to get to Marseilles to catch the boat and that my ticket had already been purchased. He said that it was government regulations. I went in high dudgeon to complain to Mrs. Stevelynck, but she told me that it was no problem and that she would take me to France the next day. So the following day we set out and when we reached the border, she showed the Belgian police her ID card and the authorities saluted her and asked no questions, allowing us to proceed. Once I was inside France, I caught a train to Paris.

I very much wanted to see Rev. de Lubac, whom I have already mentioned; about him I will now say a bit more. I had met him at the Catholic University of Lyon. He was a priest full of both faith and learning who taught religion at the University of Lyon. At that time the Church had a number of theologians noted for their real talent and ability, who emphasised that theology should on the one hand return to its roots in the Bible and Sacred Tradition, with special regard for mining the deep veins offered by the study of God the Father, while on the other hand theology should abandon the rigid framework of scholastic theology and emphasise the dialogue between various religions and contemporary society. In the Jesuit and Dominican Orders there were many eminent theologians, in particular a group of teachers at the Catholic University of Lyon. Their essays and published speeches all have this tendency. This movement unsettled the conservative wing of the Church and the inner thinkers of the Church influenced Pius XII to issue the encyclical *Humani Generis* on 12 August 1950, striking out at what had become known as the 'New Wave', but had not yet become a current.

Rev. de Lubac became one of the main targets of the attack. The Church authorities moved him from Lyon and sent him to manage a library with only two bookshelves at the Jesuit house in Paris. They banned him from teaching and from writing articles or meeting with young students. He obeyed and silently went to work every day in the library, taking up a feather duster to clean the shelves and then concentrating all his efforts on reading and waiting for other Jesuits to come and exchange books. When I saw him I felt my heart ache and, covering my head, couldn't find the words to express my admiration. Finally, I managed to say: "Father, your silence and your obedience are even greater than your written works." He smiled and asked me to sit and asked after my situation. I explained how I was about to return to communist-ruled China. At that time the persecution of the Church in Eastern Europe was reported nightly on the television. He looked at me intently and said: "Obey? Very good! No doubt you will also be silenced, but the Holy Spirit is always within your heart. My prayers go with you." On leaving, I kneeled and asked for his blessing. After saying his blessing, he also kneeled down and asked for my blessing.

One of the priests who had been criticised along with de Lubac was a Dominican named Rev. Marie-Dominique Chenu (1895–1990). He couldn't take it and went to see the then cardinal archbishop of Paris to complain. But the cardinal said to him: "Little priest, don't cry in this way. You should consider that after less than twenty years, the whole Church will think the way you do." This forecast was realised early. When *Humani Generis* was issued in 1950, the conservative Dominican Garrigou-Lagrange and Jesuit Dhanis were at the height of their influence. Who would have guessed that by 1962, when John XXIII opened the Second Vatican Council, Chenu, de Lubac and Rahner and their young fellow-thinker Ratzinger, among others, would be invited to the council as expert advisors? They had a huge influence on the progression of the council. Many of the documents issued by the council, including *Lumen Gentium*, *Dei Verbum* and *Gaudium et Spes*, were obviously owing to them. The world was progressing and the Church was moving forward under the guidance of the Holy Spirit. It's just that progress could be delayed by half a generation or even a whole generation. The problem lies in the different perspectives of the leaders and scholars, who struggle over whether to follow the guidance of the Holy Spirit and the spirit of the age or whether to put the brakes on and prevent the Church from moving forward.

While in Paris and at the Lyon School of Theology, I had met Rev. Gu Baogu who had fled China on the eve of the Liberation. I remember that Rev. Gu's thesis at Paris University had been on the *Gongsun Longzi*, in which there were many famous sayings such as the paradox: 'a white horse is not a horse'. After graduation, Shen Saiqi, Zhu Lide, Zhou Defu, Zheng Shenchong and other seminarians had gone to Taiwan, where they took up important positions. After that I never saw any of them, with the exception of Zhou Defu (who later changed his name to Zhou Hongdao), who later on came to teach at the Chinese seminaries.

The eighth of December is the Feast of the Immaculate Conception of Mary. On that day, I boarded a ship at Marseilles that would take me back to China. On the same ship were the former president of Jingu University, Liu Nairen, and several Vietnamese priests. There was also Gu Meisheng, the eldest son of the Shanghai Catholic Gu Shouxi, who had just graduated from his father's alma mater '*Sciences Po*'. His father had summoned him back to Shanghai. On the same boat was a young seminarian named Ding. After obtaining a master's degree in philosophy in France, he had decided to leave the Society of Jesus and return to China as a layman.

The packet-steamer headed for Hong Kong, where it moored in early 1951. The Irish Jesuits came to meet us. Ding didn't have a Hong Kong visa and was detained by the immigration authorities who announced their intention to fine the captain. The priest who met us knew the head of the immigration department and gave him a telephone call, whereupon this man ordered Ding's release. Thus a small commotion was settled. I stayed a few days at Huanan Seminary in Hong Kong, prior to returning to Shanghai.

While in Hong Kong, I met Lu Yingeng, the third son of Lu Bohong, who had fled to Hong Kong, as well as the wealthy businessman Yu Qiuling. The former went to America. The latter died in Hong Kong. I also met both Madam Zhu Zhengying, then editor of the *Kung Kao Po* (Sunday Examiner). She politely called me 'Uncle'. Zhu stayed at the *Kung Kao Po* until she retired and only recently died.

At the travel agency in Hong Kong I bought a train ticket to Shanghai, while arranging for my two trunks to be sent by sea, only carrying with me a small bag and my repatriation papers. When I left Hong Kong, no one saw me off at the station. As the train left Kowloon, I thought: "Farewell Hong Kong. Farewell capitalist world. Farewell forever, my good friends in Europe." What awaited me on the Mainland? I had no idea whatsoever and put all my trust in the Lord. I simply read one verse from the Bible: "The Lord in his wisdom disposed all without error." This boosted my morale and strengthened my resolve. But my main sensation was of desolation. I thought to myself that my superiors always sent me into dangerous situations. I ought not to fear as the All-Knowing could not err. I would meet all eventualities without mishap. I would not die.

As it happened those seminarians who had been sent to Hong Kong in May 1949 by Rev. Yves Henry, the capitular vicar, had already been recalled to Shanghai (Cai Zhongxian brought back the seminarians while Zhang Jiashu and Lian Guobang led the seminarians of the Congregation of Mary). Visitor Burckhardt objected, but Henry said: "I am the capitular vicar and it's not up to you. I think that the Communists will not damage the Church. The facts of the past year prove this. I want to recall my seminarians. You may not interfere." Rev. Burckhardt then wrote letters to the director of the seminary, to Bishop Zhu Kaimin, to the general of the Nanjing diocese Li Weiguang and to the man responsible for the diocese of Anqing in Wuhu stating that the Society of Jesus opposed the recall of the seminarians. Zhu and the others wrote back to Burckhardt saying that they supported Henry's decision because the tuition fees at the Hong Kong seminary were too expensive.

27
Reporting to the Diocese

I reached Shanghai station on 25 January and no one was there to meet me. I made my way alone to the seminary at Xujiahui to report to the then rector Yves Henry. Then I went to see the Jesuit father superior Rev. Lacretelle. He said to me: "So you're back. I was just planning to write you a letter telling you not to return." I thought to myself that I had been in Hong Kong for several days, during which time, had he really wanted to, he could easily have written to me. I thought he was just hedging his bets, but I said nothing.

In August 1948, Rome appointed Gong Pinmei (aka Ignatius Pin-Mei Kung, 1901–2000) to be the bishop of the newly established Suzhou diocese and Bishop Gong Shirong (aka Rev. Joseph Kong) of Nanjing to take over as head of the Shanghai diocese. Gong Shirong had already followed the example of Yu Bin and left the Mainland for Taiwan. In Beijing Mao Zedong had published an important essay, listing the main war criminals with Chiang Kai-shek as No. 1 and Li Zongren (aka Li Tsung-jen, 1890–1969) in second place. Yu Bin's name stood out among the list of forty names and was fairly near the top. Gong Shirong reckoned that as he had been Yu Bin's secretary and was already in Taiwan, it was highly unsuitable to appoint him as the bishop of the already liberated Shanghai. Were he to return, he would surely be arrested at the train station, which would be of no benefit to the Church. So Gong wrote to Rome with his resignation. In 1950 Rome permitted Gong to resign and transferred Gong Pinmei to be Bishop of Shanghai and to oversee the Suzhou diocese. On receipt of this instruction, Gong Pinmei immediately took office and established his diocesan headquarters at the church in Sichuan South Road. He appointed Rev. Zhu Xuefan as vicar general and Rev. Li Shiyu as chancellor to the diocese. Rev. Zhou Shiliang became his secretary. Rev. Fu Hezhou became chief accountant to the diocese. This was his team, but in fact he relied not on it, but on the two Frenchmen Lacretelle and Germain.

On the second day after my arrival at the Xujiahui seminary, I went to pay a call on Bishop Gong Pinmei. At that time, according to regulations, the diocesan priests of Shanghai, Haimen, Nanjing and Suzhou were doing an annual retreat at Dongjiadu. The big bosses Gong Pinmei, Zhu Kaimin, Burckhardt and Lacretelle were also at Dongjiadu. I was able to see all four of them in one place, which was very convenient. When I arrived the four of them were chatting in the reception room after having had lunch. I knocked at the door and entered, greeting all four of them. Gong and Zhu didn't ask me to sit down before asking urgently: "When are they coming back?" By 'they' they meant Chiang Kai-shek and the Americans. I had not thought that, without even making small talk, they would blurt out such a question. Without thinking I responded: "Not for a while." They immediately asked: "But when exactly?" I replied: "Hard to say." In my heart, I thought: "The Kuomintang is in chaos; when can they be expected to return?" When they asked again, I answered: "At least several years; probably more than that." Bishop Zhu Kaimin said: "You know what? They could be back by Mid-Autumn Festival this year." They were not only bishops, but also my seniors, so I thought it better to remain silent; but I thought to myself that from the Russian revolution in 1918 until that day, 34 years had passed. The Chinese revolution was unlikely to last less time than Russia's. The very first meeting I had in China, the conversation was of this nature, far from what I had expected.

While I was in Europe, the national churches had not formed national bishops' conferences or similar organisations. Every diocese reported directly to the Bishops Department in Rome and to the papal nuncio in each country, which was most disadvantageous to the organisation and the unity of the Church in each country. Nonetheless, each national Church had some means to remedy this situation. For example in France, the regional bishops and archbishops had a meeting every three months to discuss national problems and issue directives. I considered that such an organisation could help our Church in China, which was simply too divided. Thus, I innocently went to see both Gong Pinmei and Zhu Kaimin to suggest that, given the current situation, with the Communist party likely to be in power for a long time and the foreign missionaries having either left China or been ejected from the country (and unlikely to see eye to eye with us even if had they been able to remain), we Chinese religious people should unite together to face the crisis. I said that they were respectively Bishop of Shanghai and the dean of Chinese bishops and among the first Chinese to have been appointed bishops; that they had prestige and should join forces to invite all the Chinese bishops to come to

Shanghai for a meeting to find a way for the Church to survive in China in the long term, as it were to find a *modus vivendi*. They replied politely: "Let us consider before replying." While I was waiting for their reply the Jesuit father superior Lacretelle summoned me and said: "Father Jin, you have just returned to China. Why are you going around talking nonsense? I have had a letter from Archbishop Riberi saying that you have not been behaving yourself and need to be disciplined. What do you have to say for yourself?"

I said: "All I did was offer some suggestions to the two bishops."

He said: "Stick to your lessons and don't cause problems for me. I was going to ask Riberi to appoint you rector of the seminary, but he has refused." I thought to myself that in those days it was better not to be a leader.

The books I had sent by sea arrived and I went to customs to collect them. The customs officer asked me to open the trunks. As soon as they saw the contents were not only books, but books in foreign languages, they said that the marine police would need to inspect them before they could be released and could I please wait. After waiting for half an hour, the police arrived and after having a look, they saw that the books were all in foreign languages. They asked me what the books were about. I said that they were all books of philosophy. They said nothing and signed my release form. I hired a flatbed tricycle to carry the trunks back to the seminary, where Rev. Henry asked me whether I wanted to keep them for myself (he only asked because when Rev. Wang Changzhi had returned from abroad he had refused to donate his books to the library and had obtained father superior Lefebvre's support). I thought about it. I was uncertain what the future held. I could lose my liberty at any moment, so what did it serve me to hold on to all those books? I said that I would donate them as was the rule. Henry was most delighted. In those days of my return to China, I could have been arrested at any time (now I could die at any time). This world is but a temporary abode.

I fell into a secluded life, devoting myself to my teaching, taking classes and receiving almost no visitors. The students were excellent and appreciated my lessons. It was the first time a Chinese had taught theology. Previously Wang Changzhi had twice requested to be allowed to teach theology and had twice been refused by Henry. I am Chinese; the students were Chinese; but I was required to teach in Latin. Before Vatican II, all the seminaries in the world used Latin, which saved a lot of effort. And I think Latin is very beautiful. It would be a great shame to completely abolish its use. Possibly this is just the opinion of a sentimental old man!

I went to St. Ignatius College to pay a visit to Rev. Zhang Boda. He was the only Chinese Jesuit in Shanghai to act as rector of a college and so naturally became the leader of all Chinese Jesuits. He was very polite. My former teacher Rev. Wang Fang was still teaching at the school as were my former fellow-students Rev. Zhu Hongsheng and Rev. Chen Tianxiang. We had a happy reunion. From that moment, until his arrest in August, I visited Zhang Boda once a month. After he had been arrested, my former teacher who had accompanied me on these visits said: "We were very happy to see you go of your own volition to visit Zhang Boda. Zhang always felt a bit guilty about having spoken against you many times in front of the former bishop Haouisée and Rev. Henry." Of course I already knew about this, if not for which I would never have spent a year in Subei, but I felt that I ought not harbour grievances. I said to Chen: "Let bygones be bygones. We are dealing with the present now. We should not talk of the past." Since Zhang Boda openly opposed the 'Three Self Patriotic Movement' (of which I write more below) at a public meeting, he was arrested in August and died in prison of a blood clot in the brain in November. Zhang came from a prominent family and was very brilliant and good at public relations. There had been a time when people guessed that he might be the first non-French bishop or Jesuit father superior, but this never came to pass and he died in the prime of his life, which can only be seen as a very great shame.

28
The Shanghai Diocese after 1949

After I had returned to China and had a good look around, I realised that although the Shanghai diocese now had a Chinese bishop, nonetheless the power remained in the hands of the French. After Gong Pinmei had been ordained, he had first served as headmaster of the Sacred Heart Middle School in Songjiang and then spent eight years as the head of the junior middle school department of Aurora University Middle School. He was finally promoted to be the headmaster of Jinke Middle School. He had always worked as a teacher. While he was at Aurora the nominal head of the university was the powerless Hu Wenyao, while the real authority lay in the hands of the executive director Rev. Germain. Gong had total admiration for Germain. When Germain became the chief accountant of Shanghai diocese and of the Society of Jesus, based at the church on Sichuan South Road, Gong's job was to turn Sichuan South Road Church into the diocesan headquarters and was with Germain from dawn to dusk; he sought Germain's advice on everything. Before Gong became bishop, the Jesuit father superior Lacretelle was also asked to serve as vicar general of the diocese. When Gong was instated, although he appointed Zhu Xuefan as his vicar general, the latter was based at Dongjiadu Road Church and Gong rarely met him. Furthermore Gong didn't value him. (Zhu and Gong were arrested at the same time, but because Zhu had not been used by Gong and had taken no part in diocesan decision-making, he was only jailed for five years.) Lacretelle remained advisor to the diocese in canon law and went every day to Sichuan South Road to see Gong, who discussed all matters with him. Gong had Lacretelle and Germain beside him and thus they controlled the Shanghai diocese. Gong was the public face, while the brains behind the operation were Lacretelle and Germain. Gong was in fact totally obedient to them.

After the Liberation, the whole country committed itself resolutely to land reform. Shanghai was no exception. After consulting with Lacretelle,

Gong drafted a document and disseminated its contents to all the priesthood: "Catholics are not obliged to join any struggle-sessions targeted at landowners. Those who are forced to attend may not speak out. Where the deeds and property are distributed to the poor peasants, they may accept them, but only on behalf of the owners, to whom they must eventually return them." Gong wanted the diocesan priests to spread the word to the lay people, but they said: "How can we announce this openly? Doesn't this show that we are awaiting the return of the Americans and Chiang Kai-shek, after launching a secret counter-attack?" This had taken place before I returned to China. Later on, I learned about this directive from Gong and Lacretelle and thought that it stood totally on the side of the landowners and was no doubt in opposition to the land reform. It was not a very intelligent thing to do. Land reform was a national policy and was close to the heart of the people. That Gong should oppose it from Shanghai was unimaginable.

At the end of 1950, before I had returned to China, the central government had launched the 'Three Self Patriotic Movement'. Bishop Wang Wencheng of Wanxian in Sichuan and Rev. Wang Liangzuo of Chengdu responded enthusiastically. The government energetically propounded the policy throughout China, prior to which the Protestant leader Rev. Wu Yaozong was already urging all Protestants to take part. Thus the Three Self Patriotic Movement proceeded quite smoothly in that Church.

Religion had to separate itself from colonial control and should be taken in hand by the Chinese: this was the national policy after Liberation. The Three Self Patriotic Movement was initiated by the central government and because it was first responded to by the Sichuan bishop Wang Liangzuo, and because of the status of the Shanghai Catholic Church in the whole country, these two places became the main objects of attention. The papal nuncio Archbishop Riberi immediately announced his opposition to the Three Self Patriotic Movement. After discussing the matter with him, Gong Pinmei and Rev. Lacretelle also announced their opposition. The Shanghai government felt that since the Shanghai Church had opened many schools, the Three Self Patriotic Movement should be initiated in the field of education. At a meeting of the Shanghai Catholic Headmaster's Conference, under the direction of Rev. Lacretelle, when the proposal to approve the Three Self Patriotic Movement was tabled, Zhang Boda stood up and opposed it, as did Brother Bai of the Congregation of Mary and headmaster of Suidai Middle School, and so the proposal did not pass at that time. Later on both Zhang and Bai were arrested.

Bai was transferred many times; he was finally released from jail when Deng Xiaoping came to power and the Congregation of Mary took him to Paris where he died in peace at the mother house.

By contrast, Zhang died in jail in November 1951. The prison contacted the Xujiahui parish priest Cai Shifang to collect the body, which he placed in the Chapel of the Virgin Mother at Xujiahui, where thousands of St. Ignatius students and parishioners from the area were drawn to pay their last respects. Gong also held a magnificent funeral mass for him at Xujiahui Church. Zhang was buried in the Catholic cemetery at the Catholic Country Church in Hami Road. Many young people went there to pray and gather. The Church abroad also spread the news and put Zhang on the list of candidates for sainthood, much to the irritation of the Chinese government.

Because of Gong's opposition to the Three Self Patriotic Movement, the response of Shanghai religious and lay people was extremely unenthusiastic and very few people signed up for it. The first to respond was the president of Aurora University, Hu Wenyao, and the medical professor Yang Shida. Gong Pinmei invited Hu to dinner and urged him not to join, while Henry had a meeting with Yang (Henry had previously been president of Aurora), but with no result; both men joined the movement. The government had more success in recruiting new members among the corps of teachers. Tang Ludao and Gu Meiqing of Huishi Elementary School and Yuan Wenchang of Yaoming Girls Middle School joined up one after another. Among the higher class Catholics, the fifth son of Lu Bohong, Mr. Lu Weidu joined up. Other famous Catholics including Zhu Kongjia, Gu Shouxi and Dong Guimin among others steadfastly refused. Later on they were all condemned as rightists and became the primary targets of struggle sessions. Gu Shouxi was arrested and sentenced to a long prison term.

The other centre of activity was Sichuan. Riberi sent the Sichuan-born aristocrat Rev. Dong Shizhi to broadcast Gong's instruction. At the Catholic lay meeting held in Chongqing with the intention of passing the Three Self decision, Dong suddenly appeared and gave a speech on the 'Two Wholes and Their Beauty', opposing the Three Self Patriotic Movement. As a result the motion was not passed. After the meeting broke up, Dong was arrested and died in jail. Dong's speech was widely distributed among the faithful, caused much fevered discussion and became known to almost every family in Shanghai.

29
Various Political Movements

On the eve of the end of WWII, Stalin, Roosevelt and Churchill gathered for a summit meeting at Yalta and Roosevelt made a large concession to Stalin, allowing Eastern Europe to fall into the Soviet sphere of influence, so that when the war was over the anti-fascist political parties in Eastern Europe all fell into the hands of the communists and the various Eastern European countries became Soviet satellite states, while the communist parties of Western Europe all grew in strength. On the eve of the 1948 Italian election, the Communist party was at the height of its influence and Pope Pius XII called on all Catholics to vote for the Christian Democratic party. As a result, the Christian Democrats won and the political atmosphere in Western Europe calmed down.

On 30 June 1949, when the Chinese Communist party was close to achieving total victory, the Vatican Congregation of Rites proclaimed an anti-communism decree, stressing that the materialist communist ideology would certainly oppose Christian faith, even though the Communist leaders had made no speech opposing religious activities. Indeed, events did prove that the Communist party opposed Catholicism, opposed religion, opposed the Christian Church, wherefore according to paragraph 1399 of the decree, it was forbidden to publish, broadcast or read any communist publications, newspapers or listen to any radio transmissions. Also it was forbidden to write for these publications. Catholics were forbidden from participating in any activity that promoted communist theory and also could not argue in defence of anti-Christian heresy or they would be seen as abandoning their Christian faith.

At that time, I considered that such a blanket instruction would be hard enough to enforce in capitalist countries and among believers, where support for communist parties was not insignificant. In fact, most churches around the world did not pass this order down to the junior ranks. Who would have thought that when I returned to Shanghai, I would discover that Gong Pinmei and Rev. Lacretelle had in fact disseminated every word and detail of this decree? At that time I thought that from then on it wouldn't be easy to be a Catholic in China.

The Chinese Communist party really liked to hold meetings and, especially in the early days of Liberation, they held meetings almost every day, sometimes all day. Schools, factories, various work units, all the neighbourhood committees were ceaselessly holding meetings. Rev. Lacretelle forbade Catholics from attending meetings at which the public was required to chant the praises of the CCP. At the meetings, as several thousand people raised their voices and chanted slogans, there were a few Catholics—teachers, students and workers—who could only lower their heads and not join in, not raise their fists, not chant the slogans, so that people looked threateningly at them. In the schools, students were all required to wear the red neckband and to consider this an honour, while teachers organised the students to join the communist Young Pioneers, but Catholics were told that they were not permitted to wear the red neckbands. Catholic workers were allowed to go to work, but not to join labour unions. When the neighbourhood committees organised residents to read the newspaper, Catholics would not join in or would attend without listening. To be a Catholic meant paying a huge price and the consequences were terribly severe.

During the Korean War the US became the primary enemy of New China. Several hundred thousand volunteer soldiers full of bravery and energy crossed the Yalu River to fight the Americans alongside the North Korean army. Gong consulted Lacretelle and then instructed Catholics not to join the volunteer army and not to take part in the anti-American pro-Korean movement, nor to contribute funds to build planes and artillery guns. Nonetheless, the Vatican had just appointed an American to be Bishop of Yangzhou in 1949. The Vatican wanted the Catholics to prostrate themselves before an American. It really was tough to be a Catholic. Meanwhile, we the priests were living in comfortable rooms, drinking milk and eating steak while both instructing and propagating these callous and unfeeling instructions, not sparing the faithful from a hopeless outcome, causing them to miss school, become unemployed, or even risk losing their liberty. While I was in jail, I thought these things over, and felt that we had let down the faithful. We ought to have given more thought to the great numbers of the faithful and the common people, allowing them to survive under communist rule, to study hard and to work alongside the rest of the people.

New history books were being published, setting out how the Vatican was a counter-revolutionary organisation and an ally of American imperialism. Gong Pinmei announced that teachers or Catholics in Shanghai were not permitted to teach from these new history books and should resign their posts rather than teach. One teacher said to me: "Father, I followed Bishop Gong's instructions and lost my job, even though at home I am responsible for my children and elderly relatives who rely on me to make money. Since I've resigned my teaching post, we have only ten taels of gold left, enough to keep us for just over a year. What will happen after that? I trust in the Lord's providence." I felt aggrieved listening to him. We bishops and priests had no families to look after; we were provided for, but what about the ordinary laity?

Faced with the opposition of Shanghai Catholics, the government set to work harder, organising Catholic Patriotic Associations around the country and putting pressure on key figures. On 27 April 1951 the Shanghai authorities arrested counter-revolutionaries. Among them were the president of the Aurora Students' Union Dong Songling and Ying Mulan and Lin Mou. Under the leadership of the Hungarian Rev. Havas and Rev. Zhu Shude, the Aurora Catholic students united in obedience to Gong and Lacretelle's instruction to oppose all government instructions unfavourable to the church, causing them to be more and more isolated from the rest of society.

Next, the Chinese Catholic Religious Affairs Promotion Council and the Catholic Central Bureau (CCB) on Yueyang Road were investigated and Rev. Chen Zhemin was arrested (he was secretary to Archbishop Riberi) along with Rev. Shen Shijian (reverend director of the Legion of Mary) and the Irishman Rev. McGrath (leader of the national Legion of Mary), and all the Legion of Mary's activities were proscribed. CCB stands for Catholic Central Bureau, but the government changed its name to Catholic Intelligence Agency.

The CCB had been established by Riberi. When Cardinal Archbishop Spellman of New York visited China in 1948, he brought an important delegation and on his return to the US left Bishop Walsh behind to take up the post of secretary general of the CCB and to support the work of the CCB. In his youth Walsh joined the Maryknoll congregation and worked as a missionary in Guangdong, later becoming Bishop of Jiangmen, before returning to work in the US. He returned to China in 1948, was arrested in 1958 and sentenced to 20 years in jail with exceptional treatment which he served in Tilanqiao Prison, receiving regular deliveries from the Red Cross. On the eve of Nixon's visit to China, the government announced that he had been reformed, had demonstrated good behaviour and thus released him early and allowed him to return home, where he died at the main house of the Maryknoll congregation. When Walsh was arrested, many other Catholics were detained with him, among them my friend Rong Dexian's husband Zhu Yisheng, who died in prison, while Walsh was released.

In early 1951, the CCB held an emergency meeting, which Gong attended, to discuss the fact that while Riberi was unable to execute his authority, Gong would act as papal nuncio to China. Gong believed that this was a genuine appointment. In 1954, he naïvely told me: "Why does the Vatican delay formally appointing me?" In my heart, I considered that it was hard for foreigners to hand over power to Chinese. In all the time since Catholicism had first arrived in China, from the late Ming dynasty, only one Chinese, Gregory Luo Wenzao O.P. (1615–91) had been appointed as apostolic vicar of Nanjing, and even then he had to wait for over ten years to be ordained. From that time, for over 200 years, there were only foreign bishops, until 1926 when six Chinese priests were made bishops of small dioceses. On the eve of Liberation in 1948, the vast majority of bishops were still foreigners. Out of over twenty archbishops, only three were Chinese. To take me as an example, while there were foreigners in China, the father superior and the Visitor were always foreigners. Only once the foreigners had left did these positions fall to me. The Church is built of men and the thinking of most men is conditioned by their background: the controlling force of nationalistic thinking places a heavy limitation that is not easy to overcome.

In 1951, Riberi was expelled from China. He first moved to Hong Kong and then to Taiwan. In 1947, when he was acting as papal nuncio to China, I was in Europe; my return to China came just before his expulsion. I never had an opportunity to meet him or talk with him and so know little about him. Later on I heard these two stories about Riberi.

First, in the days after Liberation, he wrote a letter to all the bishops in China, exhorting them to pray for the protection of Our Lady of Sheshan and suggesting that, should the Church in China overcome its difficulties and emerge unscathed, then he would build a large basilica at Sheshan to thank the Holy Mother. Thirty bishops responded to his call and wrote many letters promising their support, which he passed to Gong and Gong passed to the parish priest of Sheshan, the Frenchman Rev. Prudhomme. He placed all these letters at the feet of the statue of the Holy Mother at Sheshan. After Gong was arrested, the People's Government used these letters during his prosecution to demonstrate that the Church was waiting for a change of regime. The question I ask now is: has not the Holy Mother protected the Chinese Church? Today, the Church in China survives unscathed and is growing every day. Isn't it time for us to show our thanks to the Holy Mother?

Secondly, in November 1947 Rev. Germain succeeded Rev. Verdier as the chief accountant of the Shanghai diocese. As soon as he took over he raised the issue of Church property: "The CCP is bound to win and the KMT to fail. When the CCP comes, they will seize the assets of the Church." He sold several properties belonging to the Shanghai diocese and invested the proceeds in the stock of large American corporations and then moved the assets offshore. When Riberi heard about this, he wrote to Germain to forbid him to sell any more. Riberi said that the foreign missionaries could leave, but the Chinese religious would have to stay and their situation should be considered. After Rev. Germain was expelled, he returned to Europe for a while before taking over the financial affairs of the Chinese Jesuits based in Hong Kong. In 1967, during the 'Cultural Revolution', Rome ordered that all the assets of the Chinese mainland dioceses in Hong Kong be handed over to the Congregation for the Propagation of the Faith in Rome. So all the US securities held by Rev. Germain were handed over. Once when I was visiting the Jesuit house in Germany, an old priest told me that in those days, he had been the chief accountant at the Society of Jesus in Rome and he had handled this matter. He considered that a large proportion of the wealth of the Shanghai diocese had been moved to a safe place, not realising that the Congregation for the Propagation of the Faith had absorbed all the money and that the Shanghai diocese didn't get a single cent. In all these years, the Congregation has not returned a penny to the Shanghai diocese. As far as the properties that remained in China are concerned, they came through unscathed, without loss. The CCP didn't confiscate them and the Shanghai diocese relies on them for its existence. I provide these ironic observations in the spirit of enquiry, as the matter leaves me utterly perplexed.

An even greater blow came later on when the government struck with an iron fist at the Legion of Mary as a prime target across the whole country. The Legion of Mary originated in Ireland for the purpose of venerating the Holy Mother and to encourage the faithful to pray and to do good works. When Archbishop Riberi had been papal nuncio to Ireland, he had discovered this organisation. He considered it useful to unite the faithful and raise its level of commitment. When he was transferred to China he put great effort into promoting this organisation and the Legion of Mary started from the grass roots and spread to every area, with every local group guided by a pastor in charge. In each local group there was a group leader and a head of the local groups, each responsible for prayer, training, outreach, finance, etc.

Riberi had in 1948 arranged for the Irish priest Rev. Aedan McGrath (1906–2000) to be the national supervisor, responsible for everything. This organisation developed very quickly in Shanghai, especially among school children, and various priests organised groups in their parishes. The fact that the organisation contained the word 'legion' in its name attracted the special attention of the CCP. They considered its objective to be a political one with a military aspect to it. In communist-ruled China, such organisations definitely could not be permitted to exist, and therefore had to be extinguished. The central government designated the Legion of Mary as a counter-revolutionary group and ordered all participants to declare their resignation. The written order specified that all members were landlord class, KMT members and similar class enemies, and required that they register their names as they left the group. They further asked members to expose and denounce others, seeking to crush the whole network. The police authorities across the whole country immediately set to work. In Shanghai the police established several stations for the registration of Legion members, who were required to report, fill out forms, produce a membership card and booklet, declare that they had come to their senses, announce their departure from the organisation, write about how they had been the victims of trickery and so on. After Liberation, any instruction of the party elite was carried out like a hurricane by the lower ranks, but, when they outlawed the Shanghai organisation, they met with setbacks as the Shanghai members obeyed Bishop Gong, according to whose instructions they nearly all disobeyed the orders of the police department and persisted in refusing to treat the Legion of Mary as a counter-revolutionary organisation, thus making the government extremely angry.

The central government considered that the Shanghai police had not made enough effort and transferred the Tianjin police chief, Xu Jianguo, to Shanghai based on his success in crushing the organisation in Tianjin. He used iron-fisted techniques to crush the Shanghai Legion of Mary. The original police chief Yang Fan was demoted to deputy. Later on Yang was arrested at the same time as Executive Vice-Mayor Pan Hannian as an anti-party activist and served 20 years in jail. When Pan was released, the Cultural Revolution saw him arrested again and he eventually died in jail. As for Yang, after the fall of the Gang of Four, his case was rectified and his record expunged and he returned to Shanghai completely blind. Xu Jianguo went on to become vice-mayor of Shanghai and later on deputy minister of the Ministry of Public Security in Beijing. His style was unyielding and murderous. During the 'September Eighth' events, he personally directed the arrest of the members of the Gong Pinmei anti-revolutionary clique (at that time Mayor Chen Yi had been transferred to the central government to be deputy premier and minister of foreign affairs). I don't know for what reason, but later on Xu Jianguo was made a diplomat, and became ambassador, first to Romania, then to Albania, whereupon he was ordered to resign and return home, was arrested at the airport and immediately jailed in the Qincheng No. 1 Prison near Beijing, where he died. (I learned about his later life from an article his daughter wrote for the *People's Daily* entitled 'In Remembrance of My Good Father'.)

In 1951 when I returned to China, Rong Dexian's son Zhu Enrong came to see me and told me that he was a member of the Legion of Mary and was an officer responsible for the library. At the time the political climate was already dangerous, so I told him to make getting to Hong Kong a priority. He obviously could not stay in the Mainland. His parents agreed that he should go. He went to Hong Kong and improved his English at Huaren College and then followed the Lord's calling and joined the Society of Jesus, working constantly among young people in Taiwan. He made a big contribution to the Church in Taiwan and was greatly loved by the university students there. Had he not left, he would certainly have been arrested and sentenced to reform through labour in the north-east or north-west of China.

While crushing the Legion of Mary, the Shanghai authorities arrested the priests who led the organisation, such as the French Jesuit Jean de Leff. De Leff was from an aristocratic family, with two younger brothers in holy orders and three younger sisters in religious orders. While in prison he wrote poetry which he published to great acclaim after he had been expelled and returned to France. Also arrested was Rev. Yao Jingxing. Yao had been the headmaster of Jinke Middle School. After serving several months in jail, he was released and transferred to Zhangjialou as parish priest. Later on he became religious affairs director of the seminary and head of the Guangqi Research Centre, doing a great many translations. Among the better known is his translation of *Sous le Regard de Jesus*. Although under very great pressure, these young Legion members showed great bravery and resolute faith, pious devotion to the Holy Mother and to the Church and were unafraid of sacrifice. Most of the members prepared a small bag containing a change of clothes and personal hygiene materials in preparation for arrest, which could come at any time. Among them, many lost their studentship, their employment or their liberty on 8 September 1955.

These Legion of Mary members were mostly middle and high school or technical high school students from well-off families. Many of their parents were Christians, so that when it came to their turn to oppose the orders of the police, their parents and friends understood. They were at that time prepared to go to jail, to be sentenced to reform through labour in Qinghai Province or the north-east. They worked hard and won awards for their efforts, but stuck to their faith unwaveringly. Some even continued to spread the word surreptitiously. After the end of the chaos of the 'Cultural Revolution', they gradually returned to Shanghai. Their living conditions cannot compare with mine today, even less with those of men like Gong Pinmei who went to the US, but they feel no resentment about the past. They are truly the Lord's good children. I admire them from the bottom of my heart. I feel inadequate in comparison with them.

Among the Jesuits at the time were seven or eight younger men who felt that the priority was to strengthen the spirituality of the lay people and to deepen their faith. These members of the Society of Jesus were Wu Yingfen, Chen Yuntang, Cai Shifang (aka Cai Chongjian), Wang Rensheng, Zhu Shude, Zhu Hongsheng, Chen Tianxiang and myself.

We decided to rotate among the various parish churches to deliver sermons; seven sermons would make up one lesson. Each priest would make a sermon; each lesson would have a main topic such as Christ, the Ten Commandments, the Seven Sacraments, the Church, Faith and so on. Speaking from the pulpit had many attractions; for instance, each sermon would be attended by a full congregation. Apart from the sermons, we also arranged for groups of parishioners to do the spiritual exercises of St. Ignatius, with good results. Most of those who attended were students, who became known as Catholic Youth. On New Year's Day 1953, some 2,000 were led by Rev. Zhu Desheng and Rev. Zhu Hongsheng to gather at the square in front of the Church of Christ the King to wish Bishop Gong a Happy New Year. The Catholic Youth was not in fact an organisation. It had no constitution and no leadership. It was only a popular name, such that all the children of Catholic families were known as Catholic Youth, just as all young people were known as 'educated youth' during the Cultural Revolution. But then some people gave the Catholic Youth a bad name and treated them as counter-revolutionary activists. After the events of 8 September the young people almost all came under suspicion as Catholic Youth activists. Those who resisted were thrown into jail for the crime of belonging to the Catholic Youth. Those who didn't recant were sent to the north-east, Anhui, Qinghai or Xinjiang to work on state farms and some of them are still there.

In 1949, the KMT was defeated and withdrew step by step from the Mainland. On the eve of the Liberation of all China by the People's Liberation Army, Catholic missionaries were full of anxiety and could not face the changeover. Earlier on I have explained how one solution was to send youngsters abroad, thinking that the CCP would destroy the Church by making the Church the brunt of its attack. Yet others thought that the CCP would respect the activities of the Church and transfer Church assets to the various Catholic enterprises and schools, only leaving a little land attached to each church. The CCP protected religion, kept the churches and took over the Church enterprises. In Shanghai, for example, they first took over the observatory and the weather forecasting station since these had a national security function and could not be managed by foreigners. Next, they took over the schools. In Shanghai diocese there were originally Aurora University and Aurora Ladies' Academy. Among middle schools, there were St. Ignatius in Xujiahui, Xuhui Girls Middle School, Qiming Girls Middle School, Jinke Middle School, Xiaoming Middle School, Fangde Girls Middle School, Zhongfa (later known as Guangming Middle School), St. Francis (later known as Shidai), Yixin Middle School, Zhengxin Girls and Boys School in Songjiang, Tangmuqiao Girls and Boys School in Pudong, Shigao Trade Middle School, Kunming Road Girls Middle School, Datong Road Middle School, Nanqiao Middle School, Zhangjialou Middle School and many, many elementary schools. All were confiscated. Among charitable activities, Guangci (now known as Ruijin) Hospital, Renai Hospital (now known as Luwan Central Hospital), Sacred Heart Hospital in Yangshupu District, Muxin Hospital in Zhabei, St. Joseph Hospital in Songjiang, Leiting Hospital: all were taken, one by one.

As Gong Pinmei said, every day he heard the bad news of the nationalisation of such and such a facility, just like the Prophet Job in the Old Testament. After each nationalisation, Gong and Lacretelle would rearrange the staff, moving Zhu Shude and Zhu Hongsheng to the Christ the King parish church and Wang Rensheng to St. Peter's parish with Qian Shengguan and Cai Liangshen as his assistants; he moved Ding Shuren, Xu Jiangu and Lu Peiyuan to the parish church in Sichuan Road and Zhang Jiashu to the parish of Hongkou with Wu Yinfen as his deputy. He moved Chen Tianbao to manage liaison with senior parishioners and serve as pastor of the Chongzhen Church on Wuyuan Road. From now on, the focus of work was the parish and in the parish, the youth and children; to raise a younger core group of acolytes and to proselytise the children. These young acolytes the children termed 'elder brother' and 'elder sister'; they totally obeyed the parish priest. Of course, there were those who did not do so, such as the female Catholic named Zhong who followed the government's call and applied to leave the Legion of Mary, but the government wanted her to go on being a parish acolyte and to be even more enthusiastic than before so as to gain the trust of the priest and report back to the government secretly. Zhong was very successful and in her alter ego, she accused Gong Pinmei during the 'September Eighth' event so that we finally saw her stand up and reveal her true nature. Later on in the 1980s, she went to the US and applied for refugee status, saying that she had been persecuted by the Communists.

During the period when Gong and Lacretelle orchestrated resistance to the government, the government never found an opportunity to seize Gong. On 1 October 1951, which was National Day, Mayor Chen Yi sent Gong an invitation to be his guest at the celebration, but Gong didn't go. When he came to the Xuhui seminary, I asked him why he didn't go, as it seemed impolite. He said: "If I go there, how could I face them, should they return my visit? They are targeting the US and Chiang Kai-shek." In his mind, he was still waiting for the US and Chiang Kai-shek to return to the Mainland. The city government also targeted the senior Catholic laity, inviting Zhu Kongjia, Gu Shouxi, Dong Guimin and others who were influential to be members of a political consultancy committee. Deputy Mayor Pan Hannian invited Gong and others to the city government to discuss matters, but these efforts were unproductive. Gong Pinmei was controlled by the Frenchmen and didn't trust the CCP. All the people closest to him were zealots such as Chen Fumin and Zhang Xibin. Chen Fumin especially was thoroughly anti-communist, stubborn and hard-nosed. They persuaded Gong that he was bound to become cardinal archbishop. They also said that the government would do nothing. As for me, I had returned from Europe, where the East was already red and the Western European workers and intellectuals all tended towards communism; thus I had no illusions about any return of the US and Chiang Kai-shek. Hungarian Cardinal Archbishop József Mindszenty had had great prestige both in Hungary and abroad, but he was among the first to be arrested in 1949. The CCP would not be afraid of Gong. I said to others: "Don't support Gong too much, even if he does become a cardinal archbishop, for thousands will suffer to make one man famous." And many did indeed pay a heavy price, especially among the young. They told me the spirit is strong but the flesh is weak. When met with the circumstances of that time, my voice was rather small and I was ashamed to be unequal to them, yet didn't make common cause with them. They would make impassioned statements such as: "Heads may fall and blood may flow, but our resolve cannot be abandoned." I was not as brave as they were. I had just returned to China, was quite young and unqualified to join the ranks of the diocesan decision-makers. Before the government dealt with Gong, some people suggested to Cardinal Tian Gengxing that he should return to China to lead the Church; the government supported this suggestion and sent people abroad to secretly win Tian over, but he declined the invitation.

30
Xuhui Seminary

In August 1951 Archbishop Riberi was expelled from China. Just before leaving, he authorised Rev. Lacretelle's application and appointed me new acting head of the Xuhui Regional Seminary. I took office on 16 July 1951 and put all my energy into the affairs of the seminary, a role I played as well as I could for four years, during which time the number of seminarians increased to 303. The priests working at the seminary had all once been my teachers and my leaders, such as Rev. Yves Henry who had once been Jesuit father superior and seminary rector and Rev. Peter Lefebvre who had been both my father superior and seminary rector (and whom I regarded as my benefactor). The rest had all taught me and were my teachers. I was only 35 years old, thus the youngest among them had become the rector of the seminary, which made me feel rather inadequate. They all greatly respected me and permitted me to take on this heavy burden without undue concern; I was deeply moved by their spirit of obedience and humility.

At that time some of the older students such as Ding Gaoming from Haimen and Zhang Zhenhua from Suzhou were already 30 years old, not much younger than I was. My first important directive on taking up my position was that the junior seminarians should do a month of spiritual training. This was fairly successful. I realised that for seminarians, the most important thing is spiritual training and that, without gaining a good understanding of spirituality, it is not possible to be a good priest.

My most exciting challenge was that, on the day after my appointment had been announced, the entire staff of twenty workers came to my office in an uproar, asking for higher pay and better benefits. After a long talk, they still didn't listen and continued to scream and shout. The two Jesuit brothers who were coadjutors and thus responsible for managing the staff had both hidden themselves away. I thought that as long as a foreigner had been rector, there had been no fuss; but now a Chinese had taken over, the fuss started. Just as I was wondering how to deal with the situation, a seminarian appeared in my office and said to them: "What's all this fuss about? The rector doesn't oversee these matters. It's my responsibility; come with me," and he led the staff out of my office, rescuing me from my predicament. This seminarian was named Wu Caisheng. I was most grateful to him and from then on gave him genuine responsibility for the staff. A district government cadre named Zhao had been egging the staff on; he was a hard nut to crack. Seminarian Wu managed the staff very appropriately, so he earned my respect. After he was ordained a deacon, other seminarians such as Lu Peiyuan, Shen Baochi, Ai Zuzhang and Zhang Tingjue among others organised the staff and I concerned myself no more with these matters.

The food in any establishment is most important. In Latin the saying is *'Bona Culina, Bona Disciplina'*, meaning that if the food is good, discipline will also be good. I handed over the management of the feeding of the 303 people of the seminary to the seminarians and they set up a management committee. I set the standard and they organised the refectory according to that standard. In those days, the seminarians still had a snack at 4 p.m. for which I set the budget at 20 yuan per month. The catering was managed for the longest time by a seminarian named Yu Chengxiang, who went to great trouble to satisfy everyone, but at some cost to his studies. The man in charge of the catering accounts was Zhuang Jianjian, while Zhu Yude was responsible for purchasing and so on. On 8 September 1955 Yu was also arrested, only 28 days before he would have been ordained a priest. While in the labour camp, he maintained his faith and remained single. In 1982 when I returned to Shanghai I sent people to find him and arranged for him to return to the seminary, where he was finally ordained a priest. He became a very good priest. He is from Haimen and is a very kind man. Because he was from Haimen and had been trained by the Bishop of Haimen, Zhu Kaimin, he was obliged to offer his services to Haimen diocese; but when he went there and met with Bishop Yu Chengcai, he was rejected on account of his poor health. On returning, he said to me: "I've had a stroke and it may happen again. Are you afraid to hire me, Father?" I replied: "If you fall ill again, the diocese will support you for the rest of your life." He quietly stayed on to work at his studies. He worked as a missionary in the Shanghai diocese for 10 years and made a good contribution to the diocese, before falling ill and dying.

After Liberation, the seminaries in many areas ceased operating one by one, while the Xuhui seminary was a rare survivor, so students were sent there from all over. For example Capitular Vicar Su of Wenzhou himself delivered Zhu Weifang; Guangxi Province sent Huang Xiongcai; from Guangdong Bishop Walsh sent Zhang Jiajian and Liu Dejun; Jiangxi Province sent You Guojie, Xie Yunsheng and Wu Guosheng; the Capitular Vicar of Fuzhou, Zheng Changcheng, personally delivered He Dunqian; Hebei Province sent Li Zhongyuan, Zhang Shangzhi and over ten others. All these had already completed part of their studies and were also hard working; all passed the entrance test and with few exceptions all became good priests.

Capitular Vicar Zheng had another purpose in visiting Shanghai, which was to ask Gong and Lacretelle to send a priest to Fuzhou to conduct a retreat and teach the spiritual exercises of St. Ignatius. Gong and Lacretelle sent Rev. Wang Zhe who taught canon law at the School of Theology. This action brought great troubles upon Rev. Wang. After the start of the Anti-Imperialist Patriotic Movement, the military representatives made him a focus of their investigations, wanting him to account for this journey as having anti-movement intentions, which lead to Wang jumping from a building to his death; but all this happened later.

It was in that year that I met Bishop Zheng and he became a very good friend. He was both patriotic and loved the Church. For the sake of his loyalty to Rome, he was condemned to 30 years of labour reform. When he finally got out of the prison, he stayed at home quietly and seldom went out. After many kinds of persuasion, he came out to look after the faithful and to work in the parish. Finally he was chosen to be Bishop of Fuzhou diocese. Before his ordination Zheng applied to Cardinal Filoni, at that time papal nuncio to the Philippines (based in Hong Kong), for the approval of the Vatican, which application Filoni did not respond to on the grounds that Fuzhou already had an underground bishop. However, Zheng's predecessor the Franciscan Pieraccini, who greatly loved the Church in China, wrote a letter to Zheng saying that he could accept ordination in order to provide pastoral care to the Fuzhou flock of some 300,000 faithful: so Zheng accepted. However, since he had not been trusted by the government for many years, nor recognised by Rome, he felt very ill at ease. He did many great things for the Church, among which was the restoration of the Rose Hill Resort with its large church, library, hotel and sculptures of the fourteen Stations of the Cross, which is now one of the famous pilgrimage sites of China. Recently he died of cancer of the oesophagus.

Just before he died, he received the notification of Rome's recognition, which allowed him to leave this world in peace.

In my opinion raising the commitment of the laity is an essential task and cannot remain at a level of making responses in church. The laity needs food for spiritual improvement. In 1951, there was a printing press at Tushanwan that was still in the hands of the Church. I wanted to use the opportunity to publish more books and applied to Rev. Lacretelle for permission, which he immediately granted and also gave me 2,000 yuan to get started. I chose Mr. Rao Ke'an as my first assistant. He was a graduate of Aurora University's Literature Department and was gifted in both Chinese and French, as well as being a devout Catholic. From then on he never left my side, working hard until my arrest. I also asked Lacretelle to send Revs Lu Dayuan and Yan Yunliang to teach at the seminary and serve as editors. Our intention at that time was to get out as many books as possible to form a 'theological library'. Then we invited Messrs Zhu Xisheng and Zhang Fanxing to do translation and with all the hard work of these few people published more than thirty sacred books in four years. During the 'September Eighth' movement we were all arrested one after another. The 'theological library' came to a premature end. All the books were disseminated and transcribed; among them some are still useful today. No doubt some lay people still have copies of the 'theological library'; if so I hope that they can bring them out so that we can republish them.

31
Anti-Imperialism Patriotic Movement

The conflict between Gong and the government was coming to a climax. Gong and Lacretelle issued an order refusing communion to all who joined the Catholic Patriotic Association. This was a very severe measure, almost equivalent to excommunicating all the members of the CPA. Pious Catholics could not join the CPA or attend its meetings. Some CPA members were not intimidated and went to church as usual and went up for communion along with everyone else. The zealots of the parish, especially the younger people, would inhibit them. The conflict was coming out into the open. Gong came and said to me: "It would be best if the Pope just excommunicated the CPA." But the CCP, which was behind the CPA, was certainly not going to give in and Gong had made his final and fatal move.

To prepare for an emergency, the Church prepared to go underground. Rev. Lacretelle ordered the establishment of a secret novitiate for the Jesuits to train up successor priests, appointing Yan Yunliang as the master of novices. The admitted novices publicly maintained their original identity, whether student, teacher or seminarian. Each man would meet with the master every week for an hour or two and make his report. Among those admitted were Lu Dacheng (a seminarian who now works in Taiwan), Yang Donghua and Wang Yiru, both graduates of the Aurora University Science Department. They were chosen to be future seminary teachers. Yang is now a priest in the Shanghai underground Church. Wang's whereabouts I don't know. The others were Zhu Xifan (now an underground priest in Shanghai), Chen Longzhang (a student who returned to lay life), and Dong Jiping who also became a layman and has since died.

At Aurora University, the French priest Rev. Emmanuel de Breuvery (1903–70) recruited several gifted female students to become nuns and form an underground convent. They were as follows. Alice Pan (Dr. Pan Yingsheng), whose mother was French. She was arrested; then released, going to Canada to work as a doctor. She died at the end of the last century. Wu Rui, who taught mathematics at a middle school after graduating; Li Qinggui, who graduated from No. 1 Medical School and stayed on to work there. Lu Shuxiong of the Legion of Mary, who, when arrested, was sent to Qinghai for reform through labour, then returned to Shanghai, taught foreign languages at Second Technology University and at the same time worked at Guangqi Press as a volunteer, translating the Psalms and some of St. Paul's letters. She was good at Chinese, English, French and her translations are accurate and elegant. She is a rare talent, has great love for the Lord and is a very respectful person worthy of admiration. Dong Jiman, who went to live in Hong Kong after her release; Xie Shirao, who later married Ren Dapeng and went to live in the US; Jiang Zejin, who teaches at Shanghai Foreign Languages University and Chen Peishen, whose later life is unknown. After de Breuvery went back to France, he passed his role to Rev. Raguin. After Raguin went to France, Alice Pan came to see me, and asked me to be their spiritual director. I agreed. They came in turn to the seminary and I talked to them about spirituality. Occasionally I went to visit their 'home', the term they used to refer to their organisation.

Zhu Shude also set up a group called 'The Fountain of My Happiness', but it collected few members.

The government questioned the CPA members Hu Wenyao and Yang Shida about Gong and both of them said that Gong was openly manipulated by the French and for this reason the Frenchmen should be expelled. The government made great use of Yang Shida, who was promoted to be head of student affairs at the No. 2 Medical College as well as headmaster of Xuhui Middle School. His influence grew at meetings both in Shanghai and at CPAs across the whole country.

In November 1952, the police arrested Rev. Germain, detained him for two weeks and, after he had answered their questions, expelled him from China. Thus the government slowly gained a full understanding of the internal affairs of the Shanghai Catholic Church. Germain first returned to France to make speeches everywhere, then, after a year, went to Hong Kong, bought a house in Argyll Street and served as the director of the Hong Kong office of the Shanghai diocese.

The next important development was in the evening of 15 June 1953. The government mobilised the army, surrounded the Xujiahui Jesuit house, the Jesuit school of theology on Pushi Road and the Christ the King Church. They arrested Rev. Lacretelle, the American Jesuits McCarthy and Philipps, and took away Zhu Shude and Zhu Hongsheng. At Xujiahui, they also took away Lacretelle's private secretary Chen Tianxiang. They detained the head of the Jesuit house, Pelliard, and sealed the premises, putting the resident priests and seminarians under house arrest. At the Ignatius lodging on Jinling Road, they seized two Belgian priests who were advisors to Bishop Zhu Kaimin and had made regular reports to Riberi.

The next day the newspapers reported this action in the headlines and termed it an anti-imperialist movement, targeted at removing the last traces of imperialist influence. In order to attract more Catholics, they changed the name of the Three Self Patriotic Movement to the Anti-Imperialist Patriotic Movement. In the city, they organised a large exhibition of sinful acts of imperialism and arranged for the people and especially for Catholics to see it. Both actions had little effect. After Aurora University's Technical School had been rectified, it became Shanghai No. 2 Medical University. On that day, when the Catholic students learnt the news, a large number went to the Church of Christ the King and to Xujiahui, taking bread and other food items, saying that they wanted to provide food for the priests under house arrest, demanding access, being denied entry and refusing to disband.

At this point, I want to make two digressions, which taught me one important lesson. There was a priest named Wang Chunhua who was under house arrest at the theological college. One day, he jumped over the wall and escaped, running to Songjiang where he found the parish priest Zhang Ruilin. Zhang hid him on a small fishing boat, but realised that this was not a long-term solution and so introduced him to the pastor of Little Huangtang in Kunshan, Wang Youhan, who then introduced him to a fishing family named Shen, which hid him. Wang Chunhua thought he could smuggle himself abroad, but was arrested as he was preparing to steal across the border in Guangzhou. He confessed everything, which led to the Shen family, who had protected him, facing severe troubles. Wang was sentenced and upon release was to get permission to join his younger sister in the US. But after achieving his ambitions, he did nothing whatsoever for the Shen family which had sacrificed so much for him. In addition, there was a priest named Wang Jiwen who ran away and hid in the home of a Catholic named Zhang. He was picked up by the police after two years, for which the Zhang family suffered many difficulties. The lesson I want to derive from these stories is that one should be very careful, when pursuing one's own ends or attempting to protect oneself, not to sacrifice others and bring them into danger or implicate them.

After the Anti-Imperialist Patriotic Movement started, the government made Catholic students their main target. At No. 2 Medical University, the progressive students and the Catholic Youth once again renewed their fierce debate without either party willing to make any concession, to the extent that during one clash, one of the progressive students named Yang Zengnian suddenly leaped down from the upper staircase, thus breaking up the crowd by falling on his fellow students' heads, preventing the use of excessive force and earning a reward from the government. When Yang had studied at St. Ignatius, he was greatly appreciated by the headmaster Zhang Boda and was baptised into the Church. Zhang paid great attention to his development and sent him to Aurora Medical School. After Liberation, Yang quickly remodelled his outlook and was valued by the authorities who saw him as a leading cadre of the progressive students. During the 'Cultural Revolution' he was struggled against by the Red Guards on account of having been a Catholic. They said that he was an alien class-element who had infiltrated the revolutionary forces and was a spy. Under the whipping of the Red Guards, he could only reveal that he was a secret party member and that his file should be in the Special Records Office. On investigation, this was found to be true and he was released without charge. Later on he was gradually promoted until he even became chairman of the Shanghai Young Pioneers and, in 1983 he became director of the Shanghai Religious Affairs Department, finally becoming deputy head of the United Front Department. He sent his wife and son to America and later defied party instructions and travelled alone to the US and remained there, upon which he was expelled from the party. In America he had no formal position, but served as a home-care nurse and recently died there.

The government arrested many Catholic Youth members such as Long Jiaping. Li Wenzhi thought that she might be arrested and went to the Catholic church on Sichuan South Road to look for Rev. Fu Hezhou. Fu sent her to hide in the home of Zhu Xueyou (Zhu was a section chief in the Huashang Electricity Co. His daughter was called Zhu Xuejin and his son Zhu Xifan—he later joined the underground Jesuit novitiate). Because Li Wenzhi continued to maintain contact with her fellow students while living at Zhu's residence and visited them often, the government discovered what was going on and arrested Li Wenzhi. While in prison Li Wenzhi was re-educated and greatly regretted her past and fully accounted for her errors. She did a good job of reporting on and exposing others. Because of this, the Zhu family got into trouble during the 'September Eighth' events. When Gong was arrested, Li was released. At the court session, Li denounced Gong, Lacretelle and myself for our sins in corrupting youth. Li joined the CPA and became one of its most active and enthusiastic members. She really was a successful example of a diehard reformed member of the Communist party. Li has worked for the CPA for 50 years as if it was but a single day. She is now 83 years old, but still works at the CPA; she is always the first to report to duty and the last to go home.

Next the government arrested Rev. Wang Rensheng of St. Peter's Church, Cai Zhongxian of Xujiahui and Fu Hezhou of St. Joseph's Church in Sichuan South Road. There were fewer priests available, so a few young people came to see me, asking me to be their spiritual advisor. I took on a few, among them Zhu Zhengmin, Liu Tongxia and her younger brother Liu Tongfan. In 1954, Liu Tongfan was arrested, while the other two were arrested after my detention. Liu was re-educated rather swiftly and was promptly released. Zhu Zhengmin was sent to Qinghai for reform through labour after her arrest. When the government finally restored order after the 'Cultural Revolution' she was released and returned to Shanghai and was compensated with a graduation certificate from No. 2 Medical University and given work. She is now retired.

32
The Four Roles

After Rev. Lacretelle and the others had been arrested on 15 June, the Jesuit Visitor Rev. Burckhardt rode his bicycle to Xujiahui to see me. He told me that Lacretelle had been arrested and so he was approaching me to be acting father superior of the Jesuits in Shanghai. Before Lacretelle had been arrested, he had also left instructions that I should be appointed capitular vicar of Huizhou District. I thus assumed the three roles of acting rector of the seminary, acting Jesuit father superior and capitular vicar. After Burckhardt had left I went to the chapel to pray before the Holy Sacrament and, kneeling, said to the Lord: "Lord forgive me, my burden is too great. I am a step closer to prison; with all these appointments I will soon be sent to jail. Please give me courage." As I prayed tears fell without restraint—utterly unheroic behaviour.

In August the government ordered the expulsion of Burckhardt as soon as possible (he was Swiss and Switzerland had already recognised the People's Republic and so the government were relatively polite to him) and he obeyed immediately, but asked his secretary to pass me a note, saying that he had already been ordered to leave the country. I should the next day take up the role of deputy Visitor of the Jesuits and thus I assumed four deputy roles, meaning also that I had four knives hanging above me ready to fall at any moment. This appointment thus only added to the dangerous position I was in.

Once Burckhardt had left China, he immediately flew to Rome to make his report. He wrote to me saying that the superior general had authorised me to make the fourth and final Jesuit vow before the appointed time. According to the constitution of the Society of Jesus, professed Jesuits should, in addition to the three vows of chastity, poverty and obedience, make a final vow of total obedience to the Pope's instructions regarding the missions. According to the Jesuit rule, those who take the fourth vow should have completed 17 years in the order. I had entered the order in 1938 and so ought to have waited until

30 August 1955. However, under these special circumstances, an exception could be made and the superior general had permitted me to take the vow in advance, allowing me to become a professed Jesuit. On 8 December 1953 at Xujiahui Church, I and Rev. Xu Jiangu took the vow together at the hands of Rev. Xu Weizeng. Xu Weizeng was Su Jiangu's uncle. After the ceremony, Rev. Lefebvre wrote the report to Rome.

In this manner I assumed four acting roles, but felt that each additional one just brought me closer to jail. To catch bandits, you must first catch the leader. The government would certainly first arrest the heads and so I could in this manner protect others by wearing so many hats. The position of the Jesuits and of the Church was becoming more precarious with one political movement after another. We were increasingly unable to ward off the blows and able only to await the worst. Awaiting my fate with resignation, I had no need to drag others into it. Who would have thought that some Jesuits were dissatisfied and uttered many complaints, saying that I was in love with power, trusted no one and so on? I could only smile bitterly when I heard about this.

Once I had been appointed acting Jesuit father superior, I went to see Gong and report to him, and to guarantee that the Shanghai Jesuits would continue as before to cooperate with the diocese and also to indicate to him that I would follow his arrangements. But I explained to him that I was not a legal expert and would not play the same role that Rev. Lacretelle had. I also said that I ought to place my main emphasis on my work at the seminary and would not visit him frequently. He expressed his understanding.

I knew that the priests of the diocese had been dissatisfied with the Jesuits for many years; in particular they resented the fact that Gong placed more confidence in Jesuits and would not seek out the opinion of diocesan priests. Furthermore Gong relied too heavily on Lacretelle's opinions. I considered these to be historical problems and felt that I ought to quickly put them to rights. First of all, I only went to see Gong rarely, in order to avoid letting people think that I was manipulating Gong. Next I suggested to Gong that the two Jesuits stationed at the Sichuan South Road Church next to Gong's office be transferred. With Gong's approval, I sent Rev. Ding Ruren to Sheshan as dean, retired Song Zhizhen as parish priest and transferred Shen Baixun to the suburbs to serve as a parish priest. I appointed Rev. Mei Chengqi as director of the Jesuit house and concurrently as pastor in Xujiahu in the place of Rev. Cai Shifang, who had been arrested. I also informed Gong that when the situation made it possible, I would send Jesuits to work in the Huizhou diocese and that, apart from the seminary, other parish work should be handled henceforth by diocesan priests. Gong advised me not to rush into anything and to defer the decision. Later on matters took a decided turn for the worse. The 'September Eighth' events were suddenly upon us (on 8 September 1955, the government launched the massive campaign against the Gong Pinmei clique). We almost all of us, great and small, ended up thrown into jail.

The government's anti-imperialist campaign continued. They successively expelled the physicist Rev. Burgaud and Rev. Yves Henry. When they were deporting Lefebvre under escort, he had a sudden heart attack on arrival in Guangzhou and died. The police informed the Guangzhou Catholic Church. Bishop Deng Yiming (aka Dominic Tang Yee-ming S.J., 1908–95) was at that time studying and working in Shanghai and had been Lefebvre's student. Bishop Deng went himself to conduct the obsequies and bury Lefebvre's body in a public cemetery in Guangzhou. Afterwards he sent me photographs to inform me, for which I thanked him. Deng was also later arrested. Upon his release, the government permitted him to continue as Bishop of Guangzhou. He applied to go to Hong Kong for medical treatment and the government gave him permission. Vatican secretary of state Cardinal Casaroli (1914–98) made a special trip to see him and took him to Rome to see the Pope. The Pope appointed him the Archbishop of Guangdong. Before making the announcement the Pope asked the advisor at the Jesuit house in Rome, Rev. Zhu Lide: "Is this appropriate?" Zhu answered: "Wholly appropriate." But as soon as the appointment was announced, it gave rise to a wave of activism against Vatican interference in Chinese internal affairs and the government did not allow Deng to return. He could only wander around abroad. He had always handled matters in a low-key manner, was always modest and prudent, very rarely making anti-communist statements. He was very different from Gong.

When I went to San Francisco Deng asked to see me. The Maryknoll Father Raymond Nobiletti who was at that time the pastor of Transfiguration Church took me to see Deng. He knew no Mandarin and I knew no Cantonese, so we communicated in English. He said that he wished to return to China, to die in his mother country. He hoped that I would express his wishes to the relevant authorities. When I got back I made my report to the Religious Affairs Bureau and to the Public Security Bureau. They asked me to tell him that he should make a public expression of regret, asking for the forgiveness of his country. Deng said he would not accept such a condition. In the end, he died in America. Before he died, he published his autobiography with the title *How*

Inscrutable His Ways! I have always considered him a good priest, a good Jesuit, a good bishop. He was a victim of the age. When I returned to San Francisco I visited his grave and prayed to the Lord in front of the tablet in the chapel.

In the early 1950s Gong Pinmei made a secret instruction that in the event that he wouldn't be able to continue to exercise his authority as bishop, first Xu Yuanrong and then Chen Tianbao (aka Chen Fumin) should succeed him. By 1955, he had decided that these two men were unsuitable, the first being timid and the second overly authoritarian. Therefore just before Rev. Balirach of the seminary was expelled, he wrote on a small sacred image a letter for Balirach to pass to the Pope, nominating Rev. Ji Ende as his first successor and Zhang Dengshu as the second. Balirach later wrote a letter to Gong telling him that he had delivered the letter to Rome. After Gong was arrested all four of these men said that they knew nothing at all about it and refused to be Gong's successor. The diocese chose the well-known and highly respected Rev. Zhang Shilang as capitular vicar and reported to Rome, but the Congregation for the Propagation of the Faith wrote back rejecting Zhang Shilang and saying that all should be done as per Gong's arrangements.

When Archbishop Riberi had been expelled from China, he had followed Rome's instructions and stayed in Hong Kong to wait for a change in the political climate. On one occasion he wrote a letter to Gong saying: "In less than five years I will be taking my walks along the banks of the Huangpu." Gong showed the letter to me. I said: "Not likely. As the days pass, the Communist government is getting stronger and the hope that the US and Chiang Kai-shek will return gets smaller." Gong didn't share my opinion. When Riberi was expelled, the government organised a propaganda campaign, saying that he was only a citizen of Monaco who liked bossing people around and interfering with the Three Self Patriotic Movement. The whole country discussed the case of this citizen of Monaco at all levels and there were cartoons of him posted on streets up and down the country. The religious and lay people all held their peace. Only the Vicar General of Nanjing Li Weiguang responded to the party's call when attending a meeting of the Three Self Reform Committee and made a speech criticising Riberi. Riberi was very angry, and reported back to Rome when he arrived in Hong Kong, requesting the excommunication of Li Weiguang, which the Vatican permitted. Riberi wrote a letter to Gong authorising him to inform Li Weiguang that he had been excommunicated. When Gong heard this he was very upset, knowing that this move would only incite Li Weiguang to be hellbent on following the CCP, also knowing that his participation would bring on the ire of the government. So he asked Li Shiyu (the two Lis had been fellow students and were friends) to carry out the order. Li prevaricated and later on Gong informed Li Weiguang by letter. After Liberation, Li Weiguang's was the only formal excommunication. The Pope didn't excommunicate anyone else (not even those who later appointed themselves bishop).

The first anniversary of the start of the Anti-Imperialist Patriotic Movement was 16 June 1954. The government dispersed the Liberation Army units that had been sealing off the Jesuit house in Xujiahui and this fact was reported in the newspapers so that priests and seminarians were at liberty to come and go as they wished. The government also chose this movement to expel Rev. Lacretelle under escort. When Lacretelle had arrived in Hong Kong he wrote Gong a short handwritten letter that was delivered by a Carmelite sister from Hong Kong (on a tiny piece of blue paper), saying that while he was in prison he could still hear the church bells, that he had not said a single word while in jail, nor had he done anything that might bring harm to the diocese. Gong showed me the letter, expressing his relief and calling for all the priests to stop worrying about Lacretelle. Lacretelle had not betrayed anyone; he was after all a holy man. Thus we returned to normal, holding meetings and carrying out underground activities, hitting back at the CPA members, working tirelessly.

After we were arrested on 8 September 1955 and put in jail, the government showed us all the confessions that Lacretelle had handwritten, over 800 pages, exposing all our internal affairs, great and small; I also heard a recording of his confession and thus realised that we had been tricked and deceived. Later on I wondered why Lacretelle had confessed so much; why after regaining his liberty he had not told us, even going so far as to say that he had not betrayed us, all the while allowing us to continue opposing the government? That he spilt the beans, we can forgive him. After being imprisoned, there are very few people who can continue to stand out to the end. But why did he want to lie to us? He was widely recognised as a holy man; but is this the behaviour of a holy man? After he went to Hong Kong and Taiwan he closed his mouth and talked no more of the past. Later on, when the whole truth came out, people abroad still didn't believe it, thinking that this was a CCP fabrication in order to smear Lacretelle's name. Later on I realised that, had he told us the truth, we would have ceased to oppose the government and this was something he did not want to see, but this is my own guess as Lacretelle has already left this world. In the meantime we in China have once again been permitted to enjoy freedom of religious practice and can forget all about him. While I was in jail

I had ample time to consider and appreciate how each missionary had his own background and his own point of view, so that the missionaries' way of looking at things could not be like ours. Where big issues are concerned, in matters of life and death, we should rely on our own independent opinion and not be led by the nose by others. We should definitely avoid being anyone's pawn or sacrificial object.

After the Anti-Imperialist Patriotic Movement had begun, a director of the Shanghai Municipal Religious Affairs Bureau named Shen came to visit me for a talk. He had also sought out many leading laymen and many had formed a favourable opinion of him. He told me that during the Anti-Japanese War, he had been in Ningbo. When the Japanese had tried to arrest him, he had been saved by the French bishop who kept him at the church and protected him. He had always been grateful to that missionary. I told him that a great many missionaries loved China and far from all of them were imperialist agents.

A Xujiahui cadre named Li (who had been in the Liberation Army) came to see me every two months. He treated me in a straightforward manner, talking about government policy, but I just went through the motions with him. I have never forgotten him and always pray to the Lord for him. A man named Zhao who accompanied him was a native of Zhaojia in Pudong who had originally been a Catholic. This man had a very bad attitude and was very negative towards the Church. No doubt precisely because he had been a Catholic he wanted to prove himself to the CCP and so left a bad impression with me. On the one hand I played along with the man named Li, while on the other hand refusing the government's desire to send political instructors to the seminary. Thus the notions of the seminarians remained those of 1949. They had no contact with new ideas. The seminarians considered this an honour and referred to themselves as 'Little Taiwan', so you can see how backward we had become.

In order to strengthen the seminarians' commitment to the Pope, I inspired the more enthusiastic students to organise a 'total love for the Pope' activity, of which the high point was a pilgrimage to Sheshan to make an oath to commit one's whole life to the service of the Pope. The vow was very long; I have already forgotten all its contents. This oath had the effect of causing very many seminarians to resolutely resist the government and refuse to accept re-education.

It required a large amount of money to keep the seminary going with 300 students and over a dozen teachers. The seminary itself had no assets, while the students from other parts of China couldn't pay their fees. I asked Gong to provide funds and he told me that Rev. Deng Liangshen was responsible for this. I asked for assistance from abroad, especially from Rev. Germain who was responsible for the overseas funds of the Shanghai diocese, having been expelled from China and posted to Hong Kong. He had bought a house on Argyll Street and started work. He informed Zhou Chengliang that there were a few foreign businessmen who wanted to leave China and go to the US or Canada. They couldn't take their property with them so they wanted to give their renminbi to the church. With the receipt issued by Zhou, they could pick up US dollars from Rev. Germain in Hong Kong. Zhou did this, thus defying the foreign currency regulations and breaking the law of China. Zhou reported to me and I agreed. This was another of my criminal acts.

Another of my crimes was to assist people in escaping from China. There were a few missionaries who had been evicted to Hong Kong and then stayed on in Macau, Taiwan or Manila. They wanted the young people who had stayed in the Mainland to join them so that they could continue to instruct them. They found smugglers who, for a price, were able to get these young people out. A Canadian priest named Hardy spoke to me of this, so I knew all about it and agreed that he and his associates should do this. I knew perfectly well that this was both illegal and dangerous, but I thought about the four acting roles that I held. For foreigners, the punishment was at most to be expelled, but a Chinese fall guy like myself was already in deep trouble and would be harshly treated, so one crime more or one less seemed irrelevant. The individual was not important, whereas the survival of the Church in China was the vital thing.

In order to support the Anti-Imperialist Patriotic Movement, the government's Propaganda Department used novels and films to great effect to spread the news of the crimes of the missionaries, utilising every means to thoroughly blacken the name of 'missionary' and thus attack Catholicism. The government translated and widely disseminated novels like *The Gadfly* by Ethel Lillian Voynich that reveal the hypocritical and ugly side of the Church. They shot a lot of movies, the contents of which described bishops and priests using religion to poison the minds of young people, how the Church structure arranged for lay people to collect secret intelligence and carry out acts of sabotage. This kind of propaganda had a considerable effect. In 1986 we organised a theological conference at Changsha in Hunan to discuss the Second Vatican Council. The State Religious Affairs Bureau and the Shanghai United Front Department sent senior cadres to take part. Bishops Fu Tieshan, Dong Guangqing and Du Shihua, Messrs Liu Bainian and Liu Jian, and Ms. Lu Weihong were all of course invited. The governor of Hunan also gave us a talk. I asked a young service staff: "Have you ever heard of the Catholic Church?" She replied: "Yes, aren't they all secret agents sent by foreign governments? How come so many leaders are coming out now to meet you? Even the governor has come. I can't understand it."

In 1870, the Apostolic Vicar of Jiangnan (Shanghai) Adrien-Hippolyte Languillat S.J. (1808–78) had travelled to Rome to attend the First Vatican Council. While in France, he had met with the recently established Congregation of the Helpers of the Holy Souls and asked them to come and assist in missionary activity in Shanghai, including education and charitable work. The sisters arrived in 1875 and started work in Xujiahui. They set up schools and started a foundling hospital to raise abandoned infants. In 1953 they had been in Shanghai for 80 years. The parents of unwanted children would leave them at the door of the foundling hospital at night to avoid being discovered. In the morning, the sisters would come and bring them into the hospital. Some would be hardly breathing; others at the point of death. With such children they would do their utmost to save them, while those they were unable to save would be buried in the neighbourhood. After 80 years, the number of children buried there was pretty large. As for those that could be kept alive, they were baptised and nurtured, while some were adopted by lay people. The majority that had no home to return to stayed behind, were taught to read and write and learnt a craft. After growing up, the boys were sent to the Tushanwan Orphanage, while the girls stayed at the convent to do handiwork. At the age of 18, they were introduced to husbands and allowed to set up home; they were even provided with housing so that they could raise a family.

The People's Government sent people to dig up the graves of the buried infants, and took photographs of the piles of bleached bones thrown together, then published them in the newspapers with banner headlines so that the people of Shanghai could see for themselves the cast-iron evidence of how the imperialist missionaries had murdered Chinese infants. This was called the '10,000 Infants Tomb'. Students, workers, office staff and neighbourhood committees all visited the tomb. All visitors were filled with righteous indignation and called out for the fall of the imperialist agents, while Catholics refused to visit and wholly denied the crimes of the missionaries.

At that time I thought that Catholics were becoming more and more isolated from the masses and were being placed apart from other people, making their daily lives extremely difficult. At the university entrance exam all Catholics were denied admittance to university and could not find work. I had an idea that when 300 years previously the Vatican had denied the Chinese faithful the right to worship their ancestors and were proscribed, one group had gone underground, another had given up the Faith—greatly to the disadvantage of the propagation of the Faith. Now the faithful were forbidden from supporting the Communist party, joining the CCP mass organisations or reading communist newspapers and publications—wouldn't they in the end meet with the same fate as their 17th century ancestors?

I realised that the Vatican only paid attention to the reports of missionaries who had been expelled from China and had no understanding of the religious policies of New China or the challenges of the Chinese Church. At the height of the Anti-American Movement the Vatican even appointed an American Jesuit named Eugene Fahy as the new Bishop of Yangzhou, requiring the Chinese faithful to follow the instructions of an American leader, which notion leaves one at a loss as to whether to laugh or cry. I considered that the Chinese government also did not understand the Church, only relying on the advice of Hu Wenyao, Yang Shida and Tang Fudao, among others—men who also didn't really understand the Church. When they reported to the government, how could they reflect the true state of affairs? Their advice was of no use to the formulation of policy, instead leading the authorities astray with the final result that neither side could tell friend from foe.

I returned to China in 1951 and was arrested in 1955, spending four and a half years out of jail. During this period I went from being a teacher to being an acting director, acting Jesuit father superior, acting Visitor and acting bishop, feeling all the time that the noose was tightening. There was nothing for it, I was not invited to join the decision-making group of the Shanghai diocese and was unable to take control of the situation. I was fully aware that I had been placed in a perilous situation where all I could do was await my arrest and death in jail.

My point of view was a bit different from Gong Pinmei's. My activities were rather less than those of men like Wang Rensheng, Zhu Shude, Chen Tianxiang, Zhu Hongsheng and Chen Yuntang, but as a Jesuit, I was fundamentally aligned with them. To all those who asked me, I would certainly say I did not want to join the CPA. I could not distance myself from the Church. My approach was rather low-key, keeping my head below the parapet, not taking public positions. I concentrated on using the time to educate a few worthy successors so they could continue our enterprise. But events conspired to destroy our hopes. The government had already been pushed to the limit of endurance and decided to round up all the oppositionists, so the seminary could not be saved. A cadre named Zhao from the Xuhui district government set to work on the twenty employees of the seminary, endlessly calling them to attend meetings, organising a federation of Catholic workers and campaigning for benefits on their behalf. They fully collaborated with the government and made reports to the government. The working class wanted to be the leaders. The government then openly arrested two seminarians; the first was Ai Zuming, the second Shi Kuisheng, shut them up for a few months and then released the latter. From then on the government gradually understood the internal operations of the seminary, collected documentary evidence and prepared to take action.

I had a friend from Jiangyin who had been the educational director of Aurora Middle School. He worked in the Nanjing diocese. He got on very well with Vicar General Li Weiguang, the first to be excommunicated for supporting the CPA. In the summer of 1955 he went to see Li. Li said one thing: "When one wave breaks, another rises," which my friend passed on to me. From this I decided that a new campaign was about to begin. The government again started arresting people, including a young Catholic lay-person named Sun Guohua from the Church of Christ the King parish. 'When the mountain rains come, the halls fill with wind.' The Catholic Church was about to be hit by an even more powerful threat.

In 1954, the diocese seemed relatively quiet, which made me suspect that the government was just hatching an even bigger campaign. What made me nervous were the big propaganda banners exhorting the crushing of anti-revolutionary secret societies, in particular the syncretistic new religion I-Kuan Tao, and the large-scale exhibition to reveal its crimes, which the masses were organised to see along with schools, neighbourhood committees and especially Catholics who were required to attend meetings and speak out. In early 1955, the Elimination of Counter-Revolutionaries Movement was launched. Mao Zedong himself chaired the movement to criticise the Hu Feng anti-revolutionary group and materials about the Hu Feng group were printed in the newspapers. One after another, Hu Feng's anti-revolutionary speeches and private correspondence were published—the private letters having been provided by his good friend Shu Wudi. Careful reading of these abstracts and the commentary made me apprehensive, because I realised that all those who held contrary opinions and divergent views had committed counter-revolutionary crimes. The contents of the letters from start to finish constituted cast-iron evidence of criminal thinking. This was equivalent to the literary inquisition invented in the Qing dynasty. At the same time I became aware that our day of reckoning was coming soon, but I managed to maintain a calm façade, not revealing one iota, afraid as I was to affect the seminarians. (The book *Les enfants dans la ville* by Rev. Jean Lefeuvre,[1] a Jesuit who went to Taiwan from Xujiahui, describes in detail this period of history and the struggles we went through from 1951 to 1955. It's well worth reading, having been a bestseller republished many times.)

---

1. *Les enfants dans la ville: vie chrétienne à Shanghai et perspectives sur l'Église de Chine 1949-1961*, by Jean Lefeuvre, Castermann, 1962.

33
Gong Pinmei

Many people ask me my view of Gong Pinmei, so I'll take this opportunity to state it. He was a very good priest who greatly loved the Lord and strictly followed discipline. His father had served the Church all his life, working flat out, devoted to his duties and amassing a small fortune with which he bought land and became a property owner. When Gong was young, he was engaged to be married, his betrothed being a woman from Gaoqiao in Pudong, but on the eve of his graduation from St. Ignatius College he heeded the Lord's call and broke off the engagement, entering the seminary.

He entered the priesthood in 1930, becoming in succession headmaster of Zhengxin Middle School in Songjiang, headmaster of the matriculating class at Aurora University Middle School and, finally, headmaster of Jinke Middle School in Shanghai, spending a total of 18 years in education, never serving as a parish priest and so gaining no experience of missionary or pastoral work. In 1949, he was appointed by Rome to his first little diocese of Suzhou, which had only 40,000 Catholics, ten priests and one middle school. Then, because the original appointee Gong Shirong was not able to take up the post, Rome decided to appoint Gong Pinmei as Bishop of Shanghai in his place, with added responsibility for Suzhou and Nanjing dioceses.

In those days, Shanghai diocese was the most important in China (with over 100,000 Catholics, over 100 priests, 2 universities, 20 middle schools, hospitals, charities, a publishing house and scientific research institutes and a great deal of property). Since Cardinal Tian Gengxing and Archbishop Yu Bin had already fled abroad, Gong in practice immediately became the leader of all Chinese Catholics. In those days, one phrase was current in the Church: all eyes were on Shanghai. Gong had not studied overseas and had little life experience. He once told me that before 1955 the farthest west he had been was on a day trip to Nanjing to have an audience with Riberi; to the south he had only been to Hangzhou for a few days' relaxation and to the north he had only reached Wusongkou on the Yangtze River. He grew up in Pudong and had never been abroad. In the midst of crisis, he suddenly assumed a heavy burden for which he was both professionally and psychologically unprepared.

His education had been in the French manner and all his teachers had been French. He greatly respected both Rev. Germain and Rev. Lacretelle and in fact was controlled by Lacretelle. While Gong was the public face, Lacretelle pulled the strings from behind the screen. After he became Bishop of Shanghai the whole country began land reform. In truth the Shanghai diocese was a landowner and all the lands in the suburbs were lost to land reform. Gong's own family property was also lost in the reform. He often told people: "I am now without a single tile above or a single inch of land below." All the businesses in Shanghai were nationalised one by one. According to his basic instinct, Gong could not follow the dictates of the CCP and wholly obeyed the Vatican, mindlessly executing anti-communist orders.

After Liberation, the New People's Democracy period ended even earlier than anticipated; after two or three years the socialist revolution was started and a policy of using, limiting and controlling the Church began. Vigorous political campaigns followed one after another, leaving Gong at a loss as to how to withstand it all. Especially when the campaign against the Legion of Mary was launched, Gong and his fellows thought that disaster had struck and therefore resisted at all points. With the background of those times, the Shanghai diocese could not produce a personage such as the Protestant Wu Yaozong, who could stand up and publicly embrace the government.

Gong was a product of his age. He was a tragic character. Under Gong's leadership and encouragement many Catholics prepared for martyrdom, but these deaths were not achieved. Even Gong was simply jailed for life. For various reasons, the People's Government released him; they changed his sentence, finally freeing him before he had fully served his sentence. He applied to go to the US for six months for medical reasons and guaranteed that after he left, he would not pursue anti-CCP activities. The government let him go. The Vatican promoted him to cardinal so he achieved his desire and gained his reward. Good pastors should remain with their flocks, sharing their joys and their troubles, but after six months, Gong did not return to China and preferred to stay in exile under the protection of the United States, living a comfortable life and making many anti-communist speeches.

Before he left, he once said to me while recuperating in Hangzhou: "In history those who betray their country never leave a good reputation." He also said: "I was born a Chinese man and die a Chinese ghost." After arriving in the US, these words were all forgotten. People have forgiven him for his loss of autonomy in the US and for being controlled by his nephew Gong Minchuan. Gong knew no English, so while he was in America his relatives who had gone there first had a hold over him. In truth he had lost his liberty a second time. But man is born with free will and has to take responsibility for his own words and actions, for the path he chooses to take. Each one of us faces our own challenge in terms of which course to take and cannot evade responsibility. I take this example as an object lesson in life.

Photo 1 Jin Luxian (second from right in the second row) as a choir boy at St. Ignatius College. The accompanying priest is Rev. Vincent Zi S.J.

Photo 2 Jin Luxian as a young man

金瑪利亞慰萱之遺象

聖女日多達然跪中見入母獻子子得其報

況以本身獻主堂者不得其報者乎

進衣
祈禱
善終
玫瑰
會

九五变相伯

Photo 3 Funeral portrait of Mary Jin Weixuan

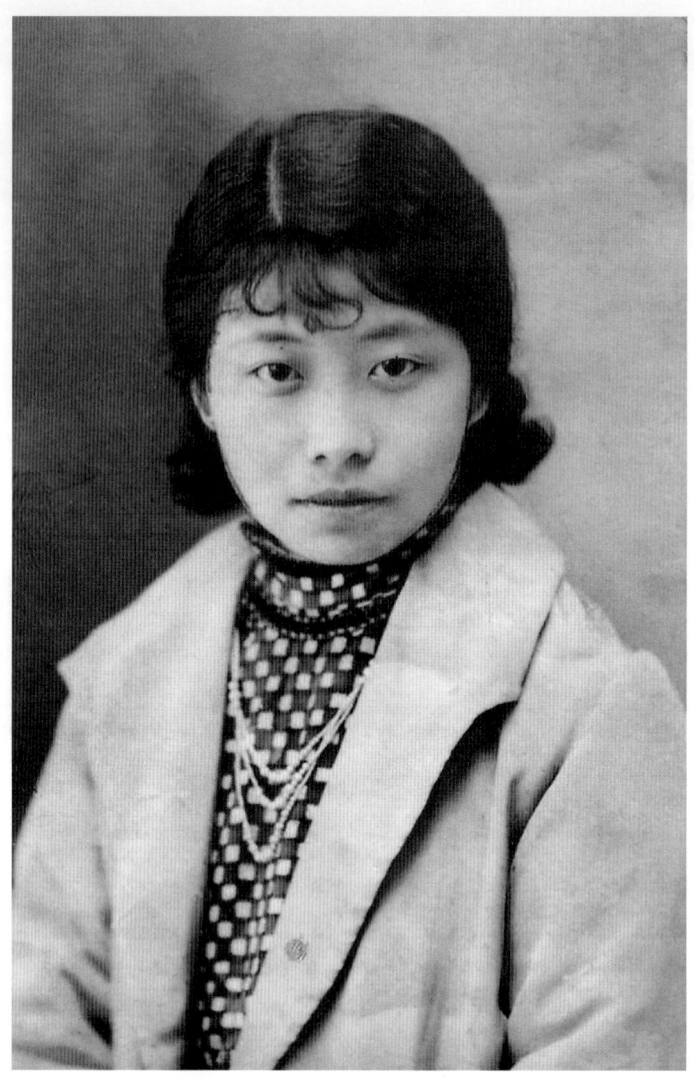

Photo 4 Rong Dexian

Photo 5　Family of Rong Dexian and Zhu Yisheng with Bishop Walsh

Photo 6   Lu Naying (third from right in the back row) with the family of Lu Bohong

Photo 7   Jin Luxian in Rome

Photo 8   Donate Seeger

Photo 9 Jin Luxian as a young priest in Beijing

Photo 10 Shanghai Jesuits with Bishop Gong Pinmei. Jin is at Gong's right. Rev. Peter Lefebvre is fourth from right in the first row.

Photo 11 Jin and Edeltrud Meistermann-Seeger 'Mami'

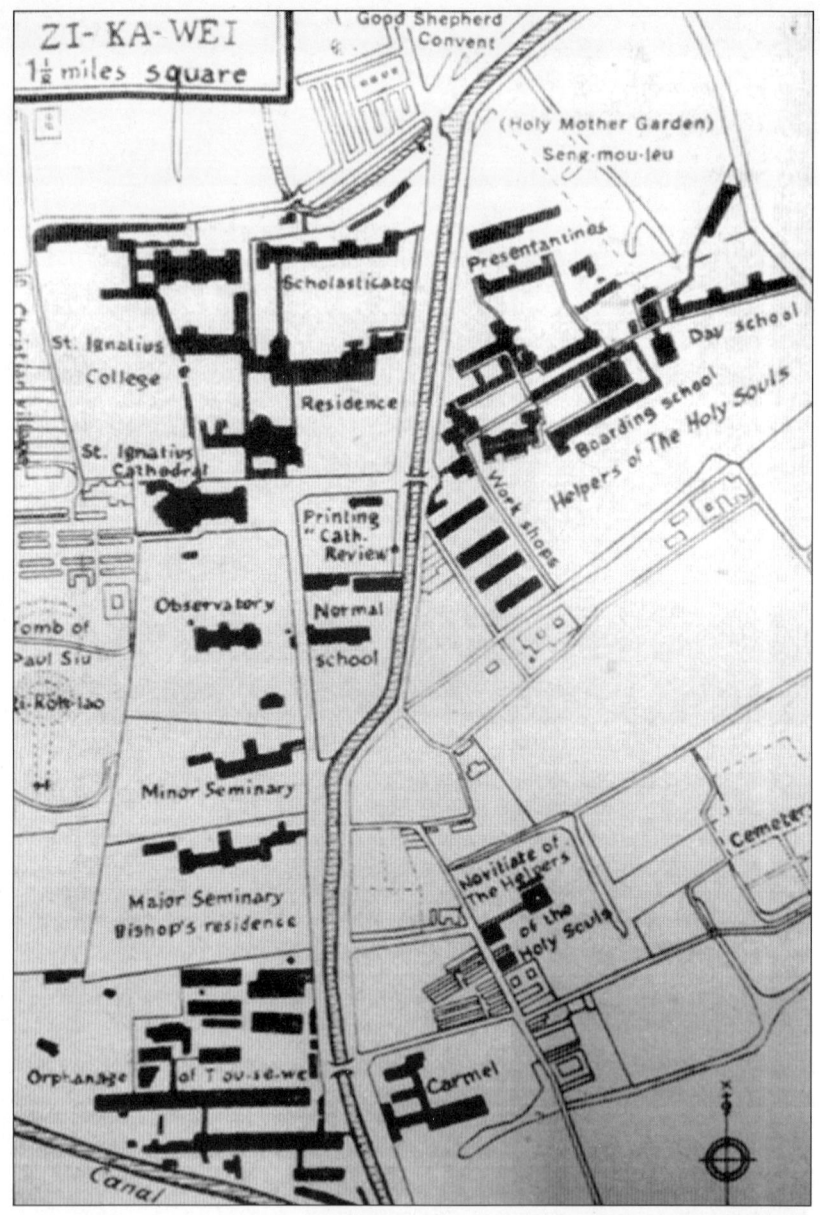

Map 1   Map of Xujiahui Jesuit buildings

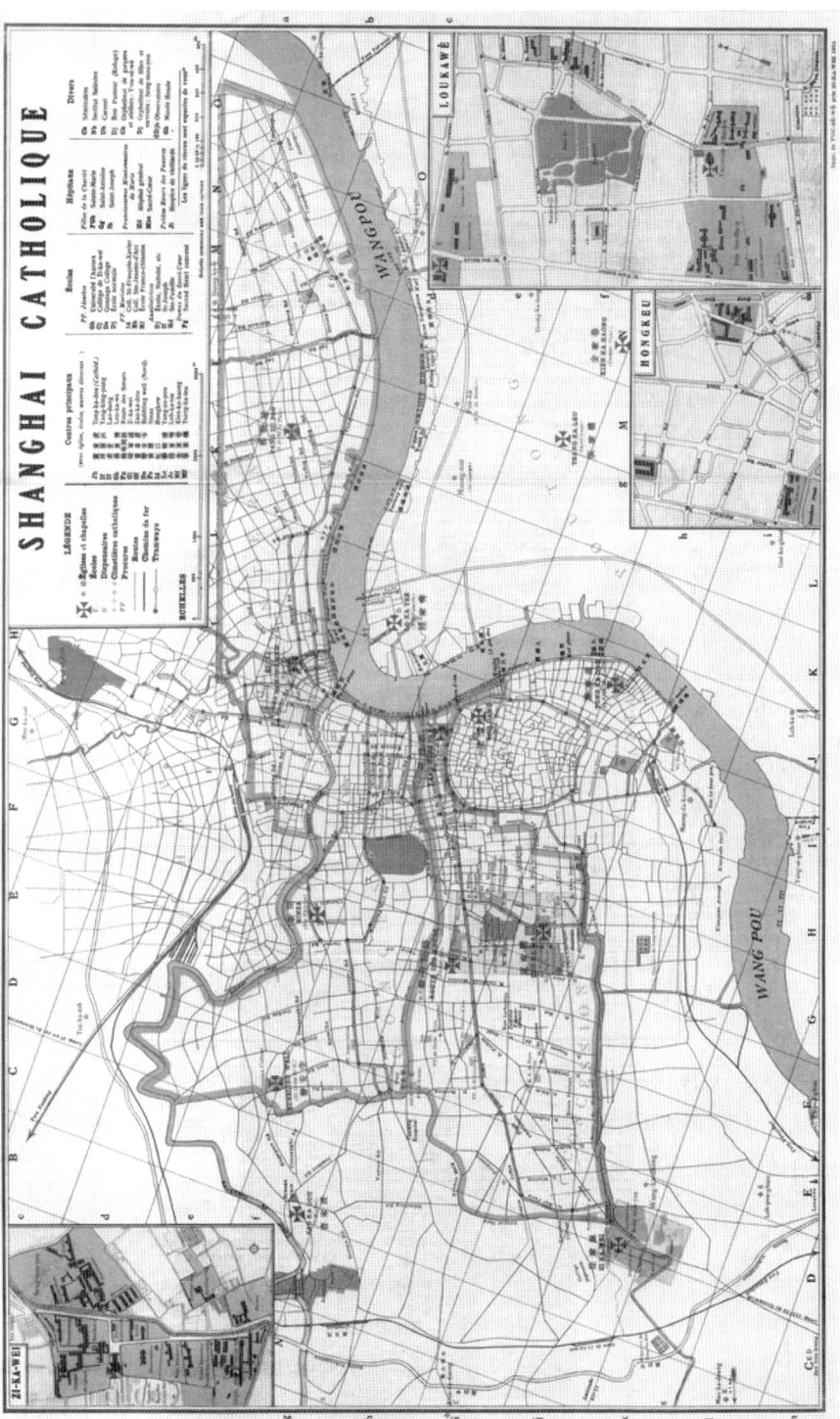

Map 2 Map of Catholic Shanghai

Map 3 Map of China showing Jin's travels

Part V

Life in Jail

34
My First Sight of Prison (1955–60)

The Feast of the Nativity of the Blessed Virgin Mary was 8 September 1955, which was also the anniversary of my first vows. At 9:30 in the evening, as I was reading in my room, the main gate of the seminary suddenly opened (the workers having been ordered in advance to prepare for this) and a group of plain clothes policemen burst in and broke up into groups to arrest people. Four men charged into my room and said to me: "You are being arrested; come with us." I was pushed into a small motor car and driven away. I saw that Rev. Yan Yunliang had also been arrested. At the time I wondered: "Why would they arrest him? He never went out or took part in any activities; to what end would they arrest even him? It must mean that this time it is going to be a large sweep." Later on I learnt that this was a national arrest warrant, from the beaches of the East Sea to the Heavenly Mountains of Xinjiang, from the border with Russia to the furthest capes of Hainan Island: everyone who was a core member of the Gong Pinmei counter-revolutionary clique and even those who had merely had real or imagined contact with Gong Pinmei were arrested; not a single one was spared. In the case of Shanghai, around 100 were arrested, while the total of those picked up later numbered in the thousands.

While I was being arrested, some 100 policemen burst into the seminary to investigate, arrest priests and seminarians and gather all the remaining seminarians together in the reception room to announce various measures. At the bishop's offices at Sichuan South Road, they arrested Gong Pinmei and in other churches they picked up other top people of the diocese—no one escaped their net.

The police locked us up in small cars outside the gate of the seminary—I was squeezed between two officers. On the road I thought: "This day has finally come! They sought to act virtuously, and they did so; what was there for them to repine about?"[1] My mission had been accomplished. The Jesuits in China and the seminary did not want me to panic. I should simply commit myself into the hands of the Lord.

The car drove to (as I later learned) the No. 1 Detention Centre of Shanghai in Nanshi District. A group of policemen asked for my name and checked my identity, made a record, confiscated all my personal belongings—including my rosary, the crucifix hanging on my chest, even the buttons on my clothes—and pushed me into a small room where there were already two men. The room had no table, chairs or bed. I was told not to give my name to anybody and was issued with a number. I was told that from now on this would be my only form of identification. Later on, I would be issued with new numbers every time I moved to a different prison, so I have forgotten them. During my relatively long period in jail I was always known by a number and nothing else.

I sat on the floor and calmed my spirit through prayer. The day I had been awaiting for over four years had finally come. I dedicated the seminary and the Jesuits to the Holy Mother and had no need to be concerned for myself. I especially prayed for the director of studies Zhou Jinghui, You Goujie and the young students Liu Danxia and Zhu Zhengmin, and asked the Holy Mother to protect them, after which I slept a little.

I was awakened at 6 a.m. A criminal in the same room was very talkative, saying he was an associate of the gangster Du Yuesheng and that was his main crime. Later on I got to know him better, learning that he was an opera fan, with a great love of Peking Opera and a friend of the opera singers Ma Lianliang, Zhou Xinfang, Meng Xiaodong and Mei Lanfang.

After two days the police came to interrogate me, requiring me to account for my crimes; they also explained the rules: confession would be treated leniently and resistance would be punished. During the five years I was in the detention centre, my main investigator (known as the interrogator) was named Li Zhen (a fact I learned later from seeing his name on the confession records I had to sign after each interrogation). The recorder was a woman named Yang.

Li was pretty good and had a fine grasp of the rules. After I had been released and returned to Shanghai, I said to Comrade Pu Zuo of the Religious Affairs Bureau and Comrade Yu Yuexin of the Public Security Bureau (PSB) that I had formed an excellent impression of Li, but they said that they couldn't

---

1. *The Analects of Confucius 7:14*, translated by James Legge, The Commercial Press, China, 1948.

understand why: the bureau had never permitted Li to join the party; his career had been unsuccessful. He had never again wanted to step inside the doors of the Public Security Bureau. Later on when I set up the Guangqi Press, I needed people to work there and Pu Zuo said that Li Zhen had a good command of the Chinese language and was at that time unemployed. I could invite him to be an editor. I said that he was welcome. Pu Zuo later told me that Li had gracefully declined and I thought: "Yes, how could an investigator work with a former subject of interrogation?" I learned that Li had had no children and had adopted a daughter, who later went to America, but remained very filial to him. Later on, I heard that he had died, having spent his last few years with severe dementia, which was a great pity.

At this point, I want to state clearly, since many people have asked me, that I was not tortured in jail. I only remember on one occasion during interrogation (with five policemen high above me on a dais and I below on a small stool) I had remained silent all along until one investigator called out in a loud voice: "Bring the instruments of torture." Two men then came in bearing handcuffs and ankle-fetters and cast them on the floor with a loud clatter. The same investigator then called out: "Put them on!" The two men were coming towards me when Li Zhen stood up and said: "Today's investigation will terminate here; take him back to his cell." Possibly they had discussed earlier that they would thus frighten me a little.

My many interrogations produced no result, so the government simply shut me away for at least a couple of months without further investigation. On one occasion they took me to another room where they had connected a wire to the outside so that I could be made to listen to the public ceremony for releasing prisoners. Among the speakers was my uncle, Dr. Jin Aide, who was originally very anti-communist, but seemed to have made a lot of progress by the time of this meeting, seeming like a new person. Then they announced the release of Liu Danxia. The next day, the investigators asked me what I thought of the ceremony. I said that Liu had made progress and was now free, which was a good thing. Li Zhen told me that I'd better abandon my fantasies: "Your followers on the outside have only two choices: one is to provide evidence and betray you; the other is to be arrested." I said that in that case they had better provide evidence against me as I had no wish to see them in jail. After the day of my arrest, I never saw Liu Danxia again. She had no desire to see me. Later on I learned that she had married a schoolmate named Liao Mingqin. Liao was a good Catholic, but I still prayed for her and asked the Lord to protect her.

On another occasion, they took me to a room where the wires had been connected and concealed so that I was required to listen to a public trial. At first there were people released and then others condemned—the Legion of Mary leader, Shen Duosen, refused to repent after many punishments and so was sentenced to death, with immediate effect. I knew Shen and his nephews Shen Shiwei, Shen Leping and Shen Letian, who were all seminarians. Shen himself was an English teacher and had a wife and children. However, he was the deputy director of the East China branch of the Legion of Mary. The director had been a female student named Chen Ruizhang. As soon as she saw the way things were going, she fled abroad and joined the Order of the Sacred Heart of Jesus as a nun. The order trained her to be an English expert, in which capacity she became a scholar of Shakespeare. In the 1980s, the Chinese government invited her to lecture at universities with a very high salary. It seems the best strategy is always flight. Chen left while Shen stayed. Their fates were as different as heaven and earth. After I heard the broadcast, Shen's appearance kept flashing in front of my eyes. I thought about his young wife and children and couldn't sleep for several nights.

At this point I should mention that in 1963 the Labour Reform Bureau chose 24 people from prisons across the country to do translation work. I was among those transferred to Qincheng Jail (of which more below). Among the same group of prisoners was a man named Zhang Yintong, who had been a history professor at Fudan University. Because he had become dissatisfied with the party secretary of Fudan University, Yang Xiguang (because Yang did not value his efforts and was not fair to him), Zhang had planned to escape to Hong Kong with his wife. His wife hid gold in her hair, but they were both arrested as they were crossing the border and sentenced together. He told me that his wife's sister was married to the sculptor Zhang Chongren (1908–88), the model for Hergé's Tchang in the Tintin story *Le Lotus Bleu*. While he had been in Tilanqiao Prison in Shanghai, he was locked in the same cell as Shen Duosen. He told me that he had reported to the jailors every word critical of the government that Shen had uttered and wondered whether Shen's stiff sentence had had any relationship to his actions. As I listened to him, I thought: "Alas, you hopeless scholar." I always had a poor opinion of him and was careful what I said to him. After returning to Shanghai, Zhang Mintai, who had been freed and restored to his former position at the same time as us, invited our fellow inmates Du Cangbai, Sun Jinggong and others to a meal. When I saw Zhang Yintong, I was inwardly disgusted. I later heard that he had died of senile dementia.

After I had heard the broadcast of the court proceedings, the investigators came more frequently. They would start their interrogation at 8 p.m. precisely, exactly when the other prisoners were going to bed. They sat up on high, smoking cigarettes and drinking tea while I sat below, both thirsty and cold. They would let me go back to my cell at 2 a.m., my mind churning so that I couldn't sleep. At 6 a.m., the jailor would wake us and require us to sit upright without any movement, every day for six months (except Sundays), exactly 180 days. These days were tough, but I got through them. As in Tripitaka's adventures in *Journey to the West*, there is no fiery mountain that cannot be crossed.

Since I resisted and confessed to nothing, the investigator gave me the evidence he had collected to look over. The first thing I saw was written by my best friend, my most respected teacher, with whom I shared every thought and discussed every matter, Rev. Chen Yuntang. I saw that the title read 'Additional materials revealing the crimes of the anti-revolutionary activist Jin Luxian'. It was a very thick volume. My first thought was: "Good Lord! If the additional materials are this many, the original ought to be much more." I also wondered what I could possibly hide from them now. I read through the document once and was greatly shaken.

The next document they threw at me was Gong Pinmei's confession, which was also a very thick volume.

Li Zhen said to me: "Now that you've had a look, what do you think? What do you imagine you can hide from us now? Why not get on with it and confess everything?"

The first confession I made were those things I thought were real crimes such as illegally trading foreign exchange and assisting young people to illegally cross the borders; but the investigator showed little interest in these things. He 'enlightened' me again and again, saying that I could not avoid serious crimes by emphasising small ones: I must confess the big crimes. He could see that I was still stubbornly unchanging, so he brought out Lacretelle's confession. I recognised Lacretelle's writing, which I was familiar with. In total he had written 800 pages: how he had sabotaged land reform, sabotaged the Korean War effort, undermined efforts to recruit soldiers and cadres and obstructed the official registration of members of the Legion of Mary and so on. The most important statement was: "I secretly organised a 'clique of priests.'" He listed Chen Tianxiang, Zhu Shude, Jin Luxian—a total of seven of us as the core group of oppositionists to the movements led by the government. Good Lord! This fellow Lacretelle! How could he invent such things? In no way had we any kind of secret 'clique of priests'. Wasn't it the case that it was forbidden for Jesuits to organise any internal groups? Why had Lacretelle, just to save his skin, dumped on us even the crime of forming an anti-revolutionary clique? What evil intention did he have in mind? Could he possibly not be aware of the serious nature of this kind of accusation? Could it be that people of a different race are always disloyal?

The main objective of the government's investigation of me was to get to the bottom of the 'clique'—the more details the better. They wanted to know the main purpose of the secret organisation, its members, its leaders, its guiding principles, internal rules, how, when and where it was planned, how communications with foreign nations were maintained, how our anti-revolutionary activity was organised both in Shanghai specifically and in China as a whole, how we reported to Gong and Lacretelle, how we incited the Catholic Youth to oppose the government. I thought to myself: "What a terrible fate has befallen me!" How could I possibly confess to this groundless accusation of forming a 'clique'?

In truth there were indeed seven of us, young, active and able preachers, with charisma and able to stir the faithful. These seven would be Chen Tianxiang, Wang Rensheng, Cai Zhongxian, Zhu Shude, Zhu Hongsheng, Chen Yuntang and myself. Today, of these seven, only I am still alive. We never set up any 'clique', let alone have any 'leaders' among us. I have thought it over many times—from where did this term 'clique' come? In Chinese the word used was *aijibo* which is derived from the French word *équipe*, meaning a crew or a team, class or group. In fact I suppose that we really could be considered a class of people. Of the seven, Chen Tianxiang was Lacretelle's secretary; Wang Rensheng was parish priest of St. Peter's parish; Cai Zhongxian was parish priest at Xujiahui; Zhu Shude and Zhu Hongsheng were respectively parish priest and deputy at Christ the King parish. These three parishes were in truth the most important in Shanghai. After the schools had been expropriated, the main focus of our attention was the parishes. These few parish priests worked as hard as they could, occasionally asking Chen Yuntang and myself to help out with the preaching. We were of course happy to escape classes and assist the parishes, especially these three parishes which influenced the whole diocese. Also, when the technical college and the universities were reformed and the successful candidates at the university entrance exam were centrally allocated, some Catholic Youth were allocated places at universities in other provinces, but still maintained contact with Chen Yuntang and Chen Tianxiang and others as their spiritual advisors—thus the Catholic Youth from Shanghai spread their influence across the whole country—this is a fact.

So I confessed my crimes:

> I had sabotaged the Korean War effort, because I had privately told people that: "It was not South Korea that first attacked the North, but Kim Il Sung who launched a surprise attack on the South, driving the Southern army almost into the sea and nearly causing them to retreat across the ocean—at which point the US had intervened militarily. It wasn't the dispatch of troops to Pusan, but the Inchon landings at the enemy's rear, thus cutting off the supply lines of the Northern troops in the South, that was a brilliant strategic move by General Macarthur." This statement obviously was against the Korean War effort.
>
> Regarding American use of bacterial warfare, I had said privately: "So the US is using bacterial weapons? The newspapers report that the American imperialists have dropped large numbers of flies from airplanes onto the snowy wastes: if this was the case surely the flies would have frozen to death. How could these be called bacteria?" I also said: "This kind of Chinese government propaganda is pretty dumb, isn't it?"
>
> I sabotaged the Three Self Patriotic Movement since I often told people: "You may not join the CPA and may not distance yourself from the Pope."
>
> I sabotaged the order for registration of the Legion of Mary since I told those members who asked me: "If you register as a member of the Legion of Mary, that will be seen in itself as a confession that you are against the Three Self Patriotic Movement and from then on you will be under the suspicion of the Public Security Bureau."
>
> I sabotaged the recruitment of soldiers and cadres, since some people asked me to help them make a decision and I told them: "Young people should rather concentrate on completing their studies and perfecting their skills."
>
> I sabotaged the Anti-Imperialist Patriotic Movement because I said: "Not all missionaries are imperialists. Some of them love China and greatly love the Chinese people, such as our ancestors Matteo Ricci (1552–1610) and Johann Adam Schall von Bell (1591–1666) and, more recently, Archbishop Costantini, Father Frédéric-Vincent Lebbe (1877–1940) and others."
>
> I sabotaged the price-control efforts of the government since I feared that if the seminarians ate only the rationed amount of food, they would go hungry, so I quietly hoarded rice.

The investigator said: "You see, you were again and again the enemy of the People. You are a criminal against the People." I replied: "I am ashamed of my crimes." The investigator said: "You cannot get away with sweeping statements.

You must confess exactly with whom, where and when or else you are acting under false pretences and your attitude is not the correct one."

Even these confessions could not satisfy the investigator's needs. He wanted me to admit that I had been sent back to China from Rome by Pope Pius XII himself with specific instructions to sabotage the CCP's People's Democratic Dictatorship, to plot the overthrow of the recently established political power of the CCP. He needed me to confess that I was an international spy. He showed me the penalty for counter-revolutionaries in the legal code: "All those who have collaborated with the imperialists to betray the motherland are condemned to life in prison or the death sentence." I said that I was not a running dog of the imperialists, even less qualified to collaborate with the imperialists and that I had no connections at all with imperialism. Investigator Li said: "You are still indulging in sophistry. We have cast-iron evidence that you are a spy."

When they arrested me, the police searched my room and confiscated all my belongings, including photos of my parents and sister, my letters, my diary and claimed all this was evidence of counter-revolutionary crimes. Among the letters was one written by a Catholic in Dongtai named Zhang in which he wrote: "This year we hope to make some money growing cotton." The investigator said: "Is that not economic espionage?" Yet another letter had been written by a French priest named de Basher from Dafeng in Subei. In the letter he wrote: "Very strange, we never have had planes flying over us here; yet today planes did fly over, which is quite exceptional." The investigator said: "What is this if not military espionage? If not a spy, what are you?"

I didn't know whether to laugh or cry at his words. They were accusing me of a very serious crime that carried the death penalty. I then made a firm resolve that if I ever got out alive I would never keep any more letters. In the 29 years from my release in 1982 until today (2008), I have not kept a single private letter. I used to keep a diary and since I found I could express myself better in that language, I had written it in Latin. One day the investigator said to me, "You are really a dishonest man. You even write your diary in a foreign language. We have asked someone to spend a lot of time and effort translating it, but there is nothing of value inside."

After my release I never kept a diary again. A diary is written to be read by oneself, but one's private thoughts are better kept in one's heart. The past is like smoke; to what end should one write it down?

So they said I was a special agent of the Pope. During the two years I was in Rome, my status was that of a student, one among the tens of thousands of foreign students, without any reason to even meet the Pope. I had only once seen Pius XII from among the hundred thousand or so people crowded into St. Peter's Square. On the basis of my status at that time, I was not considered worthy even of a private audience with the superior general of the Society of Jesus. Before I returned to China, I went to the Jesuit house and it was arranged that I should sit next to him during a meal (in those days it was forbidden to talk while eating). The fact that after the meal he stopped outside the refectory and spoke to me a little was already considered a sign of great condescension. The Church is very strict on hierarchy and the lower orders garner little respect.

The investigator said: "Even before we arrested you, we had a full understanding of your case. After your arrest we have added the confessions of your friends and their denunciations make everything quite clear. You can hide nothing from us. Your confession is of little use to us. It only serves to confirm the materials we already have and to observe your general attitude. The government does not go idly to war. We had already fully understood the case from the arrest of your predecessors here Zhang Boda, Germain and Lacretelle, as well as from those people who were sufficiently politically enlightened to collaborate with the government before we made our move."

On one occasion, the investigator came to cross-examine me, calling me a dishonest man in a very severe tone. He said that I had hidden an important matter from him and had refused to confess. When he saw that I had no idea what he was talking about, he mentioned the gold buried at Sichuan South Road. I said: "I've no idea what you are talking about." He said that Gong had confessed and had even drawn a map. They had dug up over 1,000 taels of gold. When Gong Pinmei had been released after the 'Cultural Revolution', he said to me that he would ask the PSB to return the 1,000 taels of gold, because the investigator had explained that if he confessed voluntarily, the gold would definitely be returned to him. I told the PSB what Gong had said, but they replied that the money was used as evidence against Gong and the sentence made it clear that it was confiscated. Later on I asked Gong: "Why did the government not find the gold during their initial search of the premises?" He said that Germain and he had ordered their subordinate, Brother Hang, to put the gold into wine bottles, painted on the outside with pitch so that the metal detectors had not located it.

While I was in the detention centre, the government had a full understanding of my mental development. During those five years, there were four years when I shared my cell with a young man named Lin Gengkang. His father-in-law was a paediatrician who, while studying abroad, had married a German woman, so that Lin's wife was of mixed blood. Lin could speak German and Russian. He liked soccer and had often been to St. Ignatius College to watch games. He knew Rev. Wang Fang. His father had been the director of the KMT Central Trust Fund Department and knew Lu Bohong. So we had lots to talk about. We conversed most agreeably. While the occupants of the other cells were not permitted to talk to each other, our guard didn't interrupt us. There was nothing we didn't discuss. My mood was not very even. Sometimes I was depressed. Occasionally I expressed my dissatisfaction with the CCP. After doing so the investigator was always very patient with me during cross-examinations. I was bewildered and on returning to the cell asked Lin: "How come the government knows so much about me, even knowing my emotional state? Perhaps there is a listening device in our cell?"

He looked all over and said, "Surely there can't be." After my sentencing I was transferred to Tilanqiao Prison. Next to me there was a cell that contained a Russian Jew who spoke German and we chatted in German, which pleased him greatly. He said that while he had been at the detention centre there had been a young man in the same cell who had also spoken German. Later on, he had found out that this man was sent by the government to live with him and was responsible for getting to know him. After another year had passed another Russian prisoner came, who also said that his cellmate had been sent by the government to get to know him and his description resembled Lin Gengkang—I suddenly realised that the man I had considered my closest friend was a spy. Later on I thought that he must have been seeking lenient treatment to do that kind of work, which can be seen as excusable behaviour in this light.

After I had been released and returned to Shanghai, Lin Gengkang came to see me and said that he had always thought about me. He also said that he had not been treated leniently and had had to serve 15 years in jail. Only upon his release did he learn that his wife had remarried, his eldest brother had cut off all contact and would not take him in while also swallowing up what property he still had. His remarried wife had already had a son. He taught English at a Pudong middle school, where he was very well respected. In his spare time, he did home tuition, including at the home of PSB Director Weng. I also needed an English tutor at that time, so hired him to teach English at the convent. When I saw Director Weng he said that his son had made good progress as a result of Lin's tuition. Weng also said that Lin was very pitiable and asked me to take care of him. I went to visit him at his home, in the *tingzijian* of an old house in Yangshupu District. He lived squeezed into this one room with his wife and son. When the son grew up, I asked Rev. Shen Baozhi to find him a room in Pudong, where he then moved. I also hired him as a translator at Guangqi Press. Later on he resigned the job and didn't come to see me again, but I never ceased to bemoan Lin's fate.

After receiving the confession of my crimes, the investigator wrote out a list of names and told me to write down the details I knew about those that I had had contact with. I was told to write down everything I knew, especially any problems I was aware of. The PSB had taken note of all my contacts, including people I had only met once. For example Dr. Zhu Dacheng, with whom I had no relationship at all, having met him but once on the corner of Fuxing Road and Sinan Road and exchanged a few words: the PSB even knew this. I thought: "The CCP is so detailed, so serious in its work that one can only admire them." Later I realised that I was an important criminal; I was a secret agent. How could the government not follow my actions closely? Later on, I met two senior police officials, one of whom had been director of the Political Security Department of the Shanghai PSB, the other was named Gu and had originally been with the Shanghai PSB, but was later transferred to Beijing to take up the position of deputy minister of Public Security. They told me: "From the moment you put foot on the Mainland we had our eyes on you."

I had always been in their sights, but had never had any inkling of being observed. How naïve I had been! In fact, we were all naïve. The conclusion I have drawn is that all those who think they are clever and are involved in secret activities are fools.

The list of names I had to write on was very long. Many of the people I had only met once and I had to wrack my memory for things to write about them. I wrote as best I could and at the bottom of each section, I added the sentence, "This person has no problem, but for the fact that he has met with Jin Luxian." The investigator often said to me: "We know that already. There's no need to write that rubbish." But I persisted in writing it. I thought that their meeting with me would become a problem for them. I should confess that I was a harmful pest. In later life, should I regain my freedom, I should be careful to know fewer people in order to avoid implicating them. Once I had been released and returned to Shanghai, I was at first very careful and met few people, but later on, I forgot about it and got to know many people.

In relation to three people, I do have a guilty conscience. After Rev. Burckhardt had been expelled, the Swiss consulate sent a man to see me and said that Burckhardt had deposited with them 20 bars of gold (about 200 taels of gold), which, according to his instructions, should be passed to me. I knew that it was not appropriate to keep the gold with me and so I gave some to Rong Dexian for safe-keeping. Another portion I sent separately to the houses of Gu Meisheng and Yao Dezhi. I told Chen Yuntang what I had done, thinking that were I arrested Chen would succeed me; but Chen had already made his confession so I could not hide this fact. While at the detention centre I confessed. The government took note of what I had written and asked these people for the gold, which they then took away. This brought a lot of trouble to these three people. When I got out, I made a profound apology to them. They forgave me and treated me as a friend as they had done theretofore, for which I am grateful. Gu and Rong have long gone to see the Lord, while Yao now lives in Honolulu in America. She is the wife of my good friend Li Junyi. Li was also arrested in the Gong Pinmei affair, at which time he had two sons and an infant daughter. Yao had to work hard to make a living at the same time as raising her daughter. Their eldest son studied hard and devoted himself to his work, becoming Vice-Mayor of Xuzhou city in Jiangsu Province and later on Vice-President of the Jiangsu Provincial Committee of the China People's Political Consultative Conference. He was a most filial child.

In 1957, the political climate in China changed in a manner described by Professor Fei Xiaotong (1910–2005) as 'early spring'. The government prepared to release us. First Zhang Jiashu, then Chen Fumin and Zhou Shiliang (who had both already been released) came to visit me at the Nanshi Detention Centre. They talked with me for a long time, describing the state of the Shanghai diocese. Later on, an anonymous senior cadre came to see me and we had a long talk. In the detention centre the police organised a meeting with me, Sun Zengli, Zhou Jinghai (who had been arrested at the same time as I had) and seven others. We talked earnestly about what we had learnt in prison. I have forgotten the precise contents, only remembering that Sun Zengli said: "Today is the Feast of the Pentecost. Let us rather pray to the Lord and the Holy Spirit to inspire us." Recently, I saw him and reminded him of this. He said he had forgotten, but I have always kept it in my heart. He was really a good priest. When Sun said that, the disciplinary officer said to us, "You all go back to your cells right now."

The political climate changed again and the Anti-Rightist Campaign began. Usually we didn't get to see the newspapers, but one day a newspaper was slipped into the aperture of our cell door. The leading article criticised the capitalist road of the *Wenhui Bao* newspaper. I still remember the joint trial of Zhang and Luo. Luo Longji was well known to me; he had been the editor of the *Catholic Herald* newspaper, the chairman of which had been Yu Bin. In 1945 General Marshall had come to China as the special representative of the US president to convene KMT–CCP negotiations. Luo went to see Marshall and spoke to him at length in favour of the CCP and against the KMT. Later on Marshall asked Yu Bin whether Luo's words represented the general opinion, to which Yu Bin replied that Luo spoke only for himself. Yu also said: "With Chiang Kai-shek as dictator, the issue is more or less democracy; but when the CCP is victorious, the issue will be whether or not there is any democracy at all." Marshall didn't take either side, whereas Yu Bin had used three words to sum up his whole life: patriotic, religious, anti-communist.

One day in September 1957, another newspaper was slipped in. The whole issue of the *Liberation Daily* was one long essay entitled 'Ten poisonous arrows aimed at the CCP'. The article reported how some big-name right-wingers such as Zhu Kongjia, Gu Shouxi and Dong Guimin had attacked the CCP with poison. The key piece of news was that Gong Pinmei was a good person, that it was a mistake to have arrested him and that he should be immediately set free. I thought to myself, the season of early spring has already turned into mid-winter. It might be better to just wait quietly in jail. Our rations also changed. For every single meal—breakfast, lunch and dinner—the aluminium box pushed into our aperture contained just boiled sweet potato, without salt or oil, not to mention sugar. In the first few days I was happy enough, for I liked sweet potato, but after a month of it, I got heartburn and the bile rose to my mouth; it just ran out naturally from the corner of my mouth. This went on for 92 days. When they finally gave us rice again, it seemed so delicious!

This went on for a year, after which things took a turn for the better again. In prison, light treatment and strict treatment, good rations or bad, all had to do with whatever class struggle was taking place on the outside. As Mao Zedong said: "First tighten; then slacken—this is the method of both civil and military government." When the discipline was light, the prisoners could talk in the cells, get more opportunities for exercise (which meant leaving the cell and walking around in the sun in a room without a roof), more washing times and slightly better rations. We would also ask the prison guards to buy things for us.

When discipline was strict, all prisoners were forbidden to talk, had to consider their crimes in silence, couldn't buy anything, wash or take exercise. During the first half of 1959 the mood softened again, the guards were in a better mood and the days went smoothly; but in September suddenly the broadcast announced a fierce battle to raise the three red banners up high to eliminate the anti-revolutionaries and smash Peng Dehuai, Huang Kecheng, Zhang Wentian, Zhou Xiaozhou, etc. This news was repeatedly broadcast. I thought to myself: "Wasn't Peng Dehuai the Marshal of the Korean War Volunteer Forces? Wasn't Zhang Wentian the General Secretary of the CCP?" I really couldn't make it out, but the direct consequence was that our treatment got stricter, our rations smaller, so that it appeared that class warfare on the outside was heating up again.

The treatment meted out to me was also light and strict by turns. When I didn't answer questions or refused to write materials the guards put me in a large room with twenty or even thirty others. I remember that on one occasion I was moved to a really large room, containing some thirty-two people, where I was situated right next to a large latrine. At night I of course had to lie down right next to this latrine. None of the cells had flushing toilets. With thirty-two of us squeezed in together and no space to spare, not even to stretch out, the only option was to lie in a bent position; with others coming and going to relieve themselves, trampling on my body, taking the lid off the latrine to urinate or defecate, the stench of the air filling my nostrils, the sound of urination ringing in my ears, so that it was impossible to sleep. Just as I was drifting off, another man would come and use the latrine. There was no exercise and definitely no washing.

Light treatment involved placing me in relatively small and clean cells, with washing, exercise and the ability to receive gifts including food from the outside. We were even occasionally able to watch films. Watching films was arranged like this: once all the people in a large room were sitting, the film would be played. When the hall was dark, I would be led to the front row to see the film and then fetched away to my cell before the film ended, so that I could see no one else clearly. On one occasion when I had not been seated long, a policeman brought in another man who sat down to my right. I immediately saw that he was Gong Pinmei and was overjoyed to see him. I really wanted to talk to him, but at that point another policeman immediately took him away. I don't know whether Gong noticed me or might have been perplexed as to why they brought him in and then immediately took him out again. This was the only occasion between my arrest on 8 September 1955 and my release in 1982 that I saw Gong.

In total there were three occasions when I was treated harshly and placed in crowded cells. On one such occasion I had an unexpected benefit which kept me happy for several days. In the cell was a young man named Qiu, from Hong Kong, who had joined the British navy, had been trained in Britain and come to China as an undercover agent, but had got caught and incarcerated in the Nanshi Detention Centre. He said that he had already been baptised a Catholic and subsequently been patiently instructed by his cell-mate Rev. Wang Rensheng. He said that he had total faith in Jesus. I asked him how he had been christened in jail. He said that since the prisoners used enamel mugs to wash their faces every day and that washing hair required the collaboration of two people, first to drip water onto the hair to make it wet and then to lather soap and finally to rinse the hair clean, he had asked Rev. Wang to help and that while doing so Rev. Wang had recited under his breath: "I baptise you in the name of the Father, of the Son and of the Holy Spirit." Thus Qiu had been baptised. I exclaimed in approval, adding that what they had done was very dangerous: had the government found out, their sentences would have been prolonged. Qiu said that Rev. Wang was unafraid. I thought to myself: "Wang Rensheng is a good priest, even spreading the Word of God in jail." Later on I wondered about why a young man like Qiu was placed next to me by the prison guards. Could it be that the government had sent him to lead me into a trap? I got suspicious again and later I was moved away from him and know not what happened to him subsequently. As for Wang Rensheng, he died in a labour camp after completing his sentence. Wang Rensheng sought and he found; may his soul in heaven seek great grace for the Church in China.

Whether my treatment was strict or lenient had a lot to do, not just with the overall political climate, but also with the attitude of my investigator. If I fully cooperated with the detention centre and the PSB's investigation unit and anticipated the investigator's requirements, that would have been sufficient. Instead I proved to have too little self-discipline and could not control my emotions, which led to rather more misunderstandings. As the ancients said, 'the gentleman must bend and stretch', but in jail I was no great gentleman and had become a lowly prisoner: could I not from time to time lower my gaze? Once when I was uncooperative with the investigator he said to me: "What do you think you are doing? Losing your temper with me? Don't you realise that your life is in my hands? Depending on what I write you could either be freed without a criminal record or sentenced to death." I remained silent, thinking to myself: "What kind of law do the communists think this is?" Later on I reminded myself that in the period immediately after Liberation, the CCP had only promulgated two laws: the first was a new marriage law; the second concerned the regulations governing the punishment of counter-revolutionaries. Apart from these the country was ruled by means of edicts printed with red-ink headlines. Anything the leaders said was law and I was obliged to obey whether I was convinced or not.

When a prisoner was arrested, his family members would immediately send him clothes and daily-use articles. In my case I had no family and no one sent me anything, so I relied on what was provided by the state—every month 15 sheets of toilet paper made from straw and a quarter of a bar of soap. Prisoners even had to provide their own enamel mug to use both for washing and for drinking. In the beginning the soap and paper provided by the government were insufficient. The guards told me to raise the matter with the investigator, who would find a solution. The investigator said that I should write a letter and he would send people to get the things for me. I wrote a letter to the seminary and gave it to the investigator. After a few days he told me that Rev. Zhang Jiashu had announced that he was cutting me off and would provide nothing. I replied that these things were my own property so why had he not handed them over? The investigator said: "They have a highly-developed political consciousness. You'd better write to your relatives." I had two uncles and an aunt and wrote to them all and handed the letters to the investigator, but not a single word came in reply. After a while the investigator told me that they had sent people with the letters, but my uncles and aunt had refused to accept the letters, saying that they had no relationship with me. "Do you have any friends? Write to them then." I thought it over and then wrote to Rong Dexian and after a short interval the necessary articles arrived in more than adequate quantities, along with several ten renminbi notes. According to the prison regulations, prisoners with money were permitted to ask the guards to buy things for them, while the penniless prisoners could but look on in envy. The investigator permitted me to write a letter every two months. Only after I had left jail did I learn that Rong Dexian's husband, Zhu Yisheng, had also been arrested in the Walsh affair and so she had had to send out two sets of necessities. The investigator asked her why she did not cut me off completely, to which she replied: "Politically I have cut him off; but from a humanitarian point of view I have not." After I had been transferred to Qincheng Prison in Beijing, Rong mailed the things to me, right up until the 'Cultural Revolution', when her house was ransacked; she was investigated by the 'masses' and had to spend her days sweeping the alley, with her monthly income docked to 40 yuan. Because she had no means of finding out what had become of me, she thought I had probably died in jail and finally stopped sending me money and necessities.

After I had got out of jail I learned that some priests had already made appropriate arrangements to be provided with necessities before they were arrested. Among them Rev. Wu Yingfen had the best set-up, having people send him communion, which was a great consolation to him. In the end, though, his confidence betrayed him. He had written a letter adding the phrase: "What you sent last time was perfect; please do the same next time." When the guards inspected this letter, they suspected that some written materials must have been included and searched particularly thoroughly the next time. In some bread they found hidden a small communion wafer. The package had been sent by a nurse at what had been the Puci Retirement Home in Beiqiao. She was immediately arrested, taken back to the hospital for a struggle session, lost her position and became unemployed. As for Rev. Wu, he was sent to a labour camp in Anhui and died on the collective farm there.

When prisoners got financial assistance it made a big difference to their lives. After I had been sentenced I was moved to Tilanqiao No. 1 Prison. One day when I went to collect water I ran into my former student Qin Guoliang. He called out to me: "Hello, Rector!" and appeared delighted to see me. The other prisoners who saw this reported to the guards and later I learned that Qin had been put into solitary confinement for this infraction. For three months his family could send him nothing. I felt that I had really let him down. Later on he was sent to a labour camp in Qinghai. After completing his sentence he stayed on at the camp and became an underground priest. Now he has emerged and the government has recognised him as a priest. After he returned to Shanghai he never came to see me. I sent greetings to him through others, but he ignored me. Nonetheless, I always prayed for him. Prisoners like us could easily implicate others, so we had to be exceptionally careful in everything we did or said.

Many foreigners ask me how I managed to get through such a long period in jail and whether or not I was able to say mass and whether or not I was able to read the Bible. I consider their questions truly naïve. How could anybody be allowed to say mass in a communist jail? As soon as one entered the jail all one's personal belongings were taken away. We were not permitted to carry any religious symbols, not even a rosary or crucifix. In prison one can have no books, not to mention a Bible or a missal.

Nonetheless I could say my prayers and this the CCP could never take from me. I prayed almost every day, but without uttering a sound. Any sound at all would be reported by my fellow prisoners. I couldn't even move my lips, for any such movement would indicate to the detention centre police that I was praying and they would warn me not to. I said the mass every day to myself in Latin and also said the rosary to myself, fifteen cycles in the morning and fifteen in the afternoon. On occasion I prayed the fourteen Stations of the Cross. I recited the Gospels, especially that of St. John.

As I have mentioned above, when a novice I had read the main works of the Carmelite nun, Blessed Elizabeth Catez. She greatly loved the Trinity and is famous for having said: "With the Trinity in my heart, I am as if in Heaven." When I was in the novitiate I was not very happy, but this phrase of Blessed Elizabeth's was engraved on my heart and in times of trouble I silently contemplated her words, which brought me both peace and inner strength. After going to jail I lost everything and was totally cut off from the outside world. As the investigator told me, I was in a place where the public condemned me and my loved ones abandoned me; I was all alone in the world, utterly destitute, but the Trinity had not abandoned me and remained always in my heart. No power on earth could tear the Trinity from within me. On the exterior I had been very busy and my attention seemed divided among many people and many matters. Now I should collect my thoughts and concentrate my mind on the Trinity, an opportunity given to me by the Lord and I should be grateful to Him for it. "With the Trinity in my heart, I was as if in Heaven." This phrase stayed with me for the more than twenty years I was in labour reform camps and gave me sustenance. My body and my spirit didn't give in. (When I got out of jail I learned that this nun had already been beatified. She had also sent the Holy Spirit to cure the illness of my good friend Cardinal Decourtray. The cardinal was piously devoted to her. I was delighted to learn this. When I went to Lyon the cardinal personally accompanied me to visit her convent. In 2003 I visited Lyon again and have always remained in correspondence with that convent.) After leaving jail there were once again many calls on my attention and I was unable to devote as much attention and excused myself saying: "Love of God is love of man and love of man is also love of God." In conclusion, I can say that when I said mass privately to myself in prison, I was often even more absorbed in what I was doing than when I say mass publicly today. In fact I have retrogressed. "Lord, forgive me for my sins." If I had not had to write out reports for my investigator, living among prisoners would have seemed like living a hermitic life.

Let me mention in passing that after I had made my confession, my investigator made a recording for the following reasons: first, to prevent me from retracting my confession and second, to play it back to people on the outside. I agreed that they could play this recording and in it urged those on the outside not to oppose the government. I had no desire to see them share in the bitterness of prison life. Life in prison is no joke: it is nothing like martyrdom. In prison they give you no opportunity to be a martyr. The time one spends in jail is not to deal with the question of faith, but to bring one round to the government's way of thinking, to prevent one from inciting the faithful to martyrdom. Martyrdom cannot be achieved by chanting slogans and as for those who shouted out slogans the loudest, aren't they now all in the United States?

In 1960 the situation on the outside seemed to have improved a lot as my personal treatment improved by leaps and bounds. Every day I was encouraged to relax, taken to wash, fed meat and vegetables. The investigator was affable and told me that they had already released Mei Chengqi and others. He hoped that upon my release I would lead the faithful to be patriotic and love the Church. It was at this time that the KMT crazily broadcast its intention to reinvade the Mainland so the Chinese government was on red alert and at the same time considered it unwise to release people like me. A female police officer came to see me and said: "We have missed this excellent opportunity; but don't worry, we will keep trying." At the time I thought: "Everything is in the hands of the Lord. To those who love the Lord, His dispositions cannot be mistaken."

In June the government arranged for my formal court appearance, when I was declared guilty. Later on I thanked the Lord for not having released me, because six years later the historically unprecedented 'Great Cultural Revolution' began and the Red Guards swept away all the class enemies of every description and fiercely denounced and attacked all religious workers with great violence, so that people like Mei Chengqi who had been released were gravely injured. When, after twenty-seven years, I was freed and returned to the Shanghai diocese, the Most Rev. Zhang Jiashu said to me: "You have chosen the right time to return. We have returned to good times. From my appointment as bishop in 1960 I have not left my desk." I asked: "How could that be?" to which he replied: "Since I have been bishop, the government has only asked me to do two things: write reports and make self-confessions, while betraying others."

35
Public Trial and Sentencing (1960)

The time had come: the government could enjoy the fruits of victory. In June 1960 I was given a haircut, issued with formal clothes and escorted by car to the court (I had already been in detention for four years and nine months, whereas Rev. Chen Zhemin who was put on trial with me had been first detained in 1951 and thus was in detention for nine years). For the court appearance we entered the courtroom and saw that next to the judges on the dais were Tang Ludao and Lu Weidu, who served as assessor. On the witness stand were Shen Baozhi and Li Wenzhi. Behind me were many people, completely silent. The prosecutor stood up and read the indictment; a lawyer made the case for the defence on my behalf. Then we left the courtroom and returned to the detention centre.

After an interval of a few days, they once again escorted me (this time in handcuffs) by car to a large hall on the corner of Beijing West Road in the Jingan Temple District. The public trial had begun. In the hall they had placed ten or more cages in front of the judges, with one person in each cage—Gong Pinmei, myself, Li Shiyu, Zhu Shude, Chen Zhemin, Wang Rensheng, Zhu Hongsheng, Chen Yuntang, Zhang Xibin, Chen Tianxiang, Cai Zhongxian and Cai Shifang (Cai had been arrested before me. When we were arrested he was rather swiftly released and returned to the Xujiahui seminary. Later on, when the French premier Edgar Faure came to Shanghai, he had asked to have a private meeting with Cai, which the government agreed to. When Cai saw Faure he asked him to keep the contents of their discussion absolutely secret, which condition Faure accepted. Cai then opened up to him. Who could have known that when Faure had returned to France he would reveal everything, news of which filtered back to China, leading to Cai's second arrest?). After the public trial we left the hall. Gong was sentenced to life in jail. Zhu Shude, Zhang Xibin and Chen Zemin each got 20 years. I got 18 years, plus 9 years of identification as a class enemy. Zhu Hongsheng got 15 years. Chen Yuntang got 12 years. Gong and I were sent back to the detention centre. The very next day the first independently elected and ordained Bishop of Shanghai, Zhang Jiashu, was inaugurated in a big ceremony at Xujiahui Cathedral. Gong and I were escorted to Tilanqiao No. 1 Prison to serve our sentences.

On the last day before the end of my life in the detention centre I thought things over and record here my simple conclusions. During the relatively long period of my investigation, I used the opportunity to strengthen my prayer and to contemplate my mistakes, the results of which can only be seen as to my benefit. I had truly learned my lesson. The lessons I learned are many and I record them here.

First, when we pray, we tend to ask the Lord to execute our own wishes, rather than ask ourselves to carry out the Lord's sacred will. We ought to ask the Lord and the Holy Spirit to watch over us, help us understand the Lord's sacred will and correct our mistaken way of thinking and behaving. While in the detention centre a phrase from the Prophet Isaiah kept coming to my mind. The Lord said: "My way of thinking is not your way of thinking and your way of acting is not my way of acting" (Isaiah 55:8). Our way of thinking in those days or at least the subconscious way of thinking and acting was broadly as follows: wait for the US and Chiang Kai-shek to return, oppose the CCP government and fight for time. The Lord does not think in this way: His plan is much broader. The Lord wishes to purify us, to make us face difficulties, have us repent and mend our ways. The Lord used the CCP to execute His plan. The Lord desires us to turn to Him without reservation, to rely on Him and not rely on the political powers of this mortal world or the authority of wealth or rank.

Second, the Gospel of St. John records the parable of the Good Shepherd told by Jesus. We should carry it out. Jesus said: "I am the Good Shepherd who sacrifices his own life for the sake of his own flock. The hired man is not the shepherd and the sheep are not his own. When he sees the wolf coming he abandons the sheep and runs away"(John 10:11–12). The good shepherd must watch over his flock, be prepared to sacrifice his own life and certainly must not look out for only himself. The good shepherd must not hide behind his flock, letting the sheep take the vanguard. Lacretelle hid behind Gong Pinmei. We all hid behind the faithful, in particular the Catholic Youth, letting them rush out in front of us. When danger came we sought only our own escape. Is this the behaviour of a good shepherd? We should not behave like hired men and flee at the first sign of danger, flee to a place we consider to be safe, then continue to encourage the flock to court danger by opposing the communists. We ought to consider the position of the faithful and in all matters and everywhere protect our charges.

Third, under the rule of the Communist party we definitely should not engage in any secret activities or underground organisations. Nothing can be effectively hidden from the CCP. Even during the Civil War the CCP were expert at undercover activities. If we thought of engaging in such activities, the CCP was just laughing behind our backs. From now on all our activities should be transparent, open and above board if they are to be enduring. We certainly should not think ourselves smarter, to the ultimate harm of both ourselves and others.

Fourth, do not have a high opinion of oneself or underestimate others, least of all the government. Gong thought that with the faithful and foreign support, the government would not dare to take him on, but he was wrong (a mistake later on also made by Zhu Hongsheng). Despite the international reputation of Cardinal Mindszenty of Hungary, the Communist party had arrested him. The Apostle Paul once said: "As for me, never boast of my acts, just say that I desired the cross of Lord Jesus Christ" (Epistles 6:14). In all matters we depend on the cross.

Fifth, we ought not to think well of wishful thinking, thereby neglecting or even forgiving the harm that can result from subjective thought. Our words and actions, especially the words and actions of leaders, can, in a single phrase or a single indication, cause irreparable damage for which those same leaders should bear responsibility. We are always inclined to think our subjective ideas best, when they should in fact be subjected to heightened scrutiny. We are all closely bound together so when we make a decision we should first carefully consider its effects and results. Subjective and objective points of view cannot be easily separated.

Sixth, in the detention centre the investigators made no mention of religious doctrine or canon law, but rather cross-examined us about anti-communist statements and activities that had impeded government programmes; in the final analysis simply accusing us of violations of civil law and discipline and requiring that we the clergy raise our political consciousness and avoid breaking the law.

Seven, when Gong Pinmei and I were arrested, the government also arrested all those who were associated with us or went along with us, calling them the core activists of the Gong Pinmei clique. Once you had an accusation such as 'activist' hanging over you, you were obliged to bear it for the rest of your life. Furthermore, many others were implicated, so that many had to abandon their studies or lose their jobs. Families were broken up and people perished. One certainly should not base one's decisions on individual foolhardiness or on acting without premeditation. The higher one's position, the more cautious and careful one should be.

The seven points listed here I have engraved on my heart, because they were gained as the result of a bitter lesson. When I got out of jail I used these as the principles on which my subsequent actions were based. The mistakes of an individual, which led directly to the suffering of many others, should definitely not be followed by more of the same kind.

36
Jail in Shanghai (1960–62)

After the sentencing I was transferred under escort to Tilanqiao Prison. I had been confined in the detention centre for four years and nine months. I now spent two years and seven months at Tilanqiao. There was not much difference between the two places. The prisoners were all criminals, without name and known only by number and the treatment was more or less the same, except for the fact that in the detention centre each cell had a wooden door, with a small window in the upper half to enable the guards to watch us, as well as a small aperture which could be opened from the outside, where they would place our food containers as well as a large porcelain pitcher of water to use for washing, along with another to use for drinking. The cells were of various sizes, the smallest for solitary confinement and the largest with a capacity of some thirty men. There was no line of sight between different cells, to prevent any collusion. At Tilanqiao Prison, in one type of cell, there was no door and only an iron gate.

Tilanqiao is the largest jail in the Far East, with eight high-rise buildings each equivalent to a stand-alone jail. The No. 1 Building is for severe cases. Most of the criminals with sentences of eighteen years or more were political prisoners, known after the Liberation as counter-revolutionary criminals. The No. 2 Building was for light sentences, where prisoners serving relatively short sentences were held. Another jail was reserved for the imprisonment of female criminals. Yet another building was for those prisoners about to be dispatched to labour camps outside Shanghai. One building was the prison hospital where sick prisoners were held. Before the Liberation the eight prison buildings were known by the eight Confucian concepts of: manners, ideals, health, disgrace, filial piety, fraternity, loyalty and trust.

Each building was really large, with five floors, around a central courtyard with all sides lined with cells like a dove house. Outside each cell was the corridor. The cells had no windows and the so-called door was an iron gate, with prison police patrolling—they could see everything at a glance. While at Tilanqiao I sometimes had a cell to myself, sometimes shared with one other, sometimes with four others. In the cell there was no bed, no chair and no stool. At night we slept on the floor (sometimes there were wooden floorboards and sometimes just concrete). During the daylight hours we either squatted on the floor or sat down or climbed up on the iron gateway to watch the fellow prisoners in the cell opposite. When I returned to Shanghai and people asked me what I thought of the taste of iron windows, I replied that I had never tasted iron windows and only knew the taste of iron gates.

On arrival at Tilanqiao, they took my photograph and my fingerprints and gave me a new number. I was sent to level 4 in No. 1 Building. In the small cell there was already an elderly man, named Shi, who had been arrested in 1957. He had formerly been an acolyte of the gangster Du Yuesheng and that was his most notable crime. When he had first visited Du, he had handed over 500 silver dollars. Du had laughed and asked him what he wanted. He told Du that he wanted to work in the Bank of China and after a short interval he was taken on by the Bank of China where he served as manager of the Ningbo branch (in Zhejiang Province). Shi told me: "After the defeat of the Japanese, Du travelled overland from Chongqing to Shanghai and on the way picked up several adherents, each of whom contributed 500 yuan, accumulating an enormous sum of money!" Shi had a daughter who could play the *dan* role in Peking Opera and was well known to the newspapers. He was proud of this. He was keeping himself busy learning Russian and undertook to teach me. Since I had nothing else to do, I studied with him and found Russian rather easy since the language evolved from Greek and was similar to French, due to the heavy French influence during the 18th and 19th centuries of czarist Russia. In those days the aristocrats at court considered it noble to speak French and absorbed many French words into the language. Since the alphabet is different, the words appear different, but as soon as they are pronounced they prove to be French words. Since there are several thousands of these words, it was not necessary for me to commit them to memory so that after a couple of months, it was I who was teaching him Russian. I wrote a letter to Rong Dexian and she sent me a Russian edition of *And Quiet Flows the Don* by Mikhail Sholokhov as well as novels by Tolstoy. I could read them all and thus passed my time. During the Cultural Revolution, we were not permitted to read in foreign languages so I stopped using Russian and forgot it all. For me foreign languages go as easily as they come.

The head of No. 1 Building was named Shao; he also had a deputy named Qi. Both were from Hebei. Two others named Zhou and Lu were policemen, known popularly as overseers. I was managed by Qi who was very harsh whereas the policemen had a better attitude and had a better command of the rules.

Gong Pinmei was placed in the lower floors. I was told by a prison labourer (a prisoner who ran errands and would move around as he worked) that Gong had two cells to himself, one for his bedroom and one as his dayroom, where he had a table and chair. He was served special food, with meat and vegetables every time.

The guards saw that Shi and I were getting on too well and so transferred me into another group to work on my political studies. I remember that the study group included: Du Cangbai (a Trotskyite leader); Ni Tuosheng (aka Watchman Ni 1903-72, head of the Protestant counter-revolutionary group); a man named Chen (nephew of Chen Bijun, who had been secretary of the KMT Government's Executive Yuan and governor of Guangdong Province under Wang Jingwei); Zhang Ke (deputy minister of Propaganda under Wang Jingwei) and Tan Bolu (whose father had been connected by marriage to Wang Jingwei, while his mother had been the sister of Chen Bijun). There was also a Cereals Ministry head from the Wang Jingwei puppet regime era, who had been locked up by the Japanese for expressing some opposition to their policy of confiscating rice. He was the most senior of all of us prisoners (his father-in-law had been the Qing dynasty *zhuang yuan* (imperial top scholar) Zhang Jian (1853-1926)). Each one of them had great experience, could speak of secret societies and had had their moment in history, but now they were all reduced to the level of criminals.

The one who made the deepest impression on me was Zhang Ke. He had been a Protestant. His grandmother had been the nanny at the home of the Protestant pastor John Leighton Stuart (1876-1962). When Stuart was transferred to Beijing to be president of Yanjing University, because Zhang's mother had asked, Stuart had taken Zhang Ke along with him so that he could work his way through the university. Later on he had joined the CCP and met Song Qingling and become one of her secretaries. On the eve of the KMT's Northern Expedition, he went to Guangzhou with Song. When the KMT army reached Wuhan, he followed her to Wuhan. In Nanchang, Chiang Kai-shek had started to purge the communists and wanted to put the Soviet advisors like Borodin under house arrest. Song Qingling and Borodin found out what was going on and secretly left Wuhan, travelling not by train but by car, via Henan to the north. They had to cross over the area controlled by General Feng Yuxiang, for the price of which passage Feng demanded 20,000 roubles from Borodin. Borodin said that he would pass the request onto Stalin and then left without saying goodbye, taking off as fast as he could, continuing through Hebei, Shanxi and Mongolia all the way to Russia. Song left Russia for Europe. Zhang Ke asked Song to plead for mercy to Chiang Kai-shek and ask for an official position. Song was immediately crestfallen and told Zhang to go away and that she never wanted to see him again. He then apologised to Song and even went to Germany with her.

After leaving Song, he found his way to the US. After returning to China he sought refuge with the KMT and worked as secretary to then KMT foreign minister Chen Youren (aka Eugene Chen). Chen was a Jamaican who spoke no Chinese and had to use him as a translator at every meeting and thus Zhang Ke got to know many important people in the KMT including Wang Jingwei. He followed Chen into opposition against Chiang Kai-shek and went to Fujian. After the Fujian government collapsed, he went to Hong Kong. During the Anti-Japanese War Song Qingling moved to Hong Kong so he went to see her again and worked with her, at the same time taking money from the KMT Bureau of Investigation and Statistics (the KMT's secret service) to provide them with intelligence about Song. During the Pacific War, Chiang Kai-shek sent an airplane to fetch Song to Chongqing, but Chen Youren and Zhang Ke could not board the plane and stayed in Hong Kong. The Japanese sent the two of them to Shanghai, wanting Chen to help Wang Jingwei, but Chen resolutely refused to do so. Zhang Ke however sought refuge with Wang Jingwei and became the deputy propaganda minister of the puppet regime. As the war drew to a close, he saw that the Japanese game was up and so made contact with the New Fourth Army in Subei and sent them intelligence.

After the Japanese surrendered, Chiang Kai-shek started arresting the traitors. Zhang Ke was shut up in prison, while Zhu Minyu, Lin Bosheng and others were shot. Zhang's wife went to see John Leighton Stuart (who was at that time the US ambassador to China) and begged him to help. Stuart asked Zheng Jiemin (who had succeeded Dai Li as head of the KMT Investigation and Statistics Bureau) to dine with him and asked Zheng to handle Zhang Ke leniently. Zheng influenced the court, saying that Zhang had rendered some meritorious service during the war. He was sentenced to three years in jail with early release a year later. After Liberation the People's Government learned about his relationship with Stuart who continued to send him US dollars after he left China. So they sent him to America to report on Stuart's activities. He took the US dollars and enjoyed himself in Hong Kong. After spending all the money, he returned to Shanghai and the government arranged for him to teach at the University of Politics and Law, but he considered that, in light of his services to the New Fourth Army, this standard of living was too low. He kept on complaining until they finally arrested him and sentenced him to jail.

As for Du Cangbai, he had joined the CCP as a youth and the party had sent him to study in Russia. On his return, he had been involved in labour union work. When in Russia, he had been involved with the Trotskyites and had been purged from the party. He carried on the struggle on his own rushing around from Li Zongren to Bai Chongxi (of the Guilin Clique), Feng Yuxiang (of the North-West Army) and Li Qishen (of the Fujian People's Government), collecting money from the warlords one by one, with the intention of bringing down Chiang; but the movement got nowhere. After Liberation he was arrested as a Trotskyite and sentenced to life in jail. He knew Chen Boda[1] well and had kept in touch with him. While in jail, he never betrayed Chen, for fear of bringing Chen's revenge upon himself. Once Chen had fallen, he betrayed him and won merit for this, for which his sentence was changed and he was released early to return to Shanghai, where he was very well looked after.

I stayed two and a half years at the Tilanqiao Prison in Shanghai. During one period we had to stand to attention for half an hour to one hour every day and listen to Prison Director Qi lecture us. Sometimes he boasted with big words; at other times he viciously criticised the prisoners. Seeing him so full of himself, no one dared utter a sound. I myself used the time to recite the Bible. I don't know what my fellow prisoners thought. Thus the days passed one after another. At another time I joined a Peking Opera group, among whom there was a prisoner named Wu who never stopped saying: "After each day passes, another day comes; in my heart I'd rather be fried in boiling oil." This phrase comes from the opera *Wenzhao Pass* which describes a scene in the Warring States period when Wu Zixu and his army are blocked at Wenzhao Pass. This phrase neatly expressed the feelings of frustration felt by many of us.

---

1. Chen Boda (1904–89), sometime secretary to Mao Zedong and Chair of the Cultural Revolution Group.

37
Foreign Language Translator, Qincheng Prison (1963–67)

In early 1963 I was transferred to Qincheng Prison in Beijing. It happened like this: early one day, the prison officer opened up my cell and said to me: "Bring all your belongings and come with me." All I had was my bedding, some old clothes and the few books that Rong Dexian had sent me. I entered the room to find six people already sitting on the floor. The security guard named Wu and three young policemen in military uniforms led us to a van, in which were already placed several large wooden cases, apparently containing all our files. The van drove through two large iron gates and left the prison in the direction of the railway station, where we boarded a train, entering a carriage and being made to sit on a few benches near the lavatory.

The four men chatted and laughed, while we seven just glanced at each other, silent as insects in winter, not daring to utter a sound. When we went to the lavatory, a security officer went with us and we were not permitted to close the door so that he could keep an eye on us. On the way we heard that they were going to have fun at Jinan in Shandong Province, which proved to be true, as on arrival at Jinan station we were taken off the train and taken to Jinan Prison. Three days later, Officer Wu and the others came to fetch us and escorted us onto another train to continue the journey to Beijing.

On arrival in the capital we left the train and boarded a van, which drove out of the city limits in the direction of Changping, which lies to the north of the city. We then continued north for a couple of hours until the vehicle suddenly stopped, having arrived at our destination. Later on I learned that this was the most important jail in China, used for the imprisonment of important criminals and suspects, such as the top 'capitalist roaders' during the Cultural Revolution and later on the Lin Biao group, the Gang of Four and so on. After waiting for an instant, the great doors opened and the van rolled in about 100 metres before passing through another large gate. In the courtyard were two large buildings to the right and left, each one surrounded by its own security wall. The van had stopped at the gate of the western-most of the two buildings. We were told to get out of the van and enter the building where a security officer awaited us. We later learned that he was named Ma, was about 30 years old and was responsible for the translation group.

Of the seven of us, there were two I already knew, who had previously been in same study group as I. They were the previously described Du Cangbai and Zhang Ke. The four others I later learned were named Gao, from Suzhou, who had been a spy for the KMT and Zhang Yintong, who had been a history professor at Fudan University as mentioned above. Yet another was Fang Huanru, who had joined the CCP as a youth and had been sent to Russia to study. After his graduation he was sent to organise the CCP in north-east China. On arrival in the north-east, he voluntarily surrendered to the KMT, handing over all his information. The KMT appointed him as the confidential secretary of the Central Club Clique (CC) Shanghai representative Wu Xingya, in which position he exercised some power. He later told me: "Zhang Xueliang used to send me 500 yuan every year, which sum he asked me to kindly accept." After the Marco Polo Bridge Incident, Shanghai was occupied by the enemy and the CC heads ordered Fang to remain in Shanghai to do intelligence work. After Wang Jingwei went over to the Japanese, Fang joined the Wang clique, being appointed commissioner of the Hangzhou/Jiaxing/Huzhou area of Zhejiang Province.

After the defeat of the Japanese, when Chiang Kai-shek started arresting all traitors, Fang was in a constant state of anxiety, so took all the rotten gains he had made from squeezing the People, put them into two leather cases and stored them with his best friend. When arrested, he got a light sentence and went to see his friend as soon as he got out of jail, hoping to reclaim his gold, silver and jewellery; but his friend said to him: "It has all been taken by the military dictatorship." He understood that his friend had himself taken it, but could only keep silent about it. After Liberation, he was arrested again and sentenced to 20 years in jail. He was good at Chinese, Russian and English, was widely educated and worked devotedly for the translation team. In group study sessions, he said little, betrayed no one and was always a model of polite behaviour. He had two daughters who were allocated teaching positions at the Beijing Iron and Steel Academy and who had completely cut him off. When he got sick and died the prison authorities informed them, but they didn't even come to collect his body.

Yet another in the group was a youth of some thirty years of age named Zhang Mintai, who had been a lecturer at the East China Electric Power Technical College in Yangshupu District, Shanghai. One day, on returning to his dormitory he had seen a girl crying. He asked her why she was crying so bitterly in the middle of the night and did not go home. She answered that her stepmother had beaten her. Zhang wanted to take her home, but she adamantly refused. Zhang took her back to the dorm and sent her to school the next day, giving her his name and address. On the third day, the police came to arrest him, saying that he was a rapist of under-aged women. It was the girl's stepmother who had reported him. He denied the charge and asked a doctor to investigate and it turned out that the girl's hymen had not been broken, but he was still sentenced to twenty years for acting indecently to an immature woman. He had been engaged to be married, but his fiancée was enraged and terminated the engagement.

At every single meeting Zhang talked about his situation and asked for an appeal; every appeal was overruled. He also said that he loved the CCP and would strive to join the party. He was a responsible worker and put in a lot of effort. He first learned German from me and made rapid progress. He then learned French from me as well and before long he could translate French. After the fall of the Gang of Four he was pronounced not guilty and set free. He went back to work at the Electric Power Academy. After I returned to Shanghai in 1982, he came to see me and invited me to a meal. He told me he had joined the party and been promoted to head of his department, had married a lecturer named Guan and was living a contented life. Later on he died of cancer.

Officer Ma arranged for us to live on the upper floors, four to a cell. Each cell had beds and a flushing toilet, while on the floor below was the workroom with tables, chairs, etc. We could stroll around in the courtyard as we wished. We were in the same courtyard as the KMT war criminals, but usually had no opportunity to converse with them.

The various members of the translation team were either selected from among the war criminals or brought in from prisons all over the country. From Tianjin there was Diao Peishu, a Protestant who had been sent to study in England by his pastor. On return to China he had taught English in schools. From the north-east came Wang Tiemei, who spoke Japanese. During the Japanese occupation of north-east China he had served at one time as a translator for the Japanese armed forces. From Wuhan came Xiong Shounong, a Japanese speaker, and Zhang Zhitian who said that he had been a student in

America, until we learned that he had in fact been sent to the US by the KMT to learn how to fly aeroplanes. After the defeat of Japan he had ended his training and returned to China. Facts demonstrated that he was not able to translate and could only serve as a copyist. From Guangzhou came a man named Lin, who claimed to be good at English, but his translations were useless, so he too could only do copy work. We were in total 24 men, separated into Japanese, Russian, English and French teams. I was allocated to the French team.

There were a few men who had been locked up in Qincheng as war criminals, among whom was the Russian translator Sun Jinggong. He had been a member of the CCP and a senior general under the leadership of Wang Ming, involved mainly in youth activism and taking the *nom de guerre* Qing Gong. On his arrest by the KMT, he had betrayed the party and become trusted by Chiang Kai-shek, who made him a section head of the Ministry of Finance. Yet another was named Zhu (I have forgotten his given name) who was from the same town as Wang Ming. He had become a politburo member of the CCP, but when he was arrested he had sold out all the CCPs secrets even before leaving the car he was picked up in.

The German language team also had a pair of war criminals, one named Liu, who had been a KMT police chief, first in Lanzhou in Gansu Province and then in Xiamen—he spoke excellent German. When the whole country had been liberated he had not known where to go and had feared for his life, so he went to see a fortune teller who, after checking his eight trigrams, had congratulated him, saying: "Your fate is excellent. In the second half of your life you need fear neither wind nor rain; you will lack neither food nor clothing." Who could have guessed that he would be arrested two months later? When you come to think about it, in the jail for war criminals he was indeed not exposed to the elements, nor did he need to worry about where his food or clothing came from. Yet another was named Wu. He had served as a translator in the KMT's army college. When I checked his translations, I found that his level was pretty low and asked him: "On the basis of this level how were you able to work as a translator?" He replied: "The German instructors on the dais spoke no Chinese and the KMT officers below spoke no German, so it wasn't hard for me to interpret for them."

This group of men spent 24 hours of every day together (even in a family, most people go to school and to work during the day and only spend the evening together). That we spent 12 years together is really quite an achievement.

The People's Government declared that among KMT civil officials, department heads and, in the military, major generals and above were all classified as war criminals and needed re-education in Beijing, Fushun, Yucheng in Shandong and Chongqing in Sichuan, with the most senior war criminals being held in Beijing. In principle we were supposed to refer to each other by our numbers, but because we studied together, worked together and did self-criticism together, we could not fail to get to know a bit about each other. Among the war criminals were many lieutenants-general and majors-general. There were also the heads of various departments in the KMT Bureau of Investigation and Statistics run by Dai Li. Thus, about half of the KMT ruling class was represented. One could only feel sorry for the pre-Liberation society.

Among the war criminals, some had money and others had none. The circumstances were thus: after the battles of Liaoshen, Pingjin and Huaihai, a large number of KMT officers and civil officials fled before the victorious communists, many dressed and made up as peasants, workers and merchants, with gold, dollars and gemstones stuffed into their belts. When they were arrested, having failed to escape, they were gathered in large open spaces so that the Liberation Army could take stock of them and register them one by one. Some of the war criminals thought that to be found carrying large amounts of money would be evidence of their crimes and so, while they were sitting on the ground listening to instructions, many of them secretly deposited the gold and dollars in their belts on the ground, while only a minority held on to their money and didn't toss it out. When they were body-searched by the Liberation Army the money was taken and registered; it was not confiscated, but rather held on behalf of the prisoners. During their time in jail those war criminals could ask the guards to buy them things and use these deposits as payment. Meanwhile those who had dropped their money had plenty of time to regret what they had done.

Among the war criminals were officers and also spies who, as soon as you met them, appeared to be branded. The spies of the KMT Bureau of Investigation and Statistics were spies on the outside and while in prison thought that they were still spies. When we were taking a break or strolling in the courtyard, it only took two of us to walk together for one of these spies to sidle over and listen in. Once they had caught a word or two of what we were saying, they would report it at once to the guards. The most conspicuous of them was a fellow named Yuan Xiaoxuan, who had originally been a communist, even rising to be deputy head of the Xi'an office of the Eighth Route Army before he fled to the KMT. On one occasion Director Sun Shouyi was giving us all a lecture when he pointed to Yuan and said: "Yuan Xiaoxuan, you are here to reform yourself and yet you still spy on others. Every day you tell me stories about such and such people and matters, but when I check them out I find that your reports are all wrong. Work harder at reforming yourself, I suggest." But Yuan couldn't help making a report every day—truly he was a hard nut to crack. Among the translation team the spies who couldn't change their nature were Gao (see above) and Zhang Zhitian (of whom more below).

Most of the military officers who were locked up were straightforward characters and very few of them told tales on others. For example Lieutenant-General Huang Wei (1904–89) refused to plead guilty, made no false self-criticisms and did not admit defeat, saying that his whole army had been annihilated and that he had not failed to fight hard, but that there had been CCP sleepers in the KMT headquarters command who had secretly sent the battle plan to the CCP and that it was due to this that the CCP had won victory. On one occasion the guards arranged for us to have a tour of Beijing. When we reached Tsinghua University where Huang's daughter was working as an assistant professor, the disciplinary officers called her to see her father and he asked her in front of all the prison staff: "There are rumours that the KMT will soon return to the Mainland; what will you do?" She replied: "I am in the militia. I will fight them off."

Most of the war criminals had blood debts, such as Xu, who had been responsible for the torture and execution of the Communist martyr Sister Jiang (Jiang Zhujun 1920–49); Zhou who had assassinated Yang Hucheng (1893–1949) and his family; and Yue who had headed up the Operations Department of the Bureau of Investigation and Statistics (his subordinates were all involved in assassinations).

There was also Xu who had been very senior in the CCP. He had been sent to Xinjiang to work, but after his arrest by the KMT had betrayed everything, including the exact location of Mao Zedong's cave-dwelling at Yan'an so that KMT planes could bomb it. After WWII, when Zhou Enlai represented the CCP in talks with the KMT, Zhou had asked the KMT to release Xu. Also there was the man who had been an apprentice from Jiangyin. The Central Committee had reckoned that he had a good class background, was honest and reliable and asked him to be a communications officer. Although he was quite junior, he nonetheless knew where the leaders lived, so when he went over to the KMT he was able to tell them where to arrest people, leading to a rather big setback for the CCP. Later on he became the head of the KMT Secretariat in Jiangxi Province, at which time the CCP decided to assassinate him to avenge the revolutionary martyrs he was responsible for. On the eve of Liberation he had fled to Hong Kong, but had failed in speculation and been unable to survive there, so asked his friends to intercede on his behalf with the CCP and arrange for him to return home, while also asking for a guarantee of safety. He was arrested on his return to Guangzhou and sent to Beijing, but they did not execute him. In 1975 when all the war criminals were released, he was also let go. On one occasion the doorkeeper at Xujiahui told me that someone had come to see me but would not give his name, only the number 1073. I said to let him in and recognised Xu immediately.

These war criminals and traitors were all released following an order from the central government in 1975. Furthermore, they were all given official positions (Huang Wei became a member of the National Committee of the Chinese People's Political Consultative Conference, while others joined local committees). The Politburo arranged for all those who wished to go abroad to travel for free. Various relatives of Chiang Ching-kuo (1910–88) such as Cai Shengsan who wanted to go to Taiwan were given the cost of their travel, first to Hong Kong and then on to Taiwan. On arrival in Hong Kong they sent letters to Chiang Ching-kuo expressing their enduring loyalty to the KMT, but Chiang rejected them out of hand, so they returned to the Mainland and the government still arranged for them to sit on local committees of the CPPCC. Cai Shengsan preferred to stay in Hong Kong where he could work freely as a columnist, which he did with great success. Later on he returned to the Mainland and the leaders came out to meet him. He told people that he wanted to see me, but at that time I was abroad and so missed him. This is a good moment to let you know that my nickname among my fellow-prisoners was 'Foreign Monk'.

The translation team was located at Qincheng Jail and Qincheng was directly administered by the 13th Bureau of the Ministry of Public Security. It was used to incarcerate all nationally important criminals as well as suspects awaiting sentencing. Above, I have already described that there were four buildings (later on two more were built). Apart from our building, all the others were solitary cells, which we learned about on the rare occasions we were required to do janitorial work. Each cell had a flushing toilet, but the flush-lever was outside the cell and the each time the toilet was used the prisoners had to ask the guard to flush it for them.

We also saw that some of the cells were lined with rubber, both the walls and the doors to prevent prisoners from committing suicide. However much the prisoner might yell and scream no one outside could hear a thing. One time, when we went to clean out a storeroom, we found a suitcase bearing the names of Pan Hannian (1906–77) and of his wife Dong Hui and another with the name of the writer Ding Ling, from which we learned that they had once been locked up at Qincheng. On one occasion we were called out of jail to clean out some single-storey buildings where we learned that, before Qincheng had been built, Rao Shushi (1903–75) had once been detained.

After the 'Cultural Revolution' had started all the war criminals and the translation team were transferred to the Fushun War Criminals Management Centre (leaving behind a small number of the most prominent ones), while Qincheng was devoted to the imprisonment of the Liu Shaoqi and Deng Xiaoping subordinates known as 'capitalist roaders'. In the 1980s the Catholic Church convened a meeting, paid for by the government, and I was allocated a seat at the top table along with Wu Xuelian, Xi Zhongjuan and Yan Mengfu, among others. It was only then that I learned that they too had been locked up at Qincheng. On one occasion Minister of State Security Ling Yun told me that he had been responsible for the construction of the No.1 Building at Qincheng, not then knowing that he would soon be locked up there himself. Once I saw an essay in the newspaper entitled *In Memory of My Good Father* that had been written very movingly. It had been written by the daughter of the 1950s police chief of Shanghai, Xu Jianguo. The essay mentioned that Xu had died at Qincheng. After Lin Biao had died in the plane crash at Öndörkhaan in Mongolia, his generals Huang Yongsheng, Li Zuopeng and others were all incarcerated at Qincheng. After the downfall of the 'Gang of Four' Jiang Qing, Wang Hongwen, Zhang Chunqiao and Yao Wenyuan were all locked up here. But this all happened much later on.

Every day we did translations for eight hours, after which we were free to do whatever we wanted. I studied Japanese with Wang Tiemei, while Shan Jiaxiang and Zhang Mintai studied French and German respectively with me. Shan Jiaxiang was from Henan Province and had been sent to work in north-east China, but during the 1957 'Hundred Flowers Movement' he had volunteered a few suggestions and been marked down as a rightist. His wife and he divorced, but then, as he was always complaining about his treatment, he was promoted from rightist to active counter-revolutionary and sentenced to reform through labour. I liked to walk alone in the courtyard, doing my spiritual exercises, reflecting silently, reciting the mass and saying my rosary. Thus the days passed rather quickly.

Early in 1965 Director Sun and Officer Ma had a talk with us, in a rather politer tone than usual, telling us a lot of things to encourage us, reassuring us that our translations were of high quality and that our attitude to the reform of our political consciousness was excellent. They also told us that we had a bright future and should not be depressed and so on.

Once, the war criminals and the translation team were gathered in the assembly hall where Director Sun and other leaders were accompanying an old man who entered wearing a dark blue Mao suit. He was introduced to us as Pu Yi, the last emperor of the Qing dynasty and the puppet ruler of Japanese-occupied Manchuria. After the victory over the Japanese he had been captured by the Red Army and imprisoned in the Soviet Union. Later on he was freed and sent back to China where he and members of his small entourage were locked up in the Fushun War Criminals Management Centre. Later on he was given a special pardon. He had come to tell us about how he had been reformed and encouraged us to work hard at reforming ourselves to try to achieve awareness of the value of reform through labour. I remember him saying that he had been imbued with thoughts of how "everything under heaven belongs to the sovereign; all troops are at the disposal of the sovereign." This concept was deeply imbedded in his psyche and led him to dream of becoming emperor again.

Next, the Penitentiary Administration of the Ministry of Public Security arranged for the war criminals to tour the sites of socialist construction in Beijing and we translators got to go along with them. We visited the History Museum, the Army Museum, the Cultural Palace of Minorities, Beijing Railway Station, the Heavy Industry Factory, Tsinghua University, the Great Hall of the People and so on. Everywhere we went we were received by the leaders of that work unit who gave us a detailed introduction, warm hospitality and in sum treated us as if we were honoured guests.

While we were visiting the Great Hall of the People we all felt overwhelmed by the magnificence and grandeur of its conception and acclaimed it as the height of perfection. I could not at that moment imagine that I would later be invited to sit at the top table at banquets there. After touring for ten days, Officer Ma organised a discussion of our impressions and suggested that we might want to write a thank-you letter. The English translator Zhang Xiaohu (who had graduated from the Journalism Department at Fudan University) wrote a draft which we discussed. He, however, refused to alter a single word in the most arrogant manner. One of the war criminals quietly commented that the tails of the intellectuals appeared to be standing upright again.

On 1 May (Labour Day) and National Day the war criminals and translators were driven to the Public Security Ministry (next to Tiananmen Square) where we were escorted to the roof of the building to watch the display. At this point the war criminals finally got the message that perhaps before too long they might be pardoned.

Who could have predicted that the political climate would suddenly change again as Mao Zedong personally launched the historically unprecedented 'Great Proletarian Cultural Revolution'? The newspapers reported that the capitalist roaders would be brought down, in particular the close confidant of Mao, the illustrious Liu Shaoqi. The very first 'Big Character Posters' were stuck up. Mao declared that he resolutely supported the revolutionary activities of the Red Guards, even saying: "He who fears not being cut to pieces dares to unseat the emperor." The translation team ceased translating. The guards took us to collect cans of paint and go everywhere in the compound writing the slogan: "Persist in protecting the Great Leader, Great Teacher, Great Helmsman, Great General." After a short period we were gathered on the dormitory floor of the prison block and forbidden from coming downstairs and totally forbidden to leave the compound. We were ordered to seal up all the bookcases, leaving only one copy of Mao Zedong's quotations. We held no meetings, the guards did not come and we just studied the 'Little Red Book'. On the wall there was still a map that had not been taken down, so I spent the whole day looking at the map, memorising the place names.

In mid-November, after dinner, when it was already dark, guards suddenly arrived and instructed us to immediately gather our possessions. We were to be transferred at once. After coming downstairs we saw that the war criminals were already gathered by the doorway, while outside were parked several large vans. The guards told us to load our baggage onto one van, while we all got into the other one. The vans drove out of the main gate, but we didn't know where we were going. An hour later the vans stopped at a small railway station. The station was full of soldiers armed with loaded rifles. A train was already in the station, but there was not a single passenger to be seen. We boarded the train in single file. In the carriage the windows had already been sealed with wooden boards. It was very dim inside the carriage. Once we were seated the carriage doors were shut and guards posted at the front and the rear. We just sat as still as we could, not uttering a sound, silent as insects in winter. The train started, picked up speed, didn't stop at any station along the way—it was a special train. The next morning, the train slowly decreased speed and then suddenly stopped. We got off to see that it was yet another small station, the platform covered with armed soldiers. Once again we boarded vans and after half an hour entered a compound full of single-storey buildings and stopped in front of a large assembly hall. We lined up in order to listen to the instructions of the prison authorities. Only then did we learn that this was the Fushun War Criminals Management Centre. Next we were informed of the rules, that the translation team and the war criminals were forbidden to converse with each other and we were forbidden to speak a word of any foreign language. Anyone caught using a foreign language would be severely punished.

38
The Fushun War Criminals Management Centre (1967–73)

I spent nearly six years at the Fushun War Criminals Management Centre, from the autumn of 1967 to the autumn of 1973.

I'll give you a simple description of the management centre. It had been built during the Japanese occupation of the north-east of our country, specifically for the imprisonment of Japanese military offenders. On the eve of the Japanese surrender, the Soviet Red Army had invaded the north-east and the camp had fallen into their hands. After the Liberation of the north-east the People's Government had taken it over and used it for the incarceration of Pu Yi and his court. The reformed Japanese war criminals were sent back to Japan and then the government transferred a number of Chinese war criminals to Fushun (the top KMT war criminals were separated into ranks, with the senior ranks sent to Beijing and the lower ranks to Chongqing, Yucheng in Shandong and Fushun).

The Fushun War Criminals Management Centre was located next to the provincial jail. It consisted entirely of single-storey buildings, set out thus: the dormitories were all large rooms; two rows of open beds each sleeping five people, with a very large space between each one. In the study room each person had a desk and a chair. There was a barbershop, decorated like a salon on the outside with mirrors on the walls and special chairs which were very comfortable. There was a large bathhouse, surrounded by shower equipment. We washed once a week, one group at a time. After undressing we could soak in the first bath, then climb out, lather ourselves with soap, rinse off with the showers and then jump into a second bath full of clean water. Each group could stay in the bathhouse for an hour. After washing our bodies we could go to the washroom to wash our clothes in hot water. The dining hall was huge and could seat all the prisoners at once, with four to a table. There was a clinic, with doctors and nurses. I remember a doctor called Zhang and one of the nurses named Liu. The latter could do acupuncture and had a good attitude. Her husband was a guard named Xu Zhe, who also maintained a very high standard. One time I went to the clinic with high blood pressure, about 180 high and 110 low, and saw another doctor who was a friend of Dr. Zhang's. I told him that I had piles and that it was occasionally painful to defecate. He said that he knew how to cure me. He could poke up and break a tendon in my back and that would solve it. He asked me if I would be willing to give it a try and I said yes. So he pushed up and my piles were astonishingly cured and have never given me a problem since that day.

There was an assembly hall that was decorated like a cinema. It was used for assemblies and for watching films. On the dais were hung several characters for 'loyalty' which one could not fail to notice.

There was a large playing field, surrounded by fruit trees. In sum, the facilities were very good.

The original director was named Jin and was of Korean ethnicity. Early on in the 'Cultural Revolution' he was named a 'capitalist roader' by the revolutionaries at the centre and sent off to do hard labour. The head of the revolutionary faction was named Li. He had a glib tongue. After him came the military supervisors; the revolutionaries were dismissed and the new head was a company commander. The guards were all promoted to supervisors, but had not the training for it. During the lectures they would say things like: "You have heavy blood debts to pay. I'll make a report to the leaders and shoot a few of you!" According to the original instructions of the central government, war criminals could not be body searched, could not be struck or abused, but these men even searched through our luggage and so on. Not long after, the company commander asked the original director Jin to return. Later on Jin was transferred to Beijing to become principal of the Public Security University.

As soon as we had arrived at Fushun, the acting director gave us a stern lecture. We were allocated our beds and separated into three groups. Morning and afternoon we studied how to make self-confessions and betray others in order to atone for our crimes and obtain clemency for ourselves. Some people betrayed others and one was not permitted to defend oneself or explain one's actions. My fellow prisoners often stressed that I was a running dog of the imperialists, a slave of the Vatican, could never reform myself and so on. The man who criticised me the most freely was Zhang Zhitian, who usually was the first to make a report to the guards. While we were in Beijing, his translations had all been rubbish and useless. I don't know why, but while at Fushun he was put in shackles and handcuffs and treated as a model reactionary.

By the middle of the 'Cultural Revolution' they had ceased to lecture us on how wonderful the situation was and let us work on a farm. In the beginning we walked there, accompanied by Liberation Army soldiers with loaded rifles and fixed bayonets. The local people along the road would say: "They are being taken off to be shot." Many of the war prisoners were generals who had surrendered in 1948 or 1949 and were now over 60 years old and so found the work hard going and for this reason our group was not very orderly. Later on they transported us by truck. On the farm we carried water, spread manure, planted seeds, did weeding, dug the soil, gathered in the harvest, etc. I carried water for the first time in my life. We carried two pails of water hanging from a shoulder pole which rubbed my shoulders bare. I found this exceptionally painful, so I was reduced to carrying the pails of water by hand, swinging back and forth in such a way that the water spilled out and there was only half left by the time I had reached the objective. After two months my shoulders hardened and I got used to carrying the shoulder pole.

Spreading the manure was like this: in the depths of winter when the temperature was minus 20 degrees Celsius we had to open up the outdoor septic tank, collect the run-off and pour it on the fields, then dig out the bottom layer of the septic tank and spread that on the fields as well. Of us all the most enthusiastic worker was Zhang Mintai. He would leap into the middle of the septic tank and dig away until the muck froze solid. Then we carried the muck piece by piece to the waiting truck and transported it to the farm, before spreading it out on the fields and leaving it to melt and fertilise the ground. Muck stinks and, after picking it up with one's hands, even washing them several times with soap cannot remove the pungent smell.

In the beginning weeding was tough for me. I was already nearly 50 years old and couldn't tell the sprouts and the weeds apart. I was terribly afraid that I would pick the sprouts and leave the weeds. When we worked my progress lagged behind the others, so that the soldiers berated me saying: "You stinking old nine [intellectual], you parasite, you can't tell sprouts from weeds." They also called me an imitation foreign worker who looked for excuses to slack off. Prisoners were not permitted to complain and could only hang their heads and admit their crimes. Among the prisoners was a supervisor of the labour team named Sun Huancai, who had been a KMT divisional commander. When he allocated work, he specifically gave me light work, for which I was most grateful. When he was pardoned, he went to live in Beijing in the same building as Shang Chuandao (former head of the KMT Civil Administration Bureau and joint finance chief in Jilin Province). When I was released, I went to his home to thank him for his kindness and he insisted that I join him for a meal.

In early spring it was time for sowing. I was selected along with others to carry muck into the hills. I slowly got to the point where I could carry 100 pounds up the hill. When the time came for the trucks to collect the grain, our job was to carry it from the trucks to the kitchen. In the beginning I could only carry one sack of flour; later on I could manage two and by the end I could carry three sacks as well as one of rice, together weighing some 180 pounds (I could only manage this on the flat ground; I never learned to manage hills: when I tried the sweat would pour from my brow and my legs couldn't manage the climb).

Sometimes we went to the distant suburbs to a labour camp with a brickworks, where we carried bricks to the waiting trucks in minus 20 degrees Celsius. When the trucks had driven off we were left to the mercy of the northwest wind and our cotton clothes felt like paper on our bodies. It was so cold that we soon were shivering. We carried the bricks in a hod on our backs, with two straps to attach the hod to our bodies, a bit like the backpacks that young people carry today. The most I could carry was 20 bricks. We carried them onto the trucks where someone would stack them until the truck was full and ready to take them back to the centre. When unloading, we used pouches that could carry six bricks and piled them up neatly on the ground without losing a single brick, unlike some drivers and loaders who when raising the flatbed of the truck, just dumped the bricks in a heap, causing many of them to break.

During the slack season I was sent to a small factory that did subcontracting for a big work unit to work in the tool shop with some 20 machine tools. I couldn't master the work and so was employed as a general factotum, delivering raw materials to the lathes. Later on they asked me to operate a little punching press, which was easy to manage.

While studying abroad in Germany the war prisoner Huang Wei (see above) had got the idea that he could create a perpetual motion machine. He applied to the authorities in the centre for permission to construct such a machine to his own design. In order to keep him happy or in order to win him over, the centre leaders surprisingly assented. He spent several months on the effort and wasted a considerable amount of materials. All he could manage to produce was a non-functioning perpetual motion machine. To have a machine that can move perpetually without electricity is unscientific. In the end Huang had to admit defeat.

Working in the compound itself we mainly had to tend the fruit trees. I have to confess that I am an ignoramus and that it was only while at Fushun that I learned that grape vines must be buried in winter or they freeze to death or that fruit trees eat meat and that any fish guts or dead cats should always be buried at the roots of fruit trees so that they will produce an exceptional crop. When we did this we were allocated a small share when the harvest time came.

The centre's war criminals had something in common: old age. All of them were well on in years, having been captured in 1948 or 1949 when they were already senior officials in the KMT and thus had already served long sentences. From 1948 to when I met them was already 20 years. None of them had received sentences and so they could only wait to be pardoned. During study sessions they would all praise the government's policies in a formulaic manner. They were all smooth talkers and capable of winning the guards' confidence. Our senior team leader was named Cai Shengsan: he was very able, having been a trusted subordinate of Chiang Ching-kuo. Another named Duan also made rapid progress. He had been a senior official in the KMT Bureau of Investigation and Statistics. When pardoned all these men were asked where they wanted to go and Cai, Duan and some others wanted to go to Taiwan. Of course Taiwan rejected them, reckoning that they had already been brainwashed by the CCP and were being sent as spies. Cai stayed in Hong Kong. Duan went to the United States and wrote a book critical of the CCP. We translator prisoners were also elderly, with only one youngster called Zhang Mintai, whom I have already described.

In October 1971 all the large and small 'loyalty' characters hanging in the large assembly hall were taken down, leaving me perplexed. Next, we were told that the first-ranking vice premier of the PRC and deputy chairman of the CCP, Lin Biao, had betrayed his country and died in Mongolia while fleeing abroad. A bit later on, the soldiers withdrew and Director Jin returned to his former position. The mood cleared and the food slowly improved. I still distinctly remember one day when I was eating breakfast and the kitchen brought out a plate of stinky beancurd, the odour of which permeated the entire dining hall, bringing a smile to the faces of all present. After a few days we were served noodles which we hadn't seen for many years. My tablemate Wang Tiehan swallowed down a large bowl of noodles with the speed of a monkey and then downed another. He was just about to take a third, when he regurgitated the first two. From his mouth streamed forth noodles. It seems that he hadn't chewed, just gulped them down. His vomit filled two bowls and included a few traces of blood showing that he had damaged his stomach. Our food cost had been reduced from 20 yuan per man per month to 8 yuan, but now the standard was gradually raised again. We ate more refined grain: each month 70% refined and 30% coarse, while people in the cities were at that time getting 70% coarse and 30% refined (the rough grains included millet, sorghum and maize—and were mostly used to make porridge).

We also got to watch more films—at least once a month and sometimes twice. We got to go out and tour around. Each of us was allocated a new suit of clothes—Mao suit of course. We visited the famous Fushun open pit coal mine (which had already been dug into a very deep pit), the crane factory, the forklift plant and the No. 6 Oil Refinery. We visited the birthplace of Lei Feng and went to Shenyang to visit the Exposition of Manufactured Products, the Industrial University and the former palace of the founder of the Qing dynasty. The passers-by saw us as a crowd of old folk wearing new clothes—everyone said that we were on a day out from the retirement home. The guards once again invited some of the families of the war criminals to come to Fushun to visit their relatives and gave them a warm welcome. The war criminals said: "It looks as if the day of our pardon is not far off." In fact the pardon came in 1975. All the prisoners were released at once. Not a single one was left behind.

Following this the library was opened up, which had never happened before. During the 'Cultural Revolution' we were not allowed to read anything other than the 'Little Red Book'. For me the opening of the library was a truly happy piece of news. I read the collected works of Lu Xun through twice and also carefully read the published works of Marx and Engels. Mao Zedong had said: "First destroy, then construct," which has a certain common sense about it. When reading Lu Xun I of course enjoyed his writing, but didn't admire him. I judged his contribution to Chinese literature less than that of Hu Shi. Lu Xun always takes the frontal attack, destroys and never constructs. While reading Marx and Lenin, my mind was full of the theories of Plato, Aristotle, Kant, Hegel, Confucius, Laozi and Zhuangzi. I regularly brought to mind these thinkers to compare with Marx. I reckon that Marx's theory of economics, in particular his theory of capital and theory of surplus value, are certainly new ideas, but to call this the only truth, to be judged accurate in every country, I cannot accept. My mind kept thinking of the words uttered by Zhuangzi 2,300 years ago. At the end of his book Zhuangzi wrote: "The methods employed in the regulation of the world are many; and (the employers of them) think each that the efficiency of his own method leaves nothing to be added to it."¹ In other words there are many learned people under the sky and they all think that they have discovered the only truth and that nothing whatsoever needs to be added.

I read the works of modern authors, always thinking to myself: "There is nothing new under the sun." It appears that to 'construct' you have to first 'destroy', but in what way is it easy to talk of 'destruction'? Using one contradiction to destroy another, the first contradiction had better be a razor-sharp weapon or else, while it may harm the second contradiction, it will fail to destroy it and may instead bounce back and harm itself. One of the slogans of the May Fourth Movement was "Strike down the Kong family store." Since then, have the theories of Confucius been destroyed? Destruction and construction should be undertaken at the same time. If there is only destruction and no construction a vacuum will be created, in which chaos will arise, so that after the destruction there is but desolation. Instead, construction must have victory over destruction or else there will be total destruction and the loss will be too great.

I consider that I am here on this earth to construct Jesus and to do so I have to destroy a little. When Matteo Ricci came to China in the late Ming dynasty to construct Christianity, he did not destroy Confucianism. He knew that Confucius could not be destroyed, so he used Confucius's own theories. He talked not of destroying Confucius, but of complementing him. Confucius himself said: "You are not yet able to serve men; how could you serve the spirits?"² Matteo Ricci responded with the notion that serving man is important, but that serving God is also important: "Confucius doesn't talk about serving God, so let me talk about it." Thus Ricci used Confucius to construct Jesus and used Jesus to compliment Confucius.

The War Criminals Management Centre used twenty-five years of labour, resources and energy to re-educate the war criminals. Cai Shengsan and the others studied with some success, gaining the approval of the authorities. They were able to adopt a façade of total immersion in Mao Zedong Thought, but

---

1. Translated by James Legge in *Sacred Books of the East*, ed. Max Müller, Oxford University Press, 1891.
2. *Analects* 11:12, translated by Simon Leys, W W Norton & Co Inc, Scranton, Pennsylvania, U.S.A., 1997.

deep in their hearts what they believed in was not Marxism-Leninism, but rather Sun Yat-sen's Three Principles of the People. They admired, not Mao Zedong, but Chiang Ching-kuo. As soon as they were freed, they wanted to go to Taiwan as fast as they could. It seems that destruction and construction are incredibly difficult.

After all the war criminals had been freed, the Fushun War Criminals Management Centre was turned into a small museum, with exhibits about the captured Japanese soldiers, the Manchurian puppet regime's leaders and the KMT war criminals including photographs of their re-education. In the 1990s I was invited by this museum to pay them a visit and was given a warm welcome; but all this happened much later on.

39
Return to Qincheng and Resumption of Translation Work (1973–75)

In 1973 Deng Xiaoping returned to power, taking up the post of deputy premier of the State Council and chief of the general staff. He bravely set about reorganising government departments, with quick results. In the summer the deputy director of Qincheng Prison came to Fushun and said that they intended to re-establish the translation team and wanted to take us back. Not all were welcome and those who had no real talent in foreign languages stayed at Fushun—including Zhang Zhitian, Diao Peishu, Xiong Shounong and a certain Lin whose given name I have forgotten. This time we got to travel by sleeper car and en route they bought watermelons for us and were exceptionally polite. Thus we returned to Qincheng Prison.

After we had entered the main gate of Qincheng, we immediately noticed a big difference. The original four blocks of the jail were now six, which implied that there were more prisoners and that the original cell blocks were insufficient to accommodate them. We were locked up in the same compound as before, but there was no sign of Director Sun or Officer Ma; the disciplinary officers had been changed and the new ones were very polite. We started to translate all over again.

On one occasion we were led to another compound, where we saw many fruit trees, in particular peach trees. The peaches were already ripe, but we didn't dare eat many, while old man Fang Huanru wolfed down about 20 of them. In the middle of the night we heard his groans as his stomach was in agony. He was sent to Fuxing Hospital in Beijing to be saved. Two days later we were informed by the guards that Fang had died. He had previously been operated on for an intestinal obstruction in which they had cut away a section of his intestine and stitched it back together. When he ate that many peaches all at once his intestine was ripped open. He was only a year from completing his sentence. Thus he died for such a petty reason. The prison informed his two daughters at the Iron and Steel Institute, but they refused to collect his body.

I had been arrested on 8 September 1955 and sentenced to eighteen years in jail. After finishing my sentence I was to be designated a counter-revolutionary for a further nine years. On 8 September 1973 my sentence was completed, but the prison authorities forgot all about it. My fellow prisoner Liu Chunxiang wrote a report to the authorities, asking why they were not allowed to release me. The authorities then sped up the formalities and I was released on 20 September. The disciplinary officer told me: "You should tell people that you were released on 8 September." He took me to the gate of the prison, along with some of my fellow-workers who had also been released: Zhang Ke, Zhang Xiaohu, Shan Jiaxiang and Wang Tiemei. They also told me that I would be registered as a counter-revolutionary activist for nine years, was not a citizen and was thus different from the others. I was given 50 yuan and told that this was my monthly salary. In those days 50 yuan was not too bad. Reform through labour, re-education through labour and employment by the Ministry of Public Security were three different categories, all being targets of the dictatorship of the People, while designation as a counter-revolutionary activist necessitated even more careful supervision: my movements and freedom of speech were thus carefully circumscribed.

We were permitted to go to the cadre's dining hall to eat. Vegetables were 3 fen (0.03 yuan) a dish, while meat dishes were 1 mao and 8 fen (0.18 yuan). It would be hard to spend 20 yuan a month. The cadres were all prison guards and their families. Apart from a few individuals, they kept their distance from us.

About 7 km from Qincheng is a place called Little Tangshan where there is a hot spring. Every Sunday I went there to take a bath in the hot spring, which cost 2 mao every time, which was very cheap. We had to report to the guards if we wanted to go to Beijing, but we were not permitted to spend the night there. Rong Dexian had a niece named Zhang Bochen who had graduated from the Biology Department of Fudan University and been allocated work at the No. 25 Middle School. She lived near Deng Shi Kou. When I went to Beijing I dined at her home. Rong Dexian had five daughters, one named Zhu Zhaofang and another Zhu Zhaorong. When they came to Beijing they also met with me. When I had lost my freedom, Zhu Zhaofang had been only seven years old and her sister two. They had both grown into mature women in their twenties. When I first saw them again I could not prevent myself from weeping. Zhang

Bochen was assigned by Rong Dexian to treat me very well, knitting sweaters for me and giving me padded cotton garments, treating me like a close relative and making me feel cared for. Later when I was transferred to Baoding in Hebei Province, we got three days off over Spring Festival and so I went to her home. Every time I could I went to Beijing. There were three people in Zhang's family: her husband Duanmu Yi was a surgeon who worked in the Temple of Heaven Hospital and their son who was named Ming. She lived together with her mother in one small room so that when I paid a visit she had to sleep elsewhere, leaving me to sleep in the same room as her husband and son. I am eternally grateful to them.

40
The No. 4 Re-education through Labour Camp in Henan Province (1975–79)

In 1975 class warfare broke out again in China. The senior leaders indicated that it was not a good idea to keep the translation team so close to the capital and said that we should be separated. The No. 13 Department of the Ministry of Public Security decided to break up the team. Meanwhile the team administrators told us that they would be going back to their hometowns. At the same time they told us: "As for Jin Luxian: you are not permitted to return to Shanghai. There is no work unit in Shanghai willing to accept you. Your fellow translators are going to north-east China, to Shandong Province and to Henan Province, so you can choose any one of these destinations." I considered that the north-east was too cold, that Zhang Ke was going to Shandong and I had no wish to remain with him, so I said: "I'll go to Henan." After a month a cadre from the No. 4 Xinxiang Production Brigade in Henan Province arrived and took Shan Jiaxiang and me back with him.

The No. 4 Production Brigade was a really big work unit, with 2,000 prisoners and 200 employees. It had a factory, known as the Fire Prevention Machinery Works, which altered Liberation brand trucks and fitted them out as fire engines. There were three workshops, a farm and a brick works. Shan Jiaxiang and I were allocated to the design team, all of the members of which were employees who had stayed on after serving their sentences, about 20 of them. I remember some of their names, such as Sun Haochuan, Song Jinxiang, Zhang Chunxiang, Li Kexian and Lin Guorong. These employees had been technical staff, but in the Anti-Rightist Campaign had been designated rightists and sentenced to jail. When they had completed their sentences they were released, but chose to stay on.

I was not a technician and was not able to do design work, so I was sent to manage a small library. The work was very easy and I could read. We were managed by two men named Li and Zhao who were both section heads. The factory director was also named Li. I remember his name because every time he gave a speech, he would first stand up; but when they provided him with a chair he would not sit down on it, but rather squat on top of it. I learned that Henan people liked to squat. In fact Director Li was illiterate. He kept a diary in his pocket where he recorded things in a script that only he could understand.

Once there was a rainstorm and there was a danger that the library might be flooded. The leaders told me to move the books to the third floor of another building. Since this was quite far away I used a truck to move the books. A former KMT officer named Liu Shuzhen, who had been pardoned and, since he had no relatives or family to return to, had been allocated a position in the factory, was detailed to escort me. He saw that I was over-burdened with unloading the books and carrying them up the stairs, but just watched me with folded arms. When I reached the third floor a young female cadre saw what was going on and immediately came downstairs to assist me in moving the books, going up and down several times. This was my first sight of Wang Chunxian. In comparison with that of Liu, Wang's behaviour made a good impression on me. I later discovered that she was a graduate of the Workers, Peasants and Soldiers Education Programme and had a degree from the Department of Engineering at Zhengzhou University. After graduation she had been allocated work as a designer in the factory. Her father was the deputy commander of the Henan Provincial Police Bureau. In Henan she could be counted as a 'princeling' or privileged child of a senior cadre.

After I had been at Xinxiang for several months, a manager who was also an employee named Hu Weiping asked me whether I would like to go to Shanghai to visit my relatives. Employees were permitted to make home visits. The Beijing authorities had given this permission to others, but not to me. I said that I'd like to go. He said: "Write an application to me." I was aware that the Shanghai diocese had cut off all relations with me and that my own relatives had done the same, so I put down Rong Dexian's name, saying that she was my elder sister. I then immediately wrote to Rong Dexian and she replied welcoming me to visit her. Just before I set out some cadres asked me to bring back some 'White Jade' or 'China' brand toothpaste for them. At that time these could only be bought at the special counter for foreign visitors at the Xinxiang Department Store. Hu Weiping asked me to get him a lady's watch, which could be bought with a coupon in Shanghai. I agreed to do all these things.

On arrival in Shanghai, Rong Dexian's family received me most cordially, just as erstwhile. In the early part of the 'Cultural Revolution' Rong Dexian's house had been smashed up and 90% of her belongings lost. Every day she had to sweep the alley. The only positive thing was that her younger brother Rong Deshen and his wife Xu Jie were in business in Hong Kong and could send her money every month. In those days everything was cheap, so she could live quite comfortably. She had five daughters and one son. Her son had joined the Society of Jesus in Taiwan and it was over twenty years since she had last seen him. Her second daughter had moved to her in-laws' home after marriage, leaving the eldest Zhaoyi at her mother's side, along with the fourth and fifth daughters. While in Shanghai I didn't visit any friends or relatives and anyway they didn't want to see me for fear of implication in my crimes. Rong Dexian invited me to several restaurants and bought me meals. She also threw a formal banquet to celebrate my 60th birthday.

While at her home I watched television, read magazines and listened to music. I very much enjoyed listening to a song from the film *Waterloo Bridge*. I could listen to it a hundred times without getting bored. On the third floor of Rong's home was an empty room where I could sit alone and read the Bible and meditate silently. It had been many years since I had enjoyed such peace and quiet. The days passed very quickly and in a flash the weeks were gone.

On return to Xinxiang I took a large case of toothpaste, several packets of 'Double Happiness', 'Peony' and 'Da Qian Men' brand cigarettes (bought with ration coupons) and also the lady's watch. I gave the toothpaste and cigarettes to the cadres, while Manager Hu gave me the money for the watch. While at Xinxiang I was able to go back to Shanghai every year. On the last occasion, I went to the home of Rong Dexian's elder sister Rong Rouxian. She lived in Wuxi, about 100 km west of Shanghai. I still remember her address: No. 91 Shangtang Street. She had four daughters, named in order Bo and then the character for the year of their birth. The second daughter was Bochen, whom I had met in Beijing, so named because she was born in the 辰 year. The third daughter was named Bowu since she had been born in the 午 year. She worked in Wuxi. The youngest was named Boyou and lived in Wuhan. Bowu had a little girl who was both lively and cute. Hu Weiping one day said to me: "You are still designated a counter-revolutionary activist and as a low-rank convict. Why don't I apply to the provincial Public Security Bureau to change your status?" He wrote the relevant application and asked me to make a careful study of the works of Chairman Mao, so that I knew them by heart and could apply their teachings. The PSB authorised me to drop my criminal status three years ahead of schedule.

I have already described how I was first allocated a job managing the library. In the beginning I did this job alone. Later on another employee was sent over. This man was named Cao Chengxiu. He was already elderly. He knew English and had once been involved in editing an English–Chinese dictionary, which had been widely disseminated. Before his arrest he had been enlisted in the army and had been a battalion-level cadre. He was always making appeals, claiming that he had been unjustly treated. Once when we were at the library the disciplinary officer accompanied a court official to announce to him that his appeal had been rejected and the original sentence sustained. After the court official had left Cao fainted on the spot. I was frightened and didn't know what to do, so I rushed off and told Wang Chunxian. She arranged for people to take Cao to the clinic. After he had recovered he became a very taciturn person, let his hair grow long and wore patterned shirts and make-up like a woman. When the disciplinary officer told him to cut his hair, he said: "Didn't Marx also wear his hair long?" He also said that he wanted to buy a *qipao* to wear. I said to him: "When you are walking around and need to go to the toilet, do you go to the Men's or to the Women's?" He said: "The Women's, of course." I said: "You will get yourself arrested as a pervert." He still insisted on wearing his hair long and wearing clothes with bright patterns.

Our team was later on managed by Wang Chunxian. She said to me: "I've looked through all seven volumes of your file. There's nothing of importance in there. You yourself confessed to your crimes. What you were accused of by other people was nothing more than loyalty to Rome and opposition to the Catholic Patriotic Association." Every time I had moved to a new prison, my file had accompanied me. I suspect that it is still stored somewhere in the archives of the Shanghai Public Security Bureau.

Wang Chunxian really looked after our team of 'stinking old nines'. Director Li loved to lecture us. Every time he was long-winded and disgraceful. He sat on a chair while we sat on little stools, a bit lower than his. He always made us late for meals. When Wang was present, as soon as she saw the time she would announce that the meeting was over for the day, giving us time to get to our meals.

Sometimes we went out to labour in the fields and assist the farmers. When she led the team, Wang would always allocate the light work to me. At the factory she would send me to manage the blueprint machine and the blueprint paper. I would sit alone in the room, separate from the other employees, with a bit more freedom. I could read books and pray.

Wang wanted to learn English and I patiently taught her. After I had been transferred from Xinxiang I stayed in contact with her. Later on she married her fellow student Xu Xiang. Xu's father was a department head under Fang Yi at the Academy of Sciences in Beijing. Wang Chunxian told her father-in-law about me, asking whether or not I could be transferred to work in his department. Her father-in-law agreed; but later told Wang that I was an important criminal and could not be transferred. When I was first arrested I greatly feared the PSB, but among the people of the PSB there were many who looked out for me. Later on I'll refer to another such person named Liu Jun.

I stayed at Xinxiang for four years. During that time I tried to find a church by any means, but could not locate even a small chapel, nor could I find anyone who considered himself to be a Catholic.

The 'Gang of Four' fell from power. The cataclysm of the 'Cultural Revolution' was over. The Third Communist Party Central Committee Plenum was held and Deng Xiaoping returned to power for the second time. The new policy of the central government was reform and opening up. All the rightists had their cases reviewed and the disciplinary treatment of employees was less severe, with less political study. The mood of the whole jail became easier.

41
The End of the 'Great Proletarian Cultural Revolution'

In the annals of our country 1976 was a most unsettled year. Early on Premier Zhou Enlai and Marshal Zhu De both died, after which the great earthquake at Tangshan occurred, in which some 200,000 residents died. Following this Mao Zedong, after a long period of illness and every medical effort to save him, departed this life. Just as Jiang Qing and the others in the 'Gang of Four' hatched their plan to seize power, Hua Guofeng and Ye Jianying moved quickly to launch a surprise attack and arrested them all, thus crushing their plot, to the huge relief of the whole People. After the 3rd party plenum, Deng Xiaoping was again returned to power and Hu Yaobang was selected as general secretary of the CCP.

Bold and resolute action had overturned chaos and restored order. The unjust and mistaken cases were reviewed. The whole nation gave a collective sigh of relief as the ten years of disorder came to an end. The great damage the 'Cultural Revolution' caused our country must be thoroughly investigated by history. Right now, however, I wish to set down my own thoughts relating to this unprecedented and unrepeatable human disaster. During my time with the war criminals we were all long-term prisoners and thus had no contact with the outside world—in fact we were particularly isolated. It was only after I was transferred to Xinxiang that I got to meet some younger and newly imprisoned people and through them learnt more about what had been happening on the outside and got fairly up-to-date information.

At the beginning of the mighty and historically unprecedented 'Great Cultural Revolution' we were permitted to read the newspaper, which read: "The situation is excellent; not just good, but excellent." At first we believed this, but then we doubted it. We mouthed the word 'excellent', but in our hearts wondered how this could be so since our personal experience told us that the situation was not good.

As I have explained above, in 1965 the government had arranged for the war criminals, along with the translation team, to tour the new construction projects, universities and research institutes of Beijing. We were very well treated, received by leaders and hosted by them. Then, at the start of the 'Cultural Revolution' we were transferred to the Fushun War Criminal Management Centre, where things were quite different. While escorting us the Liberation Army had loaded weapons and sent us to a small station, which was deserted except for soldiers, all armed to the teeth. This made me realise that class warfare had started up again and what was 'excellent' about that? Our food also was worse. Later on we found that our individual food allocation had been cut from 20 yuan to 8 yuan and that was really not 'excellent'.

At Fushun we did no translation and were not permitted to take out books. Each of us was issued with a 'Little Red Book' of Mao Zedong's sayings and all other books were banned. Political study was resumed with vigour and we did endless self-criticisms, while being required to expose and betray others. There was nothing to do, so our minds were full of thoughts and imaginings! Before leaving Qincheng we had gone out to do janitorial work and seen the big character posters saying: "Strike down the slogans of Liu Shaoqi". Others had said: "Strike down the slogans of the prison leaders", which left us completely confused.

The Red Guards appeared and struck down feudalism, capitalism and revisionism and seized power everywhere, sweeping away class enemies of all descriptions, smashing the 'four olds', destroying cultural assets, national treasures, creating revolutionary uproar, making brutal attacks, arresting people everywhere, making them suffer, doing everything on a huge scale. It really was a world-shattering change. Everything was taken to its extreme and then returned to its diametrically opposite expression, so that the 'Great Cultural Revolution' in turn became the anti-cultural revolution.

Day and night we had to learn the 'Little Red Book' by heart. At one's first breath on waking up, one had to dash to the exercise ground to pay respects to Chairman Mao. The last thing before bed, one had to make self-criticisms. We had to confess our sins to Chairman Mao, all of which resembled our religious ceremonies. It appeared to me that a new religion had made its appearance. But a true religion is freely expressed by its adherents, while this man-made religion was enforced with military power.

This made me suddenly realise why in the Old Testament it describes how when Moses went up the mountain to pray to God for a mere forty days, he came down to find that the people of Israel had built a golden calf to worship. This demonstrates that humankind needs a god. When a true God is destroyed, a false one is made in His place. I realised that I was actually witnessing the people of my country create a false god. For better or for worse, the facts demonstrated their own conclusion. The God announced by the Lord requires that we humanly acknowledge Him, while the man-made god, being but man himself, is incapable of human recognition and can only reduce man to his primitive state. When Mao Zedong launched his deification programme, I remembered Laozi's words "Those who strive for something fail; those who grab hold lose what they desire." When Mao Zedong died he gave himself the assessment that he had 70% succeeded and 30% failed. In 1975, I was still at Xinxiang and heard the prisoners who were undergoing reform through labour say: "The Great Cultural Revolution? From that moment Mao Zedong irrevocably lost his heroic reputation." This was the judgment of ordinary people. It really was a case of the folly of the elite and the clear-sightedness of the mean and lowly.

I believe that over a million years ago we evolved from the animals, from animal nature to human nature and then to reason. Human beings have never ceased to improve, from walking on four legs with bowed head to standing erect and walking forward; from eating animals raw and living in the trees to the formation of tribes, making tools, inventing and manufacturing; from murdering each other to pursuing benevolence, to overcoming human nature, pursuing association with the Creator of all things, all the time aiming for divine nature. But humans are also capable of excavating our animal nature, using our animal nature, inciting enmity and advocating hatred, taking pleasure in destruction. Humans can also preach benevolence, peace, harmony. Humankind's progress is like the ocean tides—the waves advance and recede. Humankind recedes one step and advances two steps.

We should have faith that humankind will progress further, that any setbacks are in fact temporary. However, while undergoing a setback, people are unfortunate. Nonetheless, I consider myself fortunate to have witnessed the setback of the Chinese people, to have witnessed the misery of the Chinese people, to have undergone misery and grieved for the Chinese people.

During the 'Cultural Revolution' I was very pessimistic about the future of religion and especially of the Catholic Church. Religion would now be underground, under the police surveillance of the CCP, so that it could not sustain itself, so that eventually there would be no sound of church bells in China, no sound of the striking of wooden fish in Buddhist monasteries. Religion would simply disappear from the face of the earth. I was even more pessimistic about my own future. I considered that people like me would never be released after completing our sentences. Even were we to be released, we would always be spied on by the masses, always working like dogs with our tails between our legs, with only a miserable future. From now on, I could only take one day at a time.

I have described above my state of mind during the ten years of 'Cultural Revolution'. I was depressed, deeply depressed. As things turned out, I learned that this depression was mistaken.

42
Hebei No. 1 Jail (1979–82)

In May 1979, the Public Security Ministry (PSM) sent two cadres to have a talk with me. One was named Wang Xiang and the other Li Jing. Wang spoke English and asked me several questions in that language. Then they went back to Beijing. Since Deng Xiaoping had again returned to power, the PSM needed to set up the translation team again. Wang Chunxian congratulated me, saying: "It seems that the government has a use for you. In the place you are going, the conditions will surely be better." I certainly had no such notion in my mind.

In August the No. 4 Production Team sent a policeman named Zhang to take me to the Hebei No. 1 Prison in Baoding City and handed me over, putting me to work with another group of employees. In a long row of single-storey buildings, the employees could have their families with them, one family to a room, while I shared a room with two other employees without family. Each room had two separate chambers. The one at the front was large and faced south; the one at the back small and north-facing. I got the small room, with a bed as well as a small stand on which a chest could be placed. There was nothing else except for a small table on which I wrote and ate my food. There was a small stool to sit on. After I had lived for a while in this small room I realised that my conditions here were worse than at Qincheng, Fushun or Xinxiang. The people who had been transferred to do translation work were as follows: Miss Song Tianying, whose father had been awarded a doctorate in chemistry in America and had become a Christian and a well-renowned pastor (in those days the saying was that, among the Protestants, it was Wang in the north and Song in the south); Zhou Bingjin, who had graduated from the Foreign Language Institute of Furen University (her husband Zhao Chundeng came with her); a Protestant named Xue and a woman who was also a Protestant (these two later on registered to be married).

There was a Taiwanese named Lin—it was said that he was a special agent. He had completed his sentence and had been released into employment. Later on he was introduced by Dr. Zhu to a female guard named Wang and they got married. Wang already had two daughters from a previous marriage who refused to call Lin 'father'. Four years later, Lin's brother in Japan came to see him. The brother had been successful in business in Japan. He arranged for several Japanese companies to invest in Hebei, so the Hebei provincial government made him a standing member of the People's Political Consultative Conference. Later on he was promoted to the national CPPCC. These two stepdaughters then changed their attitude and were very filial to him. Lin sent them to Japanese universities.

There was also a Eurasian named Ce Shaoming who spoke French and a man named Mao; these two made endless reports and earned the trust of the leaders. Chen Shiliang knew French. Chen Huanzhang was from Tangshan, had been seminarian and studied philosophy and so knew French. Wang Jiliang knew German; his father had been the general commanding the Japanese puppet government's army.

A man named Bai knew Japanese, was often loaned out as a translator and spent a lot of time with Japanese businessmen, through whom he could get hold of things including pornographic magazines (from the start of the Open Door Policy, foreign objects were extremely sought after) which he gave to the cadres. Some of the cadres were happy to get these things; but when the superiors found out about it, Bai was accused of corrupting the cadres and was brought back to the translation team and no longer allowed out.

There was also a couple named Shen and Qian, who brought a 12-year-old son, who still needed his mother to wash his face and brush his teeth every morning; a man named Peng who brought his wife and daughter; one named Xu; and another named Zhao.

A man named Xie had been a stockbroker before Liberation. When the Shenzhen stock exchange was started up, he went there and earned several tens of millions of yuan. Once he was rich, he became corrupt again.

Wang Xiang had previously worked at the PSM, but after being accused of being rightist, he had kept silent and so they accused him of being a rightist sympathiser. He left the PSM and was sent to Qinghai to manage labour reform camps, where he had met the Shanghainese Shen Baoyi and Shi Yaodi and transferred them also to Baoding. In total there were twenty-four of us. When there were enough of us, the deputy prison head gave us a lecture and emphasised: "We are neophytes leading experts. I know no foreign languages, but am still able to lead you. Intellectuals must not wag their tails," and so on *ad infinitum*.

We were divided into four teams for Japanese, Russian, English and French. Each team had its own leader. I was leader of the French team. I didn't translate myself, but edited the team's work and took responsibility for any mistakes.

In my team was Shen Baoyi, a Shanghai man who had been one of Gong Pinmei's secretaries and had been implicated and sentenced to reform through labour. Shen had a very close relationship with Rev. Zhu Hongsheng and kept up a steady correspondence with Rev. Zhu. Zhu had been released and gone home after completing his sentence. He became the (secret) representative of Rome and the Society of Jesus, staying in touch with the priests and lay people and making reports to Rome. Shen wrote to Zhu saying that I was trusted by the Communist leaders, who had made me a team leader, etc. Zhu reported to Rome that I had betrayed the Church, had surrendered to the CCP and had become a member of the party and that's why they valued me. In Hong Kong and in Rome this report was taken at face value. I was regarded as a traitor. The Hungarian Jesuit László Ladány wrote an article vilifying me in his newsletter *China News Analysis*, which was picked up by other newspapers, having a huge impact. After my adopted mother came to see me in China, she tried to go to the Jesuit house in Rome in order to tell them my true situation but the deputy to the superior general of the Society of Jesus told her: "We don't recognise Jin Luxian; he is a traitor." After I came out of jail and went abroad on trips, the Jesuits cut me off, a situation which endured until 1993. This caused me great mental anguish. What is really worthy of ridicule is that Rev. Zhu Hongsheng was arrested again in 1981 and was assigned to translation work, which he did so well he won a shortened sentence as a reward. Oh, my dear God!

We originally had thought that Wang Xiang would manage us, but we were wrong. After Wang was rehabilitated he returned to Beijing and remained on the margins. The PSM sent a man named Zou Yuan, a deputy director, to manage us. He was very harsh: under him the translation team members could only claim 4 yuan of medical expenses at the end of each month and had to use their own money for the rest. When the translation team members went on trips they had to account for their expenses. Zou lived in Bejing and came to Baoding every ten days to settle our accounts and chide us and loudly rebuke us. Zou Yuan was just as tough with other people. He used the money we earned from translating as his contribution to his superiors and bought a van for his sole use. After he had used the van and it was no longer needed, he used chalk to draw a line on the ground in front of the tires. The next day he asked the driver, "Did you use the van last night?" The driver said he had not, so he took the driver to the van and asked him, "Can the van move on its own? Look at the chalk line." The driver had nothing to say for himself and could only make a self-confession.

In the late 1970s and early 1980s there was a great shortage of foreign language skills in China. I was also hired out as a German translator. The Ministry of Metallurgy had a branch company in Baoding with a telemetry factory which had bought an instrument for underground monitoring from a German company, which sent engineers to install it. There was not a single person in Baoding who spoke German, so I was hired out to act as an interpreter. Had the foreign engineers not come, we would definitely have failed to install the equipment successfully. The German engineers opened up the cases and took out the equipment, but put two elements in the wrong place. Since there was no mobile phone in 1980 and Baoding city had no international exchange, I had to accompany them to the Long Distance Telephone Office at Xidan in Beijing. How science has made progress since then! Today even small children have mobile phones and can talk to their family and friends in Europe and the US as they walk along the street.

Later on I was hired out to teach French at Hebei University, while Shen Baoyi was loaned out to Hebei Provincial Museum to sort through the files of Xianxian diocese. In Shanghai the files of the diocese had all been destroyed by Lacretelle, but those of Xianxian had been preserved. Later on Shen Baoyi and Chen Shiliang were hired out to the Mancheng Helicopter Factory to translate the operation manual of the Wasp helicopter they had imported from France.

All those who hired translators from the translation company had to pay for them. Even though we didn't make a penny ourselves, we were happy to be hired out, since we were treated as guests by the customers and were respected by them. How different from Zou Yuan, who didn't treat us as human beings at all. In my 27 years of labour reform the worst conditions of all were at the Baoding Translation Company. While working at Qincheng, we could claim all our medical expenses, whereas at the translation company we could only claim 4 yuan a month and had to take the rest out of our own wallets. At that time I had diabetes and my blood pressure was high so I needed a lot of medicine, the cost of which exceeded 4 yuan. But heaven does not leave us without recourse. In the jail was a female doctor named Zhu Kaiyi, who was a generous-hearted person. She had originally worked at the Xiehe Hospital in Beijing. Her husband was named Wang and had worked at the PSM, but had refused to criticise people during the Anti-Rightist Movement. He was told that he had a bad attitude and so had lost his job at the PSM and was sent to work at the Baoding Prison. His wife Dr. Zhu had gone with him. She said to me: "You are intellectuals. Why is Zou Yuan so harsh towards you? Your treatment is no better than the regular employees. You need a lot of medicine, at least 200 yuan a month. You also need to eat! How about this: I will charge the medicine you need to my family account. After I pick it up, I will have people deliver it to you." What an escape from disaster! I thanked her heartily. She had two sons and one daughter. Dr. Zhu and her husband were both high-grade intellectuals, but owing to the 'Cultural Revolution' none of their children could go to university. They were all three workers. One son made shoes, the other was a cook. Their daughter Wang Jinghan worked in the harmful products section of the photographic film factory.

After leaving Baoding I always kept in touch with the Wang family. Once Dr. Zhu, her husband, and their daughter Wang Jinghan all came to Sheshan to visit me. When I went to Beijing to attend meetings of the CPPCC, Dr. Zhu and Wang Jinghan frequently came from Baoding to see me. They are my friends in adversity. They delivered me fuel in deep snow and I will not forget them all my life.

At the No. 1 Prison in Baoding there remained one person doing reform through labour named Liu Guandong. He was a priest. When sentenced to labour camp he became a carpenter. Another was Rev. Zhou Shanfu who had been a medical doctor and acted as doctor to the prisoners in hospital. He had an electrocardiogram taken of me and diagnosed that my left aorta was blocked. He advised me to be very careful and not to exhaust myself. There was also Rev. Shi Enxiang from Xuhui as well as the Bishop of Zhangjiakou, Zhang Kexing, among others. They were released one after another. Zhou Shanfu travelled around widely in the guise of doctor and came across many Catholics. He used the opportunity to preach to them while providing them with medical care. The cathedral of Baoding is in the busiest section of the city. The church had already been opened, but the self-proclaimed Bishop Wang Qiwei had already got married. The government gave him a salary of 200 yuan a month (which was a very high salary at that time). He didn't work hard and used to travel around with his wife, which the lay people found unacceptable, so that only about ten to twenty people attended his mass every Sunday.

Zhou Shanfu made contact with a family named Shi, who were better off than most. They had a large home in the north of Baoding, which was very commodious. Zhou did a deal with the head of the household that he would turn it into a missionary centre. He took me along. I saw that the house was decorated like a church and there were more than 100 bicycles parked in the yard. The house was full of Catholics, piously reading the scriptures. There were many young people there. I was very moved at this sight, the like of which I had not seen for over twenty years. Zhou Shanfu invited me to say mass, while he heard confessions. While saying mass, hot tears streaked down my face. After a month the original Bishop of Baoding, Fan Xueyan, completed his sentence and returned home. He was greatly venerated by the faithful and many more came to his masses. They added a mass on Saturday evening, but it was still not enough.

On one Sunday afternoon, I went to the Shi family home in Beiguan and saw Bishop Fan. He was most delighted and showed me a small sacred image on the back of which were written various lines of Latin script. Fan said that it was a secret message from the Congregation for the Evangelisation of Peoples in Rome to the faithful in China and read: "Any Chinese bishop who is loyal to the Vatican can ordain any loyal priest as bishop and such a bishop can have jurisdiction all over China, without previous authorisation", etc. I said: "This power is just too great." Fan said: "This is an extraordinary authorisation for extraordinary times."

As I understand it, Fan went on to ordain Zhou Shanfu, Liu Guandong, Shi Enxiang, Lian Xiusheng, Chen Jianzhang, Jia Zhiguo (who at that time was not even a priest) and others as bishops. These men then travelled secretly around the country ordaining bishops. Thus the underground Catholic Church was born. From then on, the underground bishops all operated independently, without any common leader. All over the country, there were several underground bishops active at the same time. They had no need to seek the opinion of others and organised no meetings to discuss matters. They each decided secretly to ordain any priest they considered suitable as bishop. In some dioceses there suddenly appeared as many as two or three bishops, creating chaos. Naturally all these bishops secretly ordained priests, who had no need to devote themselves to the study of theology or logic or any other subject, let alone undergo a long process of assessment. They said that it was a race against time—while all the time the Chinese Church was falling into chaos, a situation that the Vatican had not anticipated.

Every Sunday afternoon I went to Beiguan to hear confessions and sometimes to say mass, while at other times joining other priests for the mass (at that time none of us had heard of the Second Vatican Council, so we knew nothing of liturgical reform). I met many committed Catholics, among whom the ones I knew best, apart from the head of the Shi household, were the Zhao and Song households. Mr. Zhao lived next to the bridge in Beiguan. He was a metalworker, a very honest and upright person, open-hearted but also of irascible temper. He was very filial to his mother and in his home she had the final say. Zhao's wife, named Wang, was virtuous. She was respectful to her mother-in-law and had to raise her four girls and the youngest, a son (who was greatly loved by his grandmother), on top of which she had to serve her husband, working hard and not bearing grudges or grumbling. She was truly a model woman. The eldest daughter was named Jianxin and was very mature. After school she would go and collect broken bricks and tiles and sell them to people for fixing up their homes. The youngest daughter was called Yaya and the middle girl was named Xiaohong. I can't remember the other one's name. After mass the whole family would invite me to go and eat *jiaozi* (dumplings) at their home.

At the Song family home, the husband was a truck driver at the flour factory. He had seven daughters, of whom the second was called Cuimei and had only just graduated from senior middle school. At that time I was teaching French part-time at Hebei University, two lessons a week. Every time I got off work this girl would wait with her bicycle at the school gate and invite me home to eat at their house. It was plain cooking, but they were full of respect for priests. I really loved these two families and have never forgotten them.

After returning to Shanghai I kept in touch with them. Because of their faith in God, Song Cuimei and Zhao Jianxin were not allowed to go to university. Nowadays all their children have been to university. It was such a shame.

43
Friends Come from Afar

At this time I received an up-to-date German dictionary from Rong Dexian as a present. When I read it through I saw the name of my friend Georg Meistermann. I was glad to see that he had become a well-known abstract painter, but there was no address in the dictionary. I only knew that he came from Solingen in Germany. So I wrote him a letter, addressed to G. Meistermann, Solingen. Surprisingly he did get my letter, no doubt as a result of his fame. In fact, he had already left that town and moved to Köln; but, when I wrote a second time, the letter was returned to me. So perhaps it had something to do with the will of God, who arranged for him and his wife to come and take care of me. I count it among the miracles of the Lord's wisdom.

A month later, I got his reply. He said that they had always thought about me. He also said that their daughter Donate, who had so patiently taught me German, had died of cancer in 1968, leaving two children, a boy and a girl, who had already grown up. He also said that his wife was at that time in Egypt. Once she had returned they planned to come and visit me in China. After another month, a letter came from his wife, saying that they planned to join a tour group to come and see me in China. A month later, a letter arrived saying that they had fixed their plan and would land in Beijing in two weeks with a Swiss tour group. I reported to Zou Yuan. Zou said: "What's going on? It's not easy to keep abreast of all your social connections. Why are you falsely claiming that Germans are coming to see you? Not permitted!"

I replied: "They are famous people, making a special trip to see me. If you don't allow me to see them, it would not be very appropriate."

He said that he would have to report to his superiors. Later on Zou told me: "It has been approved by Deputy Director Liu Jun of the Political Security Department of the PSM" but since at that time Baoding was not one of the cities open to foreigners, they couldn't come to see me.

Zou said: "Why don't you go to Beijing and spend three days with them?"

I first went to Beijing. Zou Yuan told me to report in detail everything I observed. When Liu Jun received me he said: "When meeting foreigners you should be natural and graceful, without any artifice. No need to be reserved. Speak the truth. They know about us, so when they ask about your experiences, just tell them the truth. When they ask about China, don't talk up the situation. If you exaggerate, people won't believe you anyway. I believe that you have national pride, so won't describe the situation in our country too negatively. Relax! I trust you. If you are given anything, just politely accept it." I formed a good impression of Liu Jun and respected him.

When they arrived I went to the airport to meet them. It was exactly thirty years since we had last met. As soon as we met, we were overjoyed. They hugged me tightly saying, "For so many years, we have tried to get information about you. When our younger daughter Monika was working at the German Consulate in Hong Kong, she also tried to get information, but everyone said that they didn't know where you were." They stayed at the Beijing Hotel. I said: "I can only spend three days with you."

They said, "No way. We have come 10,000 miles especially to see you; you must join us for the whole trip. We have already paid for your tour."

I reported back to Zou Yuan and he passed the message to Liu Jun. Liu said: "Since they have come, accompany them."

I went to the International Travel Bureau and asked them to make arrangements, but they immediately refused saying that all air tickets, train tickets, and hotel rooms had already been booked and it was not possible to add another person. I told the painter and his wife that the travel agents had refused to include me in the tour group. They then suggested that we all go together and talk to them, so we went along with the Swiss tour guide and when the travel agent saw that it was foreigners he was dealing with, he stood up with a smile on his face and said: "This is easy to arrange. We'll simply inform each local travel agency to add one more person and that'll fix it."

They had brought a typewriter, a tape recorder, a bolt of cloth for making a suit of clothes, an old cross and a German–Latin missalette for me. They had thought of everything. I gratefully took the presents. While in Beijing, Zhang Bozhen invited them to dinner at the Beijing Roast Duck Restaurant. They very much took to her and in their subsequent letters always asked after Maomao (her nickname).

On the fourth day I set off with their tour group. In the past I had always bought hard-seat tickets, but this time we went by soft sleeper. We visited Nanjing for two days, then Wuxi and Suzhou and finally reached Shanghai where we stayed at the Shanghai Mansions. In those days, this kind of hotel only accepted foreign guests. When I was in the corridor, a hotel staff rudely said to me: "What are you doing here? Get out at once! Is this where you are staying?" I had to show him the room key to shut him up. The Friendship Store was also out of bounds to Chinese. I thought that when I was small, the Bund Park was said to have had a sign at the gate saying, 'Chinese and dogs not allowed,' which had caused us much shame and disgrace. How could it be that after so many years of Liberation, we had once again returned to foreign domination? I could make neither head nor tail of it. I had been away from Shanghai for twenty years, but when walking around it felt as if nothing had changed. There were no new buildings.

While in Shanghai, Rong Dexian gave a dinner for my friends at the Jing'an Hotel. They particularly liked Zhaoqing, saying she was exactly what they imagined a Chinese girl to be like. We then travelled by train to Hangzhou and on by plane to Guangzhou, which was the first time I had been on an airplane.

We looked around Guangzhou for two days. On the eve of our departure, they came to my hotel room and said very seriously: "We have seen you and put our minds at rest. We imagine that your foreign friends and especially those in the Society of Jesus will also be glad. When we get home, we will go to Rome and report your circumstances to the Jesuit headquarters."

I thanked them very much for their good intentions. After my arrest I had always missed the Society of Jesus and had prayed for all the Jesuits in the world. I was also deeply confident that the Society of Jesus would not forget me and would certainly pray for me. They also said to me that my complexion was not too good. I was obviously suffering from malnutrition. My clothes were too shabby. They wanted to send me 200 yuan a month so that I could buy some clothes and eat more nutritious food. Should they send me renminbi or marks? I thanked them and said that renminbi was better. After going back they sent me 200 yuan every month. In those days a section chief only got 50 yuan a month in salary and *Maotai* wine was 8 yuan a bottle, so I had become wealthy. Finally they took out 2,250 in Foreign Exchange Currency (FEC) bills and said that it was no use to them in Germany and asked me to accept it, which I did. I took them to Guangzhou Railway Station. They were going to Hong Kong.

They hugged me tightly and asked me to look after myself. I watched their train leave the station with tears in my eyes.

They had already bought me airplane tickets to Shanghai and from Shanghai to Beijing. On the flight back to Shanghai, I thought of visiting friends and relatives. I went to see Rong Dexian and Weng Fanyin at Zhu Zhaoqing's home. I stayed several days. I planned to go and see Zhu Hongsheng and tell him to be careful because his every move was observed by the People's Government, but he refused to meet me and I was very disappointed. Chen Yuntang saw me at his nephew's house and invited me to a meal. While I was there the Jesuit responsible for the Shanghai diocese came from Hong Kong to pay a visit and asked to meet with Zhu Hongsheng, Chen Tianxiang, Chen Yuntang, Cai Chongjian and others for a talk. They found a house belonging to people whom they completely trusted and held the meeting there. I have heard that after the meeting a tape recording of the whole discussion was sent to the PSB. Two months later Zhu Hongsheng and the others were arrested. Some of the Shanghai lay people said that it was the traitor Jin Luxian who had come to Shanghai to investigate and betray Zhu and the others who caused their arrests. I was once again the subject of false accusations. Zhu had a habit of keeping all his letters in a filing cabinet, keeping a copy of every letter he wrote for himself. When he was arrested, these files were searched by the PSB. Every single one of the people he had contact with was investigated and many were arrested. Before this, his friends had warned him to be careful, but he had replied: "Relax! The CCP won't dare to touch me." He was really crazy.

Accompanying the Germans for fifteen days was the greatest gift the Lord had given me in 27 years. It was also most useful to the next half of my life (which I will describe in the next volume of my memoirs). I thank the Lord.

While in Shanghai, I was accompanied by Yuan Sizhen, the younger sister of Rev. Yuan Side. We went to Sheshan on pilgrimage. The mid-level church was already open, but the basilica on top of the hill itself was still being used by others. On my return to Beijing, Liu and Zou met with me and I made a report of the key facts. Zou said that I had to hand over my FECs to my superiors. Zou wanted to take them from me, but Liu said: "Hand over what? What's given to you, you make use of." I was grateful to him.

On my return to Baoding, I bought three 'Phoenix' brand bicycles for the daughters of the Song and Zhao families who had been so kind to me (each one cost 150 yuan) in repayment for their kindness. They told me that riding

'Phoenix' brand bicycles around attracted a lot of attention. In 1981 China was like that.

After a while I got a letter from the German painter. He wrote that they had excitedly gone on a special trip to Rome and applied to see the superior general, who asked his assistant Joseph Pittau to meet them. This man sternly said: "We don't want to hear the name Jin Luxian. While in jail he surrendered to the communists. He is a traitor …." When I read this letter, my heart was broken. My friends had come 10,000 miles to see me, while the Society of Jesus treated me thus. I could only say to God: "You will never deny me. You are the most trustworthy. I believe in you."

In the meanwhile the PSM made all of us in the translation team cadres. Our monthly salary was adjusted; in my case from 50 yuan to 70 yuan. However, we were still managed by Zou. The German painter really did send me 200 yuan every month, so that I had a monthly income of 270 yuan. I bought new clothes and a few snacks, especially cakes and chocolate candies. Sadly this state of affairs did not last. I was forbidden by my doctors from eating sweets. No point in complaining. The doctors gave me medical leave, allowing me to work half a day and rest half a day; the days passed very easily.

44
My Return to Shanghai

On 1 June 1980 I was still working for the Baoding Jing'an Translation Company. The policeman responsible for me said: "Tomorrow you will go to Beijing. There's some translation business we need you to look into. Tonight you can stay at the PSM guesthouse in Xila Hutong." I was of course happy to get a change and to spend some time in Beijing. The next day I went to the PSM to pay a call on Deputy Director Zou Yuan. He told me to wait the next day for some people to visit me.

The next morning a man named Zhang Xianming came to the guesthouse to see me. He took me to a small villa opposite the Ba Mian Cao post office, where two men were already waiting. They introduced themselves as Zhao Yaping and Jiang Jiasen, both from the Political Security Department of the PSM. They knew all about me. Then a senior cadre arrived. The others immediately rose to their feet and showed this new man respect. They said that he was the deputy head of the Political Security Department and that his name was Liu Jun. The four men enquired after my circumstances and wanted to know whether I faced any difficulties in my life. They talked about the national reform and Open Door Policy, guaranteed freedom of religion and so on. They talked for two hours. Then they took me to the nearby Cui Hua Lou Restaurant, where they had already ordered a meal, after which they took me back to the guesthouse.

In early August, Zhang Xianming came to see me at Baoding City Guesthouse, where Liu Jun was waiting for me. They again talked with me. Liu advised me to keep my distance from the underground Catholic Church and then gave me lunch again before driving me back to jail.

In October the cadre responsible for me, Zhao Yutian, told me to go to Beijing the following day on business. This time I knew what it was all about and went with a light heart. The next day Liu Jun and his team talked with me, discussing the state of the Shanghai diocese. Their focus was on the activities of Zhu Hongsheng and his associates. They knew every detail of the activities of Zhu Hongsheng, Chen Tianxiang and Chen Yuntang. They said that Zhu and his associates had been naïvely engaged in sabotage with the support of foreign powers. There could be no positive outcome. They advised me to not make contact with them and certainly not follow their example. I learned that the government knew all about the activities of Zhu and his associates. I was worried for them. I planned to find a way to tell them to restrain themselves, but there arose no opportunity to put my plan into effect.

After this they arranged to meet me for a talk every two months. In the middle of 1981, they suggested that I return to the Shanghai diocese. I said that I wouldn't go, and added: "It would not be easy for me to leave my present life. I am very suited to translation work. I have no intention of returning." They advised me to think it over. They were very patient about helping me to see their point of view. Then they invited me to lunch at the hall of the CPPCC: on the table was a bottle of Gujing wine. I said something polite about it being a good wine and they immediately bought a bottle as a present for me.

Liu Jun once again set about changing my mind: "The new policy of freedom of religion is not a temporary one. It is not an expedient measure. It will not change again. However, religion must be organised by Chinese people and we will not permit foreigners to come and organise it. We realise that in future, Catholicism will need seminaries, in order to educate the next generation of religious people. Your generation is already aged. It is vital to get the new seminaries started as soon as possible. The days of foreign missionaries coming to spread the Word are over. In another twenty years, you will go to heaven and Catholicism will simply die out in China. You will bear the responsibility for that. The government has made up its mind, but you yourself refuse. You should take responsibility for the Church."

He spoke with such depth of feeling that I was moved by his words, but still remained undecided. I spoke with my fellow inmate Dr. Zhou Shanyu and he said: "You must not join the CPA; nor must you return to Shanghai. It looks as if you may have to leave the translation company. If the PSM requires it, you cannot refuse them and you will find yourself constrained to do what you at first declined to do."

"At the moment they are polite to you, but as the days pass, they will become less polite. In Xi County there is a remote village in the mountains with over twenty Catholic families who are pious and God fearing. They are all Catholics, no outsiders. The government never goes to visit them. I can introduce you to them as their parish priest."

I thought to myself that this was not a suitable solution. For one thing, I was Shanghainese. Were I to go to such a village I would be bound to attract unwanted attention; secondly, even if the government paid no attention to the village now, eventually it would and then I would be arrested. So it was not a long-term solution. Two years later the two priests who did hide out at that village were arrested and the Catholics were all locked up.

The Political Security Department of the PSM spent two years in all (two hours every month and over a meal) trying to persuade me. Even though they realised that I was just going through the motions, they still patiently and carefully educated me and earned my respect for them. Only after I had returned to Shanghai did I realise that it was all the result of the hard work put in by the deputy head of the Shanghai Religious Affairs Bureau, Chen Yiming. Chen's father had been the famous educationalist Chen Heqin (1892–1982), who had been the head of the Shanghai International Settlement United Municipal Council's Education Department. Chen had had a Western education, but became progressive and joined the Communist party. During the KMT period, he had been sent to do underground work. Later on he went to study in America and did revolutionary activism among the Chinese students there. He was expelled by the US authorities and returned to China, where he was initially responsible for religious affairs in the East China Section of the CCP, later on joining the Shanghai Religious Affairs Bureau. During the Anti-Rightist Movement, he was accused of rightist tendencies and was fired from his post and expelled from the party. He went to work in a factory. After the 'Cultural Revolution', the government needed to get a handle on religious matters and so invited him back to the bureau. He immediately obeyed and threw all his energies into sorting out the government policy. It was his suggestion that I be brought back to Shanghai to revive the operation of the seminary. The Shanghai diocese should be grateful for everything he did while he was in his post to open up churches and reclaim church property, rushing about everywhere, appealing to everyone, building a secure foundation for the Shanghai diocese.

In May of 1982, I said to Liu Jun that I was ready to return to the seminary to revive its operations. He was delighted and said: "No need to go straight back to Baoding. Why not spend a few days in Beijing?"

Next day I went to see Liu Jun, at whose office I met a new person, whom he introduced as Comrade Ding Genfa of the Shanghai PSB. Ding introduced himself and welcomed me to return to Shanghai, hoping that I would relax and work, and not hesitate to contact him in the case of any difficulty. They would help me sort out any problems. His approach seemed quite straightforward.

The next day I saw Liu Jun again, meeting yet another person whom he introduced as Comrade Pu Zuo of the Shanghai Religious Affairs Bureau. He wanted to get to know me a little so that it would be easier to work together after my return. Pu Zuo first expressed his welcome and then said: "Now, first you need to write a letter to Bishop Zhang Jiashu asking him to accept you back into the Shanghai diocese." I was extremely angry at this suggestion. I was originally part of the Shanghai diocese so why should I have to seek Zhang's permission, when I myself had no desire to go back? "I am not going back," I said. I got up as if to leave. Jiang and Zhao told me to sit down saying that I could say anything I wanted, but I wouldn't open my mouth again. In my very first meeting with Pu Zuo, our negotiations had broken down. Liu said, "Let's leave it for today and ask Old Jin to come again tomorrow."

The next day it was the same group of people. Pu Zuo opened the conversation with: "Father Jin, on behalf of the Shanghai Religious Affairs Bureau I welcome you back to Shanghai. You need not write that letter. When I go back I'll have a word with Zhang Jiashu and that will be enough."

I temporarily returned to Baoding and continued with my translation work. One day Zou Yuan sent one of his subordinates named Li Jing to find me. He gave me 50 yuan and said: "This is the money for the ticket to Shanghai. When you are ready, buy yourself a ticket and go back."

I said, "I know all about it." I returned the 50 yuan to him and refused to accept it. I thought: "Is this the right way to dismiss me?" I couldn't have cared less about the 50 yuan.

About this time the cadre Wang Chunxian, who had been responsible for me for a while, telephoned me from Xinxiang and said that her father who at that time was the deputy director of the Henan provincial-level PSB had called her urgently back to the provincial capital Zhengzhou. She went only to be confronted by her angry father who asked her: "What is your relationship with Jin Luxian? The PSM has sent people to investigate your relationship with him. I'm in deep trouble!"

Wang told me what she had said: "What relationship? Wasn't he my subordinate and I his supervisor? I was responsible for his political education for four years." Her father said: "It's not that simple. If that's all it was, why would the PSM send people to Zhengzhou to investigate me?"

She said: "Jin taught me English." To which he said: "Did you have to learn English from a serious counter-revolutionary activist? You really are confused!"

Her father was afraid that she would be implicated. Later on I asked Liu Jun about this and he replied, laughing: "Before you go back to Shanghai, just occupy yourself with routine work and make clear all your social connections." This investigation made Wang's father worry for the rest of his life, whereas Wang Chunxian herself remained unperturbed and thought nothing of it. This was the gap between the older generation and the younger one.

After another ten days or so, people from Baoding came to take me to Beijing. Liu Jun organised a dinner at the Beijing Hotel to see me off. This was attended by the deputy minister of the PSM, Ling Yun, who was very friendly, speaking *putonghua* with a strong Shaoxing accent, demonstrating how hard it is to change one's native accent. Ling toasted me and wished me success in my work. During the conversation he told me that he himself had spent seven years in Qincheng Jail, which he had been responsible for constructing. He also said that I could stay in touch with Liu Jun and that Liu would help me with any problems that needed sorting out.

A day later Cao Jingru, the deputy director of the National Religious Affairs Bureau, invited me to dinner, along with the section chief of the Catholic Section, Madam Fu Keyong. She had studied art. After Liberation she had been with Chen Yiming in the East China Bureau before transferring to Beijing. While Fu was in office she gave tremendous support to the Shanghai diocese, sparing no efforts. Liu Jun was also there. He laughed and told Cao: "Now I am handing Jin over to you. He is extremely politically reliable." Liu was from Hebei. He had joined the Eighth Route Army aged fifteen to fight the Japanese devils. His wife was also from a 'red' background. Liu had once joked: "I started out risking my life for the party; then I risked my whole life for the party. Finally I risked my own children for the party." His eldest son was in the army, his youngest son in the police, and his daughter was in the State Security Ministry. Liu treated people honestly and was uncorrupted. I went to his home once, an old house inside the PSM. His furniture was old-fashioned with no fancy decoration. He was truly a good party member. The next day the PSM sent people to take me to the station. They had booked a soft sleeper for me, which was very comfortable. In the same compartment was an old cadre, but I had just got out of jail and didn't desire human contact so we exchanged not a word during the journey.

On the platform in Shanghai waiting for me were Ding Genfa and Wang Yibai from the administration office of the city Religious Affairs Bureau, Rong Dexian's daughter Zhu Zhaorong and a few others. Ding said that he had booked a room for me at the Jinmen Hotel, but I preferred to stay at Rong Dexian's home. He said: "Zhang Jiashu and his people are on vacation at Putuo Island." I could visit the diocese a few days later. My two suitcases were sent on to the diocese ahead of me. (In my heart I deeply did not want to return to Shanghai. If I write about my return in detail it is because even now there are people who say that I betrayed my colleagues in payment for the opportunity to return to Shanghai.)

After a few days, the deputy head of the Municipal United Front Department, Li Guang, invited me to a meal along with the Religious Affairs Bureau's Chen Yiming and the head of administration, Wang Yibai, along with Zhang Jiashu, Li Ende, Shen Baozhi, Gu Meiqing, Lu Weidu and others from the diocese. We had not seen each other for 27 years and had long assumed we would never meet again. It was hard to bear the emotion of knowing that we would again be working together! Was the past as hazy as smoke or was it all as clear as yesterday? It was hard to say.

On the morning of 21 June I went to Xujiahui along with other religious and lay people to attend the birthday celebrations of Zhang Jiashu. At the gathering many people gave him their best wishes and gave him presents. I also made a speech, the contents of which I have forgotten. I was given accommodation at No. 120 Puxi Road, while the other priests and nuns were lodged at the former Congregation of the Helpers of the Holy Souls convent at No. 201 Puxi Road. The next day I went to pay a call on Zhang Jiashu and the CPA leaders Gu Meiqing and Lu Weidu. The former Catholic Youth member Li Wenzhi came to see me, saying that she had been instructed to look after me and to act as my secretary.

No. 120 Puxi Road had originally been the Jesuit house. My early education had been passed there. Later it had become a parasol-handle factory, where all those who had been priests and nuns worked during the Cultural Revolution. The factory had already been moved, but the property had not yet been returned to the church.

The churches which had already been returned to the Shanghai diocese were the Xujiahui Cathedral (where Rev. Lian Guobang was parish priest and

Ai Zuzhang his assistant), the church in Sichuan South Road (as yet without a parish priest), the church at Zhujiajiao in Qingpu, the mid-level church at Sheshan (Rev. Gong Qiusheng was parish priest) and Xinkaihe Church on Chongming Island (Yu Xianda and Zhu Shangjian)—in total five churches. I remember that at the time I was arrested there had been 392 churches, large and small. It would be a huge task to rebuild all that.

That day, 21 June, was also my saint's day and the day before was my 66th birthday. I was about to begin a new life. I made an examination of my past life. I was an ordinary person, but I had undergone an extraordinary period in my life. I had volunteered to join the Society of Jesus in 1938. I loved the Jesuits: they had made a large contribution to the Church of Christ. I had taken a vow to be a good Jesuit, to become a brick that would bear some of the weight of the great structure of our Church, wherever the Society might choose to send me. My two years of novitiate had been very tough, but I had matured. When later the Society had repeatedly posted me to work in dangerous situations, I had obeyed without saying anything, working with total commitment, always considering how to perform my duties as well as I could.

During my 27 years in jail, every day I sang to myself the song: "The Society of Jesus is my mother", believing that all the Jesuits in the world were praying for me, from which thought I derived both peace of mind and inner strength. What I could not have imagined was that when my adopted German mother came to see me and then rushed to Rome to see the Jesuit leaders to tell them the happy news that I was still among the living, the deputy superior general who met with her would sternly tell her that I was a traitor and was no longer recognised as a Jesuit. When I had received my adopted mother's letter I really felt as if a sword had pierced my heart. That was the most painful moment of all my 27 years of lost liberty. In her letter, my adopted mother wrote that her whole family still loved me, which was a great consolation to me. The truth is that she always supported me and looked after me up until the day of her death.

In passing I'll mention something told to me by Rong Dexian. When Zhu Hongsheng had been released and returned to Shanghai, he told Rong Dexian the news that he had got from his friend in Baoding, concluding that I had already betrayed my faith and joined the Communist party. On seeing Rong Dexian he had said: "As the head of the Zhu family I am informing you that you must cut Jin off completely, treating him as if he were already dead. You must ignore him henceforth." Rong didn't pay attention to his words and persisted in her faith that I would never betray the Church.

My German adopted mother, Lu Naying and Rong Dexian are the three noblest women I have met in my life. They were also good mothers. They gave me motherly and sisterly love. In Europe and America there is endless debate as to whether God might be male or female. For us Chinese, this issue presents no difficulty, since we explain everything with the concept of *yin* and *yang*, with *yin* first and *yang* second. As to whether to use 'He' or 'She' to describe the Lord, I say He is both *yin* and *yang*, above which, in China, we place the absolute principle. The Lord has in His heart both a father's love and a mother's love. When we speak of the Lord's love for us, we may say that She is both our father and our mother.

Index of Names

This index covers significant persons mentioned in the text with brief biographical details.

CCP = Chinese Communist party
KMT = Kuomintang
PLA = People's Liberation Army
PRC = People's Republic of China
S.J. = Member of Society of Jesus

Benedict XV *(1854–1922) Pope 1914–22*, 23, 82
Berchmans, John S.J. *(1599–1621) Saint*, 56
Bith, Marcel S.J. *(1883–1963) Provincial of Paris*, 82, 87, 93, 96, 105
Boff, Leonardo *(b.1938) Franciscan, liberation theologian, Professor Emeritus of Ethics, Philosophy of Religion and Ecology at the Rio de Janeiro State University, Brazil*, 123
Bonsirven, Joseph S.J. *(1880–1958) Biblical scholar and theologian*, 99
Borodin, Mikhail *(Mikhail Gruzenberg 1884–1951) Comintern agent in China*, 232
Burckhardt, Franz S.J. *(1902–2002) Jesuit Visitor to China*, 131–2, 156–58, 187, 216

Campion, Edmund S.J. *(1540–81) Priest and martyr*, 110

Casaroli, Agostino *(1914–98) Cardinal and Vatican Secretary of State*, 189
Catez, Elizabeth *(Blessed Elizabeth of the Trinity 1880–1906) Carmelite nun*, 55, 222–4
Chen Boda 陈伯达 *(1904–89) Secretary to Mao Zedong during the Cultural Revolution*, 233
Chen Guangfu 陈光甫 *(K.P. Chen 1880–1976) Pioneer Chinese banker*, 33
Chen Yi 陈毅 *(1901–72) Marshal of the PLA, Mayor of Shanghai and Foreign Minister of PRC 1958–72*, 171–4
Chen Youren 陈友仁 *(Eugene Chen 1878–1944) KMT Foreign Minister*, 232
Chenu, Marie-Dominique *(1895–1990) Dominican theologian and founder of Concilium*, 155
Chiang Ching-kuo 蒋经国 *(1910–88) President of Republic of China*, 241, 251, 254

Clemenceau, Georges *(1841–1929) French Prime Minister 1906–9 and 1917–20*, 96

Costantini, Celso *(1876–1958) Cardinal Archbishop Apostolic Delegate to China 1922–35, Secretary of the Congregation for the Propagation of the Faith 1935–53, Apostolic Chancellor 1954–58*, 106, 117–8, 125, 151–2, 211

Dai Li 戴笠 *(1897–1946) Spy, Head of the KMT Investigation and Statistics Bureau*, 232, 239

Danielou, Jean S.J. *(1905–74) Cardinal, Professor at Institut Catholique (Paris)*, 100, 139

Danneels, Godfried *(b. 1933) Cardinal Archbishop of Mechelen-Brussels, liturgical scholar and reformer*, 123

de Breuvery, Emmanuel S.J. *(1903–70) Professor of Economics at Aurora University, Shanghai*, 181–2

Decourtray, Albert *(1923–94) Cardinal Archbishop of Lyon 1981–94*, 55, 124, 143–5, 152, 222

de Grandmaison, Léonce S.J. *(1868–1927) Theologian, Director of Etudes*, 55

de Guebriant *(1860–1935) Bishop of Jiangchang, Sichuan*, 23

de Lesseps, Ferdinand *(1805–94) French diplomat and engineer*, 90

de Lubac, Henri S.J. *(1896–1991) Cardinal and theologian*, 57–8, 96, 98–100, 154–5

Deng Yiming 邓以明 S.J. *(Dominic Tang Yee-ming 1908–95) Archbishop of Guangzhou*, 189

Dezza, Paolo S.J. *(1901–99) Cardinal, Head of Gregorian University*, 113–4

Dhanis, Edouard *(1902–78) Professor of theology at Louvain University*, 95, 99, 155

Ding Ling 丁玲 *(1904–86) Chinese writer first lauded and then persecuted by the CCP*, 34, 242

d'Ouince, René S.J. *(1896–1973) Director and Chief Editor of Etudes 1935–52*, 95–6

Durand, A. *Rector of Sacred Heart Seminary*, 38–9, 44–7

Du Yuesheng 杜月笙 *(1888–1951) Chinese gangster and anti-communist patriot*, 206, 230

Fahy, Eugene S.J. *(1911–96) (absentee) Bishop of Yangzhou*, 195

Fan Xueyan 范学淹 *(1907–92) Bishop of Baoding 1951–92*, 274

Fan Zhongliang 范忠良 S.J. *(b.1918) Bishop of the Shanghai (underground) Catholic Church*, 51

Faure, Edgar *(1908–88) French premier and President of National Assembly*, 225

Fei Xiaotong 费孝通 *(1910–2005) Professor of Sociology at Peking University*, 216

Feltin, Maurice *(1883–1975) Cardinal Archbishop of Paris*, 103

Feng Yuxiang 冯玉祥 *(1882–1948) Warlord and supporter of KMT*, 18, 232–3

Fessard, Gaston S.J. *(1897–1978) Marxist thinker, philosopher and theologian*, 96

Fu Zuoyi 傅作义 *(1895–1974) KMT General who surrendered Beijing to the Communists in 1949*, 94

Ganne, Pierre S.J. *(1904–79) Theologian accused of Marxist tendencies in 1950*, 99

Garrigou-Lagrange, Reginald Marie *(1877–1964) Dominican Thomist theologian*, 95, 155

Index of Names

Gong Pinmei 龚品梅 *(1901-2000) Cardinal and Bishop of Shanghai*, 17, 157-8, 161-74, 190, 195, 199-201, 205, 209, 213, 216-8, 225-7, 231
Gonzaga, Aloysius S.J. *(1568-91) Saint*, 8, 56, 135

Haouisée, Auguste S.J. *(1877-1948) Bishop of Shanghai 1933-48*, 44-5, 74, 83, 160
Henry, Yves S.J. *Jesuit father superior*, 20, 39, 43-7, 51, 58, 61, 66-7, 74-5, 78, 83, 156-60, 163, 177, 189
Hu Feng 胡风 *(1902-85) Left-wing literary theorist who criticized Mao's theories and was imprisoned 1955-79*, 196
Huang Wei 黄维 *(1904-89) KMT General*, 240-1, 250

Janssens, Jean-Baptiste S.J. *(1889-1964) Superior General of the Society of Jesus*, 95, 131
Jiang Qing 江青 *(1914-91) Actress, fourth wife of Mao Zedong and member of Gang of Four*, 242, 265
Jiang, Zhujun 江竹筠 *(Sister Jiang 1920-49) Joined the Communist underground in Chongqing during the anti-Japanese war in 1939, working as an activist at Sichuan University. She was arrested by the KMT secret service in June 1948 and, according to Communist party history, subjected to every kind of torture before being executed in November 1949 on the eve of Liberation*, 240
Jin Dayi, David 金达义 *(1918-?) Jin Luxian's brother*, 11-4, 19-20, 26, 30-1, 37-9
Jin Weixuan, Mary 金慰萱 *(1913-34) Jin Luxian's sister*, 1-2, 10-2, 26-7, 29, 39, 40-1

John-Paul II *(1920-2005) Pope 1978-2005*, 9, 122-3

Kádár, László *(1927-86) Archbishop of Eger, Hungary*, 122
Kim Taegon, Andrew *(1821-46) Korean priest, martyr and saint*, 9
Koo, V.K. Wellington 顾维钧 *(1887-1985) Chinese diplomat who attended the Paris Peace Conference after WWI*, 106
Küng, Hans *(b.1928) Emeritus Professor of Tübingen University banned from teaching Catholic theology*, 122-3, 152

Ladány, László S.J. *(1914-90) Hungarian priest and editor of* China News Analysis, 67, 271
Languillat, Adrien-Hippolyte S.J. *(1808-78) Apostolic Vicar of Jiangnan*, 194
Lebreton, Jules *(1873-1956) Professor of the History of Christian Origins at the Faculty of Catholic Theology, Paris*, 55, 95
Lefebvre, Peter S.J. *(1883-1955) Rector of Shanghai School of Theology*, 44, 71-3, 159, 177, 188-9
Lefeuvre, Jean S.J. *(1902-2010) Priest and author of* Shanghai: les enfants dans la ville, chronique de la vie chretienne a Shanghai, 1949-55, 197
Leighton Stuart, John *(1876-1962) Protestant pastor, President of Yanjing University and US Ambassador to China 1946-52*, 231-2
Li Zongren 李宗仁 *(Li Tsung-jen 1890-1969) KMT General and President of the Republic of China 1949-50*, 157, 233
Liénart, Achille *(1884-1973) Cardinal and Bishop of Lille 1928-68*, 124

Lin Biao 林彪 *(1907-71) Communist General and Vice-Chairman of CCP 1958-71*, 235, 242, 251

Ling Yun 凌云 *(b.1917) Minister of State Security of the PRC 1983-85*, 242, 287

Liu Bainian, Anthony 刘柏年 *(b.1934) Vice Chairman of the Chinese Catholic Patriotic Association 1992-2010*, 193

Loew, Jacques *(1908-99) Dominican friar and worker priest*, 102

Loyola, Ignatius *(1491-1556) Saint and Founder of the Society of Jesus in 1539*, 37, 56, 94, 113

Lu Naying 陆纳英 *(1908-66) Jin Luxian's friend and benefactor*, 2, 31-2, 41, 45, 48, 107, 290

Lu Zhengxiang 陆征祥 *(Lou Tseng-Tsiang 1871-1949) Chinese diplomat, Benedictine friar and patriot*, 105

Luo Guang 罗光 *(Stanislaus Lo Kuang 1911-2004) Archbishop of Taipei 1966-78*, 118

Luo Wenzao, Gregory O.P. *(1615-91) First Chinese priest and first Chinese Bishop as Apostolic Vicar (of Nanjing) 1674-91*, 168

Ma Xiangbo 马相伯 S.J. *(1840-1939) Scholar and educator, founder of Aurora Academy, Fudan Public School and Catholic University of Peking*, 1, 23

McGrath, Aidan *(1906-2000) Supervisor of the Legion of Mary*, 167, 170

Meistermann, Georg *(1911-90) German painter and stained-glass designer*, 143, 152, 277

Mindszenty, József *(1892-1975) Cardinal Archbishop of Esztergom in Hungary*, 174, 227

Pan Hannian 潘汉年 *(1906-77) Executive Vice-Mayor of Shanghai, imprisoned from 1955 to 1977*, 170, 174, 242

Paris, Prosper S.J. *(1846-1931) Bishop of Jiangnan*, 44

Paul VI *(1897-1978) Pope 1963-78*, 100, 119, 129, 139

Peng Dehuai 彭德怀 *(1898-1974) Marshal of the PRC persecuted to death for criticizing Mao Zedong*, 218

Pi Shushi 皮漱石 *(1897-1978) Bishop of Shenyang 1949-78*, 66

Pius XII *(1876-1958) Pope 1939-58*, 103, 114, 118, 123, 128, 154, 165, 212-3

Rahner, Hugo S.J. *(1900-68) Dean and President of Innsbruck University*, 137

Rahner, Karl S.J. *(1904-84) Theologian associated with Nouvelle Théologie*, 138

Rao Shushi 饶漱石 *(1903-75) 1st Secretary of the East China Bureau of the CCP purged in the 1950s*, 242

Ratzinger, Joseph *(b.1927) Pope Benedict XVI from 2005*, 122-3, 155

Riberi, Antonio *(1897-1967) Cardinal Archbishop and Papal Nuncio to China 1946-51*, 33, 131, 159, 162-3, 167-70, 177, 183, 190, 199

Ricci, Matteo S.J. *(1552-1610) Missionary to China who published translations of Western scientific and mathematical works into Chinese*, 113, 211, 253

Roncalli, Angelo *(1881-1963) Pope John XXIII from 1958 to 1963. Called Second Vatican Council*, 119, 128, 155

Rong Dexian 荣德先 *Jin Luxian's friend and benefactor*, 2, 31-4, 40-1, 168, 171, 216, 220, 230, 235, 256-7, 260-1, 277, 279-80, 288-90

Index of Names

Schillebeeckx, Edward *(1914–2009) Dominican and theologian who played an active role in the Second Vatican Council*, 123
Sin, Jaime *(1928–2005) Cardinal Archbishop of Manila*, 124
Song Qingling 宋庆龄 *(1893–1981) Honorary President of the PRC*, 231–2
Spellman, Francis *(1889–1967) Cardinal Archbishop of New York*, 33, 132, 167
Suárez, Luis Ruiz S.J. *(1913–2011) Benefactor of Macau and helper of lepers*, 72
Sun Ke 孙科 *(1891–1973) President of Legislative Yuan of ROC 1932–48*, 118–9

Teilhard de Chardin, Pierre S.J. *(1881–1955) Paleontologist and geologist*, 67, 72, 95–6
Thérèse of Lisieux *(1873–97) Saint, Carmelite nun and author of* The Story of a Soul, 43–4, 118
Tian Gengxing 田耕莘 *(Thomas Tien Ken-sin 1890–1967) Cardinal and Chair of Furen University, Taiwan*, 66, 118, 175, 199
Tritz, Pierre S.J. *(b.1915) Benefactor of the Philippines*, 64, 72, 105

Walsh, James *(1891–1981) Maryknoll priest imprisoned by the PRC*, 33, 167–8, 179, 220
Wang Jingwei 汪精卫 *(1883–1944) Assistant to Sun Yat-sen who led the Japanese puppet Nanjing regime 1940–44*, 231–2, 236
Wang Liangzuo *(b.1920) Bishop of Chengdu who was among the first to join the Catholic Patriotic Association (CPA) and later Chair of Sichuan CPA*, 162

Wang Ming 王明 *(1904–74) 2nd General Secretary of the CCP who fell afoul of Mao Zedong*, 238
Wang Yangming 王阳明 *(1472–1529) Neo-Confucian philosopher, official, educationist, calligrapher and general*, 57
Wetter, Friedrich *(b.1928) Cardinal Archbishop of Munich*, 123–4, 152
Wu Jingxiong 吴经熊 J.D. *(1900–86) 2nd representative of the Republic of China at the Vatican*, 101, 117–8, 127
Wu Jingzi 吴敬梓 *Author of* Rulin Waishi 儒林外史, 16, 34
Wu Li 吴历 S.J. *(1632–1718) Landscape painter and poet, who converted to Christianity and was one of the first Chinese priests*, 108
Wu Peifu 吴佩孚 *(1874–1939) General in the Beiyang Army of the Zhili Clique*, 18, 128
Wu Yaozong 吴耀宗 *(1893–1979) Protestant minister and YMCA leader, founder of Three-Self Patriotic Movement*, 162, 200

Xavier, Francis S.J. *(1506–52) Saint and missionary to Japan, India and the East Indies*, 56
Xu Guangqi 徐光启 *(1562–1633) Chinese scholar-official who collaborated with Matteo Ricci in the translation and dissemination of several important works of science and mathematics, converted to Christianity and was an early patron of the Catholic Church in China*, 13

Yu Bin, Paul 于斌 *(1901–78) Cardinal Archbishop of Nanjing 1936–78*, 48, 118, 127–9, 157, 199, 217

Yuan Shikai 袁世凯 *(1859-1916) General, 2nd President of ROC, Hongxian Emperor*, 7, 17, 106

Zhang Boda 张伯达 S.J. *(Beda Chang 1905-51) Dean of Faculty of Arts at Aurora University, Martyr*, 44, 87, 160-2, 184, 213

Zhang Chongren 张充仁 *(1908-88) Chinese sculptor, friend of Hergé*, 208

Zhang Jian 张謇 *(1853-1926) zhuang yuan (Imperial top scholar)*, 231

Zhang Jiashu 张家树 S.J. *(Aloysius Tsang 1893-1998) Bishop of Shanghai 1960-88*, 13, 17, 25, 39, 132, 156, 173, 216, 220, 223, 226, 286, 288

Zhang Lingfu 张灵甫 *(1903-47) KMT General*, 76, 78-9

Zhang Wentian 张闻天 *(Lo Fu 1900-76) General Secretary of the Chinese Communist Party 1935-43*, 17, 218

Zhang Xueliang 张学良 *(1901-2001) Warlord who aligned with the KMT, but then kidnapped Chiang Kai-shek during the Xi'an Incident in 1936 and forced a change in policy from extermination of the CCP to resistance against Japan*, 236

Zhao Zhensheng 赵振声 S.J. *(1894-1968) Vicar Apostolic then Bishop of Xianxian 1937-68*, 65, 83, 132

Zheng Changcheng 郑长诚 *(1913-2007) Bishop of Fuzhou 1951-88*, 179

Zhu Kaimin 朱开敏 S.J. *(Simon Chu 1868-1960) Vicar Apostolic, then Bishop of Haimen 1926-60*, 33, 48, 156-8, 178, 183